THE THEATRE OF PAULA VOGEL

Lee Brewer Jones is Professor of English at Georgia State University, USA. He is the co-author, with Alyse W. Jones, of the Longman textbooks *College Writing: Keeping It Real* (2001) and *A World of Writing* (2005).

Also available in the Critical Companions series from Methuen Drama:

THE THEATRE OF SIMON STEPHENS
Jacqueline Bolton

CRITICAL COMPANION TO NATIVE AMERICAN AND FIRST NATIONS THEATRE AND PERFORMANCE: INDIGENOUS SPACES
Jaye T. Darby, Courtney Elkin Mohler, and Christy Stanlake

THE DRAMA AND THEATRE OF SARAH RUHL
Amy Muse

THE THEATRE OF AUGUST WILSON
Alan Nadel

THE THEATRE OF EUGENE O'NEILL: AMERICAN MODERNISM ON THE WORLD STAGE
Kurt Eisen

THE THEATRE AND FILMS OF CONOR MCPHERSON: CONSPICUOUS COMMUNITIES
Eamonn Jordan

IRISH DRAMA AND THEATRE SINCE 1950
Patrick Lonergan

For a full listing, please visit https://www.bloomsbury.com/uk/series/critical-companions/

THE THEATRE OF PAULA VOGEL

PRACTICE, PEDAGOGY, AND INFLUENCES

Lee Brewer Jones

Series Editors: Patrick Lonergan and Kevin J. Wetmore, Jr.

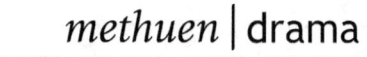

LONDON • NEW YORK • OXFORD • NEW DELHI • SYDNEY

METHUEN DRAMA
Bloomsbury Publishing Plc
50 Bedford Square, London, WC1B 3DP, UK
1385 Broadway, New York, NY 10018, USA
29 Earlsfort Terrace, Dublin 2, Ireland

BLOOMSBURY, METHUEN DRAMA and the Methuen Drama logo are
trademarks of Bloomsbury Publishing Plc

First published in Great Britain 2023
This paperback edition published 2025

Copyright © Lee Brewer Jones and contributors, 2023

Lee Brewer Jones has asserted his right under the Copyright, Designs and
Patents Act, 1988, to be identified as author of this work.

For legal purposes the Acknowledgments on p. viii constitute an extension of this
copyright page.

Cover image © (L-R) Max Gordon Moore, Adina Verson, Richard Topol,
Katrina Lenk, Mimi Lieber and Steven Rattazzi in Indecent
(Photograph © Carol Rosegg)

All rights reserved. No part of this publication may be reproduced or transmitted
in any form or by any means, electronic or mechanical, including photocopying,
recording, or any information storage or retrieval system, without prior
permission in writing from the publishers.

Bloomsbury Publishing Plc does not have any control over, or responsibility for, any
third-party websites referred to or in this book. All internet addresses given in this
book were correct at the time of going to press. The author and publisher regret any
inconvenience caused if addresses have changed or sites have ceased to exist, but
can accept no responsibility for any such changes.

A catalogue record for this book is available from the British Library.

A catalog record for this book is available from the Library of Congress.

Names: Jones, Lee Brewer, author.
Title: The theatre of Paula Vogel : practice, pedagogy, and influences /
Lee Brewer Jones.
Description: London ; New York : Methuen Drama, 2023. | Series: Critical
companions | Includes bibliographical references.
Identifiers: LCCN 2022060176 | ISBN 9781350251717 (hardback) | ISBN
9781350251755 (paperback) | ISBN 9781350251724 (epub) | ISBN
9781350251731 (ebook)
Subjects: LCSH: Vogel, Paula–Criticism and interpretation. | Vogel,
Paula–Influence. | American drama–20th century–History and criticism.
| American drama–21st century–History and criticism.
Classification: LCC PS3572.O294 Z74 2023 | DDC 812/.54–dc23/eng/20230210
LC record available at https://lccn.loc.gov/2022060176

ISBN: HB: 978-1-3502-5171-7
PB: 978-1-3502-5175-5
ePDF: 978-1-3502-5173-1
eBook: 978-1-3502-5172-4

Series: Critical Companions

Typeset by Deanta Global Publishing Services, Chennai, India

To find out more about our authors and books visit www.bloomsbury.com
and sign up for our newsletters.

CONTENTS

Preface: A "Little Jewish Play"		vi
Acknowledgments		viii
1	Early Life and Influences	1
2	Developing a Unique Voice	15
3	Building an International Reputation	41
4	The House of Paula Vogel	79
5	Vogel in the Twenty-First Century	107
6	**Critical Perspectives**	129
	The Alchemy of Influence: Paula Vogel and Sarah Ruhl, *Amy Muse*	129
	Drawing New Circles: On Paula Vogel's Maieutics, Quiara Alegría Hudes's Broken Language and the Seeds of Boricuan Inspiration, *Ana Fernández-Caparrós*	140
	"The Feminine Spirit That Really I Needed": Interview between Lee Brewer Jones and Lynn Nottage, *Lee Brewer Jones*	155
Notes		163
References		173
Notes on Contributors		189
Index		191

PREFACE: A "LITTLE JEWISH PLAY"

In February 1921, a New York Court of Special Session found portions of James Joyce's *Ulysses* obscene, fined *The Little Review* editors who had published the novel, and doomed it to several years of waiting before a US publisher would take it on. Then, two years and a few weeks later, sixteen people were arrested for performing Yiddish author Sholem Asch's *God of Vengeance* at Broadway's Apollo Theatre. As with *Ulysses*, the charge was obscenity, and once again, a guilty verdict came down. Rudolph Schildkraut, the lead actor, and others suffered not only the indignity of a conviction (eventually reversed on appeal) but also incalculable harm to their careers.

Although the newspapers of the day avoided stating directly what the jury found obscene about *God of Vengeance*, hints survive. Defense attorney Harry Weinberger (also a manager of the play and one of the defendants) likened its content to the biblical stories of David and Bathsheba, Amnon and Tamar, and the Song of Solomon, passages noted for eroticism. The apparently unstated subject matter was a love affair between brothel owner Yekel's daughter Rifke (nicknamed Rifkele) and prostitute Manke. The 1918 Isaac Goldberg translation that the Apollo production used contains the stage direction "Kisses Rifkele" (42), which indicates that prosecutors may have believed *God of Vengeance* brought a same-sex kiss—the first—to Broadway. Even as the 1920s roared, a lesbian relationship and especially such a kiss would not do.

In Asch's original Yiddish version or translations into a host of European languages, *God of Vengeance* had toured throughout Europe. Goldberg notes in his introduction that Max Reinhardt directed the play "at the Deutsches Theater, Berlin, in 1910" (viii) and that the play subsequently traveled across "Germany, Austria, Russia, Poland, Holland, Nor-way [*sic*], Sweden and Italy" (viii). Goldberg reported a 1916 Italian run as especially successful.

After the Broadway fiasco, however, fortunes turned dramatically for *God of Vengeance*. By October 1923, licensing authorities in London had prohibited any performances there. Within a decade, Nazism began closing the doors of European theatres that might have run Asch or other

Preface: A "little Jewish Play"

Jewish playwrights. Even after the Holocaust ended, a weary Asch issued both a warning and an appeal aimed at stopping a 1946 Spanish-language production in Mexico. Asch had seen and endured enough.

With Asch abandoning his play, *God of Vengeance* gathered dust on library shelves for decades. It was so thoroughly forgotten that when young doctoral student Paula Vogel arrived at Cornell University in the 1970s, *God of Vengeance* came as a revelation to her. Professor Bert States sent Vogel to the library stacks, where she stood and almost inhaled a yellowing copy. So began, for Vogel, a fascination with the sensitive way a married heterosexual male depicted lesbian love and a desire to restore *God of Vengeance* to what Vogel steadfastly saw as its rightful place.

For many writers, Vogel's appreciation for Asch and *God of Vengeance* may have led to a footnote, but for Vogel (and collaborator Rebecca Taichman) it foretold a capstone, or at least a milestone, in a major career. In 2016, Paula Vogel successfully returned to Cornell, decades after the university dismissed her ABD, to defend *Indecent*, her adaptation of and elaboration upon Asch's work, and earn her PhD. Then, in April 2017, ten actors and musicians shook the literal dust off their clothes, the words "the true story of a little Jewish play" flashed at the Cort Theatre, and 65-year-old Paula Vogel made her Broadway debut. Nearly a century after the morality police drove *God of Vengeance* from Broadway and, indeed, even the shores of the United States, Vogel brought it back, and she brought a significant portion of the original Yiddish text, particularly the kiss, with her.

Vogel's earned PhD, with *Indecent* as her dissertation, and her Broadway debut at sixty-five illustrate both the power of her vision and her tenacious independence. Vogel arrived on Broadway alongside her former student Lynn Nottage, the only woman to win the Pulitzer Prize for Drama twice. For Vogel, as much and perhaps even more than for any other playwright, these experiences relatively late in life brought particular joy and seemed especially appropriate. *The Theatre of Paula Vogel: Practice, Pedagogy, and Influences* is an account of Vogel's career through *Indecent* and beyond. It represents an attempt to place Vogel alongside those who have inspired her and those whom she has taught. Just as *Indecent* reveals *God of Vengeance* as more than a "little Jewish play," this book argues for Vogel as one of the most important figures American theatre has yet produced.

ACKNOWLEDGMENTS

Thanks go first to Paula Vogel for her plays that have held my attention since I first picked up a copy of *How I Learned to Drive* in 2013. As well, I will ever be grateful to Vogel's "gods"—John Guare, Caryl Churchill, and María Irene Fornés—for their works and their influence and similarly to such Vogel students as Nilo Cruz, Sarah Ruhl, Quiara Alegría Hudes, and Lynn Nottage for the plays they have written. In particular, I am grateful to Lynn Nottage for taking the time to give me an interview, which is published for the first time in this book.

When Matthew Roudané first heard the "House of Paula Vogel" idea, the word "book" soon followed. He has supported this project all along the way, most recently by introducing me to contributor Ana Fernández-Caparrós, to whom I am also grateful. Similarly, Amy Muse's contribution greatly enhances the volume. Pearl McHaney proved an essential proofreader of an early draft of several chapters; of course, any remaining errors are mine.

At Methuen Drama, I want to thank Ella Wilson, Lara Bateman, and Mark Dudgeon.

Esther Nelle Jones has not only served as my amanuensis and research assistant, but she has also been my supportive daughter while I worked on this project. Eli Brewer Jones III contributed proofreading assistance and insights. Ethan and Ezra Jones cheerfully abided my occasional physical absence and more frequent book absorption.

Most of all, this is for Alyse. Shortly before my fiftieth birthday, she gently suggested the time had come for me to pursue my lifelong dream of earning a PhD. Without her advice, her enduring counsel, and above all else her abiding love, this book would never have come to be. This acknowledgment only begins to repay the debt.

* * *

The author and publisher gratefully acknowledge the permission granted to reproduce the copyright material in this book:

Quotations from "Loose Screws" by David Savran. Copyright © 1996 by David Savran. Published in *The Baltimore Waltz and Other Plays*. Copyright

Acknowledgments

© 1996 by Paula Vogel. Published by Theatre Communications Group. Used by permission of Theatre Communications Group.

Quotations from *The Baltimore Waltz* by Paula Vogel. Copyright © 1992 by Paula Vogel. Published in *The Baltimore Waltz and Other Plays*. Copyright © 1996 by Paula Vogel. Published by Theatre Communications Group. Used by permission of Theatre Communications Group.

Quotations from *And Baby Makes Seven* by Paula Vogel. Copyright © 1984, 1993 by Paula Vogel. Published in *The Baltimore Waltz and Other Plays*. Copyright © 1996 by Paula Vogel. Published by Theatre Communications Group. Used by permission of Theatre Communications Group.

Quotations from *The Oldest Profession* by Paula Vogel. Copyright © 1980 by Paula Vogel. Published in *The Baltimore Waltz and Other Plays*. Copyright © 1996 by Paula Vogel. Published by Theatre Communications Group. Used by permission of Theatre Communications Group.

Quotations from *Desdemona: A Play about a Handkerchief* by Paula Vogel. Copyright © 1986, 1994 by Paula Vogel. Published in *The Baltimore Waltz and Other Plays*. Copyright © 1996 by Paula Vogel. Published by Theatre Communications Group. Used by permission of Theatre Communications Group.

Quotations from *Hot 'N' Throbbing* by Paula Vogel. Copyright © 1993, 1995 by Paula Vogel. Published in *The Baltimore Waltz and Other Plays*. Copyright © 1996 by Paula Vogel. Published by Theatre Communications Group. Used by permission of Theatre Communications Group.

Quotations from *How I Learned to Drive* by Paula Vogel. Copyright © 1998, 2018 by Paula Vogel. Published by Theatre Communications Group. Used by permission of Theatre Communications Group.

Quotations from *Indecent* by Paula Vogel. Copyright © 2017 by Paula Vogel. Published by Theatre Communications Group. Used by permission of Theatre Communications Group.

Quotations from *In the Next Room or the Vibrator Play* by Sarah Ruhl. Copyright © 2010 by Sarah Ruhl. Published by Theatre Communications Group. Used by permission of Theatre Communications Group.

Quotations from *Water by the Spoonful* by Quiara Alegría Hudes. Copyright © 2017 by Quiara Alegría Hudes. Published by Theatre Communications Group. Used by permission of Theatre Communications Group.

Quotations from unpublished text of *Dog Play* © Sarah Ruhl. Used by permission of Sarah Ruhl.

Acknowledgments

Every effort has been made to trace copyright holders and to obtain their permission for the use of copyright material. However, if any have been inadvertently overlooked, the publishers will be pleased, if notified of any omissions, to make the necessary arrangement at the first opportunity.

CHAPTER 1
EARLY LIFE AND INFLUENCES

Paula Vogel was born in Washington, D.C., on November 16, 1951, the youngest child (following brothers Carl and Mark) resulting from the union of Donald Vogel, a Jewish man from New York, and Phyllis Bremerman, a Catholic woman from New Orleans. Vogel has stated that one grandfather (presumably on her mother's side) voted for George Wallace, an electoral fact emphasizing her diverse heritage and informing Grandfather in *How I Learned to Drive*. The Vogel marriage failed, with Donald leaving the family while Paula was still in elementary school, and Phyllis Vogel brought up her children on what Vogel has described to Carolyn Craig as "the wrong side of the beltway" (214), near Baltimore. Before the divorce, Paula Vogel had already imbued the vastly different backgrounds of both parents, which left her with what Craig calls "a bit of a split personality—but a useful one in terms of a gift for story-telling" (214). Vogel told Craig, "Some people say that this is very traditionally Southern, this kind of great story-telling.... Others say it's *so* New York" (214). To PBS interviewer Elizabeth Farnsworth, Vogel identified "the Jewish gene in me" ("A Prize-Winning") when explaining how she chooses her topics and her language.

Vogel appears to have been born bold; moreover, actress Mary-Louise Parker, who originated the role of L'il Bit in *How I Learned to Drive* and then performed the part on Broadway twenty-five years later, has affectionately described Vogel as "fun to listen to, tough, relentlessly friendly, and more than a little twisted" (Parker). The sister of a man, Carl, who died of AIDS, Vogel shows an ability to see humor in even ghastly situations, telling Farnsworth, "Some of the funniest moments I think I've experienced in my life have been in family funerals." Perhaps Vogel's dogged perseverance and willingness to employ dry humor that provokes even as it stimulates emerge in what Carolyn Craig calls a "loose screw" episode (214). While struggling to rear her children in a Baltimore-area apartment, Phyllis Vogel reported a building violation and was unjustly evicted in retaliation. According to Craig, Phyllis Vogel opted for revenge rather than a legal fight. She left the apartment, but before doing so, she and her children carefully unscrewed "everything in the apartment" (214), down to the last appliance screw. Then, after directing that every screw go into "a circle in the living room floor" (214), Phyllis Vogel left a two-word note: "Screw you!" (215). This moment predicts the way the adult Paula will employ language, irony, and especially chutzpah, a Jewish concept here not derived from a Jewish gene but definitely illustrated in the inventiveness and originality typical to a Paula Vogel play.

The geography of Vogel's upbringing also may partly account for the split personality Vogel has described to Craig. In the 1950s and 1960s, the area between Washington and Baltimore did not consist of the endless suburbs of today. South of the Mason-Dixon Line, the area was part of a state that did not secede yet maintained segregation through much of the twentieth century. Neither fully Northern nor truly Southern, the Maryland of Vogel's youth comes out in *How I Learned to Drive*. At the same time, Vogel reflects her father's New York Jewish roots in *Indecent*.

Vogel learned early on to stand as a minority of one and as someone comfortable with apparent contradictions. From working-class roots, she rose to be an Ivy League professor (Brown and Yale) for more than thirty years. A lesbian married to Ann Fausto-Sterling, Vogel acknowledges attraction to men, a fact which may explain why *And Baby Makes Seven* (1984) has a woman in a same-sex relationship engage in heterosexual coitus so that she may conceive a child. A young wordsmith who lamented, "I didn't know any women writers" (Craig 216), Vogel struck out for a writing career regardless. A good speaker assigned many of the male parts in her school plays, Vogel intuited gender bending, another component of *And Baby Makes Seven*, with female characters taking Edward Albee's *Who's Afraid of Virginia Woolf?* one step further and playing their own imaginary sons.

Although Vogel has reported that when five years old, she "fell in love" with Mary Martin's portrayal of Peter Pan (Mansbridge 2) and has never recanted her love for theatre, especially musicals, she was not the first Vogel child with literary aspirations. Carl Vogel began writing but gave up the craft after he came out to his family several years before Stonewall and became the subject of relentless homophobic bullying. Carl then left the family when his sister was sixteen. This turn of events must have been troubling to Vogel, who had her first lesbian experience and in turn came out when she was seventeen, months before Stonewall, but it was significant in her development. She explains, "When he stopped writing, . . . I started" (Craig 215). Writing seems to have replaced acting for Vogel while in no way diminishing the performative elements of her work, as her writing career and teaching accomplishments show.

Vogel pursued her education, becoming "the first generation in my family that had graduated high school and the first generation to go to college" (Mansbridge 3). After earning her undergraduate degree at Catholic University in 1974, Vogel applied to several universities, including Yale, where she would have been a classmate of Wendy Wasserstein had the program not rejected her. She did gain admission to Cornell, however, where she quickly set about making her mark. Twice she won the Forbes Heermans and George McCalmon playwriting competition, a university award (Warner). She also revised one of her prize-winning plays, a feminist take on Robert Bolt's *A Man for All Seasons*, into a longer drama, *Meg*, which garnered the American College Theater Festival's National Student Playwriting Award in 1977. The prize, which came with a William Morris agent (Mansbridge 4), would be renamed for Vogel in 2002.

Vogel followed *Meg* with *Desdemona*, a recasting of Shakespeare's *Othello* entirely in the domestic sphere. *Desdemona* makes a powerful statement by giving its title character agency, but it is not clear who was able to witness it during the 1970s. Vogel's *The Baltimore Waltz and Other Plays*, published in 1996, records only one pre-1993 "production," a "staged reading October 1977 at Cornell" (174). Bigsby, however, reports that in 1979, *Desdemona* "had been successfully staged . . . at the New Plays Festival in Louisville" (*Modern* 411). While this statement is credible, Bigsby's assigning the Cornell University staged reading to 1973 is problematic at best, given that Vogel was only twenty-one or twenty-two and still at Catholic University that year. Still, Bigsby is correct in calling any small success *Desdemona* enjoyed in the 1970s "something of a false start" (411). Bigsby adds that "Paula Vogel sees her career as having started" in 1980, the year she "sent her play *The Oldest Profession* to theatres across the country only to have them reject it" (411).

While Vogel was experiencing a false start in national and regional theatres, her fortunes at Cornell were worse. "Animated by the emerging discourse of feminist dramatic criticism that she was helping forge," Sara Warner writes, Vogel was writing "a revisionist approach to theater history in her dissertation, 'Hiding Scenes in Restoration Comedy'" (Warner). Calamity struck when two members of Vogel's committee departed Cornell, replaced by new faculty who left Vogel only one option if she were to finish the degree: "start over on page one," Vogel recalls (Warner). Vogel eventually left Cornell in 1981 involuntarily and ABD; as she told a 2016 audience, "I was fired" (McCasland).

A position teaching playwriting at Brown University, where Vogel worked from the mid-1980s until Yale hired her away in 2008, afforded Vogel a secure living while she tried to build an audience for her plays. Brown also gave her an opportunity to teach such talented members of the next generation as Nilo Cruz, Lynn Nottage, and Sarah Ruhl. Even before Vogel achieved her first national success with Obie Award-winner *The Baltimore Waltz* (1991), she developed enduring friendships, including one with emerging critic David Savran. Savran acknowledged Vogel as a muse of sorts in his 1988 *In Their Own Words: Contemporary American Playwrights*, which includes a note of thanks to "Paula Vogel, who instigated the project and advised me every step of the way" (vii). Savran also recalled how, when he and Vogel "were in graduate school," they experienced the thrill of discovering new work at The Public Theater, or La MaMa, the exhilaration of seeing Stephen Sondheim's *Sweeney Todd* or Caryl Churchill's *Cloud 9* or John Guare's *Gardenia* (xiii).

The particular playwrights Savran lists among those who exhilarated him and Vogel are interesting selections, given Vogel's mature choices and acknowledged influences. *Sweeney Todd*, by Sondheim, is a musical. Many of Vogel's plays are infused with music; for example, in her "Production Notes" for *How I Learned to Drive*, Vogel writes, "**As For Music:** Please have fun. I wrote sections of the play listening to music like Roy Orbison's 'Dream Baby' and The Mamas and the Papas' 'Dedicated to the One I love'" (6) and so forth (emphasis in original). She even adds, "Other sixties music is rife with pedophilish (?) reference: the 'You're Sixteen' genre hits; The Beach Boys' 'Little Surfer Girl'; Gary Puckett and the Union Gap's 'This Girl Is a Woman Now'; 'Come Back When You Grow Up,' etc." (6). What is more, Vogel's *A Civil War Christmas: An American Musical Celebration* features public domain nineteenth-century songs, and *Indecent* includes both klezmer musicians and has the actors co-perform original compositions.

Of even greater interest is Savran's recollection of Churchill and Guare. In 1998, interviewer Elizabeth Farnsworth asked Vogel, "And who have been the most important influences on your life?" Vogel replied, "I have to say that there are three playwrights that I always list as my gods." "One," she continued, "is John Guerre [*sic*], the incredible playwright who may be best known for *Six Degrees of Separation*. He has mentored me on the page. Another extraordinary playwright, American playwright," Vogel went on, "is Maria Irene Fornez [*sic*], who is just a remarkable voice, a Cuban-American playwright. And lastly," she concluded, "there is the divine Caryl

Churchill, a British playwright, the writer of *Top Girls* and *Cloud Nine* ("A Prize-Winning").

Joanna Mansbridge notes, "To see a Paula Vogel play is to participate in a three-way dialogue with the dramatic canon, social history, and contemporary American culture" (1). As noted above, *Meg* reimagines, *Desdemona* elaborates upon Shakespeare, and *And Baby Makes Seven* employs an Albee device. *The Baltimore Waltz* borrows characters from Carol Reed's film *The Third Man* as well as the technique of squeezing an entire story into an instant in actual time from Ambrose Bierce's "An Occurrence at Owl Creek Bridge." Other canonical writers who influence Vogel include David Mamet (in *The Oldest Profession* and possibly *How I Learned to Drive*), Nabokov (in *Drive*), Thornton Wilder (in *The Long Christmas Ride Home* and *Indecent*), and of course Sholem Asch, who not only influences but appears in *Indecent*.

Although important to Vogel, neither Shakespeare, Albee, Mamet, nor any other writer has risen to the level of being deemed among Vogel's "gods" alongside Guare, Fornés, and Churchill, two of whom Savran has recorded Vogel appreciating back in the 1970s. Vogel does not employ either of her gods in the same way that she does Shakespeare and the other mere mortals she has acknowledged. Their influences upon her exist in their being older contemporaries and in analogues that we may see in her plays.

Vogel's "Gods": John Guare

Among Vogel's "gods," John Guare has enjoyed the greatest commercial success. Indeed, although the one acts "Cop-Out" and "Home Fires" ran at the Cort Theatre (where Vogel made her Broadway debut in 2017) for less than one week in April 1969, Guare was on Broadway every decade between the 1960s and the 2010s. The book and lyrics that producer Joseph Papp commissioned Guare to write for a production of Shakespeare's *Two Gentlemen of Verona*, which ran at the St. James Theatre for 614 performances between 1971 and 1973, garnered Guare a Tony Award and two Drama Desk Awards as well as "allowing him to pursue his playwriting in the enviable position as an experimental writer with a degree of mainstream acceptance" (Urban 60).

Born in New York in 1938 and brought up in the Queens borough, Guare wrote in the "Foreword" of *The House of Blue Leaves*, "I never wanted to be any place in my life but New York" (vii). Two plays generally acknowledged among Guare's finest, the aforementioned *The House of Blue Leaves* (1971) and *Six Degrees of Separation* (1990), take place entirely in New York City although in different boroughs (Queens and Manhattan, respectively) and among different milieus (the working class and what the Occupy Wall Street movement of 2011 would call the one percent).

The House of Blue Leaves, Guare's first full-length play, is a semi-autobiographical work that incorporates a historical event, Pope Paul VI's visit to New York, which took him through Queens. When Guare, who was in Cairo, Egypt, at the time, received a postcard from his parents, detailing "the wonderful experience of a lifetime they had seeing the Pope on Queens Boulevard" (Plunka 70), "Guare began writing the play that day" (70). While Guare's work on *Two Gentlemen of Verona* established him commercially, *The House of Blue Leaves* signified he had become a significant Off-Broadway playwright as well, for it ran for 337 performances at the Truck and Warehouse Theatre and won both an Obie Award and the New York Drama Critics' Award for Best American Play. Revived Off-Broadway in 1986, the play moved to Broadway's Vivian Beaumont Theater and later to the Plymouth Theatre. This production won multiple Tony Awards, including laurels for Jerry Zaks (director), John Mahoney (actor), and Swoozie Kurtz (actress), as well as the Drama Desk Award for Outstanding Revival. A second revival, in 2011, ran at the Walter Kerr Theatre and was nominated for one Tony Award (Edie Falco, actress).

What Gene A. Plunka calls the "finest theatrical achievement" (186) of Guare's career, *Six Degrees of Separation* achieved two distinctions that have eluded Vogel and her other "gods": it was adapted into a successful film, and it introduced an expression (adapted from the 1929 Frigyes Karinthy short story "Chains" or "Chain-Links") into the common lexicon. In the Karinthy story, the narrator states that technology is causing the world to become smaller. He then goes on:

> One of us suggested performing the following experiment to prove that the population of the Earth is closer together now than they have ever been before. We should select any person from the 1.5 billion inhabitants of the Earth—anyone, anywhere at all. He bet us that, using no more than *five* individuals, one of whom is a personal acquaintance, he could contact the selected individual using nothing except the network of personal acquaintances. For example, "Look, you know Mr. X. Y., please ask him to contact his friend Mr. Q. Z., and so forth."

Early Life and Influences

The discussion then demonstrates how one of the characters could contact either Nobel Literature laureate Selma Lagerlof or an anonymous employee of the Ford Motor Company in between two and four steps. Guare's increasing the number of steps to six for the title of his play has made the "Six Degrees of Separation" a common expression, even one that has evolved into a parlor game involving actor Kevin Bacon and a charitable organization that Bacon, after initial reluctance about the link between him and the "six degrees" concept, supports.

Like *The House of Blue Leaves*, *Six Degrees of Separation* draws upon a historical event, albeit one arguably less significant than a papal visit. During the 1980s, hustler David Hampton, whom Morgan Falconer has described as "an ingenious conman . . ., in his early twenties, began inveigling his way into the homes of wealthy white New Yorkers, including Melanie Griffith and Calvin Klein, often by saying that he was a friend once removed . . . and claiming that he was the son of the actor Sidney Poitier" (Falconer 4). Falconer adds, "At least a dozen people let [Hampton] stay or gave him money" (4). Hampton served as the model for Guare's character Paul, the catalyst of *Six Degrees*.

On May 16, 1990, *Six Degrees of Separation* premiered at Lincoln Center in what Urban calls "a rarity in the American theatre" (68), a production "without any readings or workshops" (68). The production, which (like the 1986 revival of *The House of Blue Leaves*) was directed by Jerry Zaks and which featured Stockard Channing[1] (Bunny in the 1986 *Blue Leaves*), was a huge success. It transferred to Broadway and the Vivian Beaumont Theater, eventually running for 485 performances. Both Guare and Channing won Obie Awards, and the Broadway production won the Best Director Tony Award for Zaks. Guare was a Pulitzer Prize finalist, and he won the Olivier Award after the play began a 1991 run in London. It has been revived many times, including a 2010 revival in London and a 2017 limited run at Broadway's Ethel Barrymore Theatre.

When Guare adapted the screenplay for the 1993 film, both he and director Fred Schepisi strove to maintain the play's "like the wind" feel and its sense of mocking posh New York sensibilities. Schepisi faced a challenge "to make a film that would be as emotionally rousing as the play while maintaining its poignancy" (Plunka 188). The filmmakers retained Stockard Channing as Ouisa, giving Channing a major film role that would countermand her 1978 *Grease* "bad girl" Rizzo persona. Donald Sutherland was added as Flan, Ian McKellen as Geoffrey, and future Academy Award winner Will Smith as Paul.[2]

The film version of *Six Degrees of Separation* seems important for two different reasons. First, it has had a great influence on John Guare's reputation. Turina writes, "The film contributed noticeably to widening the reception and the impact of Guare's seminal work and to strengthen [sic] its status as the playwright's major theatrical achievement" (57). The film has also effected a phenomenon of putting the concept of Six Degrees into the mainstream of American consciousness.

Writing in 1988, Vogel's friend David Savran acknowledged the "exhilaration" of seeing Guare's 1974 *Gardenia* with Vogel (*Words* xiii). Then, after winning the 1998 Pulitzer Prize, Vogel told interviewer Simi Horwitz, "In my mind I talk to John Guare every day and bless him for never writing the same play twice, for his stylistic leaps and bounds, and fearlessness." These examples illustrate how Guare gained his place among Vogel's "gods," and they also set a theme that recurs with María Irene Fornés and Caryl Churchill. One common characteristic of Vogel's "gods" is that each of them has been praised for having a broad range and, rather than relying on familiar and comfortable themes and tropes, for creating a unique work with each drama. Finally, at least one critical survey of contemporary American drama, while not commenting upon Guare as a Vogel "god," nevertheless acknowledges a close relationship between the plays of the two. Krasner writes, "Whereas Guare is interested in connections between people, Vogel is concerned with connecting past and present" (151).

Writing in 2006, Krasner could not have been expected to anticipate the extent Guare would plumb the past in the 2010 play *A Free Man of Color*, which premiered at the Beaumont when the playwright was seventy-two. *A Free Man of Color* explores early 1800s New Orleans and Haiti and features a cast of characters as diverse as Jacques Cornet, the character referenced in the title, as well as Thomas Jefferson and Napoleon Bonaparte. The play was a finalist for the 2011 Pulitzer, which went to Bruce Norris for *Clybourne Park*. Here, Guare both reflects Vogel's interest in history and sets an example of late-career success that could well inspire Vogel, who turned seventy in November 2021.

For at least one day in 2016, Guare may have had a specific occasion to thank Vogel. Writer Stuart Emmrich tweeted on May 21 about spotting "celebrity" John Guare picking up tickets for *Indecent* at the Vineyard Theatre box office. "That's G-U-A-R-E," the playwright explained to the woman at the window, who "didn't blink an eye" (Emmrich). To Vogel, Guare has been a god; to this anonymous theatre employee, he remained just another customer.

Vogel's "Gods": María Irene Fornés

Among Paula Vogel's "gods," Cuban-American María Irene Fornés is the only non-native English speaker. Fornés never acquired native fluency, telling interviewer David Savran in the 1980s, "My vocabulary in English is very limited. When I read a newspaper or magazine article I'm constantly finding words that I don't know" (63). The possibility, however, that as a writer Fornés thought in Spanish and then translated into English before putting her words on the page has not diminished what Diane Lynn Moroff identifies as the "lyricism" in Fornés's dramas, especially her best-known play, *Fefu and Her Friends* (33).

Fornés was born in Havana on May 14, 1930, to a family that Scott T. Cummings reports "was poor and moved often" (5). Despite their poverty, Fornés and her five older siblings "knew that their family was somehow different" (6) and reflected what Cummings calls "Bohemian roots" (5). The dyslexic child of two avid readers, Fornés "never became much of a reader herself" (6), learning instead "by osmosis" (7). The death of Fornés's father precipitated her family's emigration to New York, where Fornés, who "spoke little English when she arrived in the USA" (Cummings 7), gradually insinuated herself into the Bohemian life of Greenwich Village, where Hilton Als reports she quickly became a "femme fatale" ("Feminist"). Fornés became a US citizen in 1951 and eventually resided in the same apartment for forty years. She always had, according to Als, "her voice, which was inherently feminist and instructive without being self-serious" ("Feminist").

Before settling in on 16th Street and becoming part of what Catherine A. Shuler calls "the alternative, experimental theater of the 1960s and 70s" (218), however, Fornés lived from 1954 until 1957 in Europe. There, her major artistic interest lay in painting. During this time, Fornés experienced a Joycean epiphany in a theatre when she attended the premier of Samuel Beckett's *Waiting for Godot*. Although Fornés spoke no French and had never read *Waiting for Godot* in any language, the experience moved her powerfully. Her epiphany then took a literal Joycean turn in 1958, when she saw Zero Mostel in *Ulysses in Nighttown*, an experience she recounted decades later to multiple interviewers. Both experiences set her to thinking about drama.

Fornés did not write her first play until 1960, when she used letters written by her great-grandfather to craft a Spanish-language play *La viuda* (*The Widow*), which she entered in a playwriting contest sponsored by

Fidel Castro. Since nothing further came of the play and since Fornés never translated it into English, Cummings deems it "more a precursor than a first play" (10). Plays such as *There! You Died!* soon followed, however, and by the time Off-Off Broadway was recognized as an actual entity, Fornés was prepared to join it. By 1966, Fornés became the first Off-Off Broadway playwright on Broadway, when Jerome Robbins, best known for *Fiddler on the Roof*, was hired by The Establishment Theatre Company to bring *The Office* to Henry Miller's Theatre. The play, despite a cast that included Elaine May, Jack Weston, and Doris Roberts, ran for only ten previews before the producers canceled the show, which never officially opened. Those previews were the closest Fornés would ever come to Broadway success, and she never revised or developed *The Office* further.

Decades later, John Guare hinted at the sting this near brush with commercial success may have brought Fornés, for in 1999–2000, Fornés "became the ninth contemporary American playwright to be celebrated by New York's Signature Theatre with a full season devoted solely to her work" (Cummings "María Irene Fornés" 33). During the season, Fornés participated in a roundtable interview with fellow honorees Arthur Miller, Edward Albee, Horton Foote, and John Guare. As Cummings writes, "With unmentioned irony, Guare later referred to Fornés's 'very, very bad experience in the commercial world'—34 years earlier!—when Jerome Robbins 'pulled the plug' on *The Office* days before it was to open on Broadway" (155).

What might have been a crushing experience helped drive Fornés, instead, to pursue alternative avenues for producing her and other Off-Off Broadway playwrights' works. In 1975 she became centrally involved in INTAR (International Arts Relation). Fornés created and directed works for INTAR, and she also brought new talent into the group. Perhaps most notably, Fornés recruited fledgling playwright Nilo Cruz to INTAR and subsequently introduced him to Paula Vogel. Hilton Als almost certainly had INTAR in mind when he wrote that Fornés "had an equally influential career as a professor" ("Feminist"), a role in which she both models for and anticipates acolyte Vogel.

In 1977, after what Assunta Bartolomucci Kent calls an "inordinately long (thirteen-year) gestation period" (120), Fornés produced what remains her most famous play, *Fefu and Her Friends*. Fornés "forced herself to finish the play by slating it for production at Theater Strategy" (Kent 121), indicating a difficulty working with the subject matter that required Fornés to "set up an atmosphere that discouraged distraction and elicited more focused images

Early Life and Influences

and dialogue" (121). This atmosphere included "listening to recordings of the passionate Cuban singer, Olga Guillot" (121).

Completing the script of *Fefu and Her Friends* may have indicated that Fornés had finished the play, but the exigencies of Off-Off Broadway staging required additional creative work on the part of the playwright. In the highly experimental and innovative Part Two of *Fefu*, the directions state, "The audience is divided into four groups. Each group is led to the spaces. These scenes are performed simultaneously." As Annette Saddik explains, this staging came about directly because of "the play's first production [occurring] in a Soho loft space in downtown New York" (168). Here, the playwright illustrated on a very large scale how, as Cummings writes, "her fondness for found objects became a decisive element in her playmaking" (6). This anecdote relates the unique needs a playwright who writes for small theatres and audiences faces in bringing a creative vision to life. It also explains why Saddik does not hesitate to find something of the avant-garde in Fornés's dramaturgy.

Fornés remained a productive playwright through The Signature Theatre Company's 1999–2000 dedication of its season to her, for which she produced her last play, *Letters from Cuba*. Soon after, dementia took away her creative capabilities and forced her to leave her beloved Sheridan Square apartment. By this time, however, Fornés's reputation as one of her era's foremost playwrights was well established, as was her acknowledged impact upon Vogel's work. To *Conducting a Life: Reflections on the Theatre of Maria Irene Fornés*, a sort of festschrift as Fornés's seventieth birthday approached, Caryl Churchill, the third and final Vogel god, contributed "A Poem for Irene Fornés." In this brief poem, Churchill recalled being inspired by Fornés and also a brief meeting with the older playwright's centenarian mother before concluding simply, "Thank you for both those" (xiv).[3]

Vogel's "Gods": Caryl Churchill

Among the three playwrights Vogel has listed as her "gods," Caryl Churchill is the only non-American as well as the only one upon whom Vogel, in her interview with Farnsworth, bestowed the appellation "divine" (Vogel "A Prize-Winning"). Born in London, England, on September 3, 1938, Churchill was a small child during the Second World War and the final dissolution of the British Empire. After her family emigrated to Montreal, Canada, when Churchill was ten, she returned to England for her university education and has remained there. Best known early on for a series of BBC radio plays from the 1960s, when her sons were born, Churchill began "working with companies" such as Joint Stock and Monstrous Regiment in 1976 (Aston xi) and has written more than thirty plays since.

Churchill is best known for *Cloud Nine* (or *Cloud 9*), her 1979 drama that moved to New York and won the Obie Award in 1982, and *Top Girls*, her 1982 play that won the Obie the following year. As the 1982 Obie indicates, *Cloud Nine* offered what Amelia Kritzer has called Churchill's "first experience of solid (though certainly not unanimous) critical acclaim" (112). The success of *Cloud Nine* most likely made theatre companies and producers receptive to another Churchill script in *Top Girls*; Elaine Aston and Elin Diamond warn, however, against in any way regarding the second play as a sequel to the first. They write, "Both from a critic's perspective and from a performer's point of view, seeing or being involved in one Churchill play is not a way of being prepared for the next" (13). Echoing what Vogel has said about Guare never writing the same play twice, they cite a David Benedict comment during a *Theatre Voice* discussion that "with Churchill 'there are no repeats'" (13).

Now in her eighties, Caryl Churchill enjoys one of the finest reputations of any living playwright, not only in the eyes of Paula Vogel but also in those of many of her peers. In 1998, Caroline Egan interviewed nine writers for *The Guardian*, asking whom each considered the "playwright's playwright." Four (Mark Ravenhill, Martin Crimp, Shelagh Stevenson, and Phyllis Nagy) selected Churchill (Egan TO13). A similar 2011 survey of twenty dramatists for *The Village Voice* found that, once again, a plurality of four playwrights (Vogel, Adam Bock, Julia Cho, and Sheila Callaghan) chose Churchill (Soloski "Who Is"). The term "playwright's playwright" will resonate later in Joanna Mansbridge's assessment of Vogel.

This esteem for Churchill has also translated into action. Dan Rebellato reports that the Royal Court Theatre "held not one but two seasons of her work in the 2000s" (163). Both 2002 and, "to mark her seventieth birthday" (163), 2008 were so devoted, with 2008 featuring "ten playwrights [who] directed staged readings of ten of her plays" (163). Also in 2008, Mary Catherine Garrison, Mary Beth Hurt, Elizabeth Marvel, Martha Plimpton, Marisa Tomei, Jennifer Ikeda, and Ana Reeder gave sixty-three performances of *Top Girls* at Broadway's Biltmore Theatre. *New York Times* critic Ben Brantley gushed that director James Macdonald and the performers had "done full justice" to Churchill's text. Brantley went on, "And it's a delight to see how each settles so comfortably into different complex roles without signaling how clever she is" ("Ladies"). Churchill remains the essential writer Brantley called, in a 2015 review of *Cloud Nine*, "one of the wisest and bravest playwrights on the planet" ("Review" *Cloud Nine* C1).

Vogel's choices of "gods" give a sense of the dramatic principles and techniques she has followed throughout her long career, whether she has been adapting Shakespeare, Albee, Ambrose Bierce, Nabokov, or Sholem Asch. Defamiliarization and negative empathy are among the identifying markers for most Vogel plays, as a look at *Desdemona: A Play about a Handkerchief*, *The Oldest Profession*, and *And Baby Makes Seven* will show.

CHAPTER 2
DEVELOPING A UNIQUE VOICE

A close observer of American theatre in the late 1970s may plausibly have concluded that Paula Vogel was a potential up-and-coming important playwright. Vogel had twice won the Forbes Heermans and George McCalmon playwriting competition at Cornell University, the second award coming for *A Woman for All Reasons*, "a feminist take on Robert Bolt's *A Man for All Seasons*" (Warner). Vogel then revised this play into *Meg*, which won the American College Theater Festival's National Student Playwriting Award in 1977 and was published the same year by Samuel French. Vogel had already finished *Desdemona: A Play about a Handkerchief*, which received a staged reading at Cornell in 1977, if not more.[1] Other plays were under development as well.

A decade later, that same observer may have regarded Vogel as a playwright whose early promise had come to very little. Vogel held a prestigious faculty position at Brown University and was both friend and confidant to rising critic David Savran. Her plays, however, were rarely performed, and when they were, they played at such places as San Francisco's Theatre Rhinoceros and Edmonton, Canada's, Theatre Network. Vogel had not managed to publish any additional plays. The number of people who had read or seen a Paula Vogel play remained, of necessity, tiny.

This is not to say that Vogel was not writing important plays during this time. Three of the plays she wrote in the 1970s and 1980s—the aforementioned *Desdemona*, *The Oldest Profession* (1980), and *And Baby Makes Seven* (1984)—would eventually run Off-Broadway and make their way into print. Not until the success of Obie Award-winner *The Baltimore Waltz* (1992), however, would Vogel's plays from these decades begin to attract significant reading and viewing audiences. It comes as no surprise, then, that C. W. E. Bigsby would point to Vogel's earliest success as "something of a false start" that required "another fourteen years before a successful revival" (*Modern* 412). Vogel lived for years with the sting that followed her 1980 experience when, Bigsby adds, "she sent her play *The Oldest Profession* to theatres across the country only to have them reject it" (411).

Why Vogel languished for so long and how she persevered as a productive, if only marginally known, playwright warrant consideration. In *Desdemona*, for instance, shifting the focus from Shakespeare's Othello to Desdemona, whom Othello strangles, and giving her sexual agency would appear, at first glance, well suited for 1970s feminism. Even though Vogel has long considered herself a feminist and, in the 1970s, started a dissertation "[a]nimated by the emerging discourse of feminist dramatic criticism that she was helping forge" (Warner), feminist theatrical groups avoided *Desdemona*, just as they later would *The Oldest Profession* and *And Baby Makes Seven*.

One reason Vogel attracted so little attention early on lies in her tendency to create something rarely seen in feminist theatre of the time, namely what Joanna Mansbridge calls "female characters behaving badly" (33). Vogel, Savran adds, "reacted strongly against the first wave of feminist theatre that surfaced during the 1970s, the 'let's celebrate-ourselves-as women' brand of feminism that [Vogel] regards not just as simplistic and ahistorical but also as exclusionary because certain kinds of women (depending on their class or racial or occupational position) inevitably get left out of the celebration" ("Loose Screws" xii). Writing in 1996, Savran posited that for Vogel, "feminism means being politically incorrect" (xii), even in plays Vogel wrote several years before the term "political correctness" entered the lexicon.

Bigsby states that Vogel experienced "marginality, not least because she was not only a woman but an avowed lesbian" (*Modern* 411). Gay playwrights, up until then, Bigsby argues, "had been men and their protagonists, largely, likewise" (411). Bigsby points out that gay male playwrights "could lay claim to a tradition that went back . . . through Tennessee Williams, Albee, Lorca and Oscar Wilde" (412). Vogel, stylistically "drawn to the expressionists and the absurdists" (412), could offer "an equivalent to Virginia Woolf's stream of consciousness" (412), hardly a basis for building a dramatic career, but, Bigsby implies by omission, to few or no playwrights.[2] Vogel's response to her lack of success did not include compromising her artistic vision, but it did lead her "to develop works which required little in the way of resources" (411). Very low budgetary requirements might have increased producers' willingness to stage Vogel; alas, however, either they did not, or they did so only slightly.

Vogel's artistic vision derives from influences that are not only particular but also unusual. According to Savran, Vogel has read from Brecht and, like

Brecht, "writes from a deeply rooted political sense" ("Loose Screws" xi). "[E]ven more significantly," Savran writes, Vogel reflects the influence "of Viktor Shklovsky, the Russian Formalist from whom Brecht purloined the Alienation Effect" (xi). What Savran calls the "Alienation Effect" Vogel and most other readers of Shklovsky derive from Shklovsky's "defamiliarization," sometimes rendered as *ostranenie*. In the simplest of terms, defamiliarization means making the familiar strange. Shklovsky writes that "life becomes nothing and disappears. Automation eats up things, clothes, furniture, your wife and the fear of war." He goes on,

> And so what we call art exists in order to give back the sensation of life, in order to make us feel things, in order to make the stone stony. The goal of art is to create the sensation of seeing, and not merely recognizing, things. The device of art is the "*ostranenie*" of things and the complication of the form which increases the duration and complexity of perception, as the process of perception is its own end in art and must be prolonged. Art is the means to live through the making of a thing; what has been made does not matter in art. (80)

The artist, according to Shklovsky, should seek to make the familiar strange, and so if defamiliarization does not explicitly make the "object" (whether person, place, thing, or even idea) new, it at minimum requires a new look at the object, thereby paralleling if not following Ezra Pound's modernist dictum, "Make it new."

In addition to defamiliarization, Vogel also uses negative empathy because she believes, as she said at the 2012 Comparative Drama Conference, "The purpose of drama is to make us project ourselves into everything that we fear and everything that we resist and everything that we are revolted by" ("Paula Vogel on Negative Empathy"). Negative empathy forces us to develop empathy for people we would ordinarily expect to despise. For example, a reader may feel empathy for Humbert Humbert in Vladimir Nabokov's *Lolita*, a novel which Bigsby cites as an influence upon Desdemona (412) and which also partly inspired Vogel's *How I Learned to Drive*. Such a feeling exemplifies negative empathy, as do any positive feelings we project upon child molester Uncle Peck, a character in *Drive*.

While negative empathy constitutes a powerful tool, it has also long been a tough sell to popular theatre. In her Comparative Drama Conference remarks, Vogel continued, "What we are experiencing in the commercial theatre are models of dramaturgy that have been a purgation of negative empathy," for popular theatre today is "based on only positive empathy." Producers and playwrights, Vogel argues, exclusively ask themselves, "Do I like this character?" rather than a question Vogel frequently poses herself of whether she can make her audience, at least to some degree, like an unlikeable character ("Paula Vogel on Negative Empathy"). It is arguably not simplistic to say that the theatres Vogel approached in the 1970s and 1980s, concerned with fundraising and board members, among other matters, did not want—or dare—to find out. The same is true of many venues, none more than Broadway, today.[3]

As noted earlier, *Desdemona: A Play about a Handkerchief*, although ignored for more than a decade, eventually earned its due as an important early Vogel play. *Desdemona*, Vogel's earlier play *Meg*, and her unfinished dissertation on Restoration Drama (as well as her comment on Aphra Behn) indicate that in her twenties, Vogel was highly interested in Renaissance and Restoration England. In later published plays and in her interviews, Vogel frequently alludes to or directly mentions plays of these periods, but she has not offered a subsequent drama set in those times. She has, however, built upon the use of defamiliarization evident in *Desdemona* throughout her long career.

Desdemona defamiliarizes Shakespeare's *Othello* in a variety of ways, most obviously in its setting and its concomitant focus. Vogel moves the action backstage and limits all of her characters to Shakespeare's women: Desdemona, Emilia, and Bianca. At the end of Scene Five, the directions state that "we hear the distinct sound of a very loud slap" (186), a blow Shakespeare's Othello strikes in Act Four Scene One. What Mansbridge calls "Shakespeare's closed moral universe" (42) comes from offstage. Othello, however, does not directly obtrude upon *Desdemona* beyond the slap. We know and the characters discuss but we do not directly see or hear any other action from the masculine realm Shakespeare presents.

Like the backstage setting, Vogel's title significantly defamiliarizes Shakespeare. The First Folio title of Shakespeare's play, published in 1623 by the late playwright's former colleagues John Heminge and Henry Condell, is *The Tragedie of Othello, the Moore of Venice*. This title, which repeats all the keywords from the quarto version published by Thomas Walkley in 1622, leaves little to no doubt as to the tragic figure of the play. Vogel found this emphasis troubling. She has told C. W. E. Bigsby that:

in the 1970s, when I had read *Othello*, I was struck by the fact that my main point of identification, of subjectivity, was a man who is supposedly cuckolded, that I was weeping for a man who is cuckolded rather than for Desdemona . . . and it wounded me a great deal that Desdemona is nothing but an abstraction and that I didn't find any way of identifying with her. (*Contemporary* 299–300)

It is both tempting and facile to say that as the title figure, Desdemona is the protagonist of Vogel's play that bears her name. While trying to make Desdemona a "real" character rather than an abstraction, Vogel nevertheless toys with the notion of a protagonist in *Desdemona: A Play about a Handkerchief*. Indeed, Vogel says that the play literally is *about* the handkerchief of both Shakespeare's and her play, which Desdemona demeans as a "crappy little snot rag" (179). Referring to Tom Stoppard's 1966 *Rosencrantz and Guildenstern Are Dead*, Vogel told Bigsby that she found the play regressive because of its "reinforcement, through the Chain of Being motif, of a class structure." She added, "By foregrounding secondary characters, it was actually saying that there *are* protagonists" (300). Then, one of Vogel's "gods" intervened, for "along came Harold Pinter's *Old Times* and Maria Irene Fornés's *Fefu and Her Friends* and that made me question the whole idea of protagonists" (300). Wishing to provide a counterpoint to Stoppard, Vogel created *Desdemona*.

Mansbridge asserts that the subtitle of *Desdemona* indicates "over determination" (43) of the handkerchief. It also brings theft into the play. Indeed, Emilia and Bianca steal or accuse others of stealing. Then, too, as Joanna Mansbridge notes, "Vogel steals Shakespeare's play" (43). In stealing Desdemona from Shakespeare, Vogel lets her audience decide whether to weep for a woman murdered by her husband even while she defamiliarizes Desdemona away from the chaste wife Shakespeare presents. As Mansbridge notes, Vogel dares to ask several questions, including the possible veracity of Iago's claim about Desdemona's infidelity. Mansbridge wonders how that would affect the way we respond. How would we feel about Othello killing Desdemona? Why, moreover, are our tears for him, not her (33)?

Vogel makes Desdemona unfaithful, but her infidelity comes with a defamiliarized twist: she is innocent of any sexual contact with Cassio. Desdemona protests "and of all people to accuse—Michael Cassio!" (183) not as a declaration of virtue but rather as a dismissal of her husband's lieutenant, whom she calls a "prissy Florentine," snorting, "Leave it to a cuckold to be jealous of a eunuch" (183). We are left with no doubts about the extent of the cuckoldry. In addition to what Emilia calls "giving hand jobs in the pew" (192), Desdemona has gone so far as to work in Bianca's "establishment . . . on sheets that are stained and torn by countless nights" (194). Desdemona, thus, literally works as a whore, giving her a sexuality far beyond anything her husband suspects.

Not only does Vogel defamiliarize Desdemona as possessing sexual agency beyond the "once each Saturday night" (195) that Emilia describes with Iago, but Vogel goes a step farther in defamiliarizing the nature of sex work. Rather than making Desdemona a passive receptacle of the sweat and semen of those who purchase time with her body, Vogel presents a Desdemona whose relationship with these men is almost predatory. "I lie in the blackness," she says, where "they spill their seed into me, Emilia—seed from a thousand lands, passed down through generations of ancestors, with genealogies that cover the surface of the globe" (194). Desdemona describes herself as "*taking* them all into me" (emphasis mine), adding, "[O]h, how I travel!" (194). Desdemona's initial attraction to Othello turns out to have been sexual and a means of expressing her acquisitive desires. She recalls "the first time I saw my husband and I caught a glimpse of his skin, and oh, how I thrilled" (193). Desdemona has imagined "a man of a different color" as if he were from "another world and planet," a means by which she has once thought that "I can escape and see other worlds" (194). Then, alas, she recalls that "under that exotic façade was a porcelain Venetian" (194).

Desdemona's sexual agency is problematized by issues of class and race. This and other Vogel plays build, Mansbridge notes, "feminist claims to authority," but they also make us note "the intersection of gender, sexuality, and class" (27). Desdemona may choose to play the bawd on an occasional evening, but Bianca implicitly calls our attention to the stratifications of Venetian society that differentiate her from other sex workers. Bianca tells Desdemona that "if you weren't born a lady, you'd a been a bleedin' good blowzabella" (212). Desdemona was born and will die a lady, however. Bianca aspires to what, for a moment now and then, Desdemona casually tosses away, for Bianca dreams that Cassio will marry her and liberate her from Venice and her brothel. "Aw've got a tidy sum all saved up fer a dowry" (214), she tells Emilia and Desdemona, and she fantasizes how, as Cassio's wife, "Aw'd get us a cottage by th' sea," and "Aw'd be bearin 'im sons so's to make 'im proud" (214). Likewise, Emilia shares comments about "the curse of aristocratic blood" (190) even as she acknowledges, "I'd like to rise a bit in the world" and longs for the day Iago can "make me a lieutenant's widow" (187).

Race is problematized by comments such as Desdemona's already referenced "porcelain Venetian" remark and also by jokes about sexual potency and phallic endowment at Iago's expense and, ostensibly, Othello's "credit." We learn, by comparison, that "The wee-est pup of th-litter comes a-bornin' in the world with as much" (182) as Iago, who very likely has patronized Desdemona. When asked for details about her customers, Desdemona says, "There was one man who . . . didn't last very long" (219), to which Emilia replies, "Aye. That's the one" (219). Indeed, Emilia describes her own sexual experiences with Iago by recalling, "He'd be all through with me by the time of the third 'Hail Mary'" (220).

A hoof-pick Desdemona finds sets up more racist and phallic comments. Desdemona proclaims that "if I could find a man with just such a hoof-pick—he could pluck out my stone" (181). Mansbridge considers the hoof-pick "metonymic representation" for *Othello*, masculine where the handkerchief is feminine. Desdemona whispers to Bianca that Othello is "constantly tearing his crotch hole somehow" (205). This comment refers to Othello's libido, his endowment, and possibly even implied homosexual activity. Then, in Scene Nineteen, which contains no dialogue, at Emilia's expense, "*Desdemona holds up the hoof-pick, and Bianca and Desdemona explode in raucous laughter*" leaving Emilia "*furious*" (206). Desdemona, who derides Emilia so much as to call her "a *vessel* of vinegar" (203, emphasis mine) after Iago's "spilling his vinegar into her for fourteen years of marriage, until he's corroded her womb from the inside out" (203), dismissively tells this wife of a poorly endowed man lacking stamina, "Oh, hush, Mealy—just mend your crotches, and don't listen" (209). One woman is demeaned because of her white husband's lack of sexual prowess, while the other relies on a racist trope as she takes her Black husband's potency for granted, pining instead for Lodovico, of whom she boasts, "[T]hat was a lover!" (191).

Desdemona finally defamiliarizes Shakespeare's play through its negation of two of the play's most famous lines, "Put out the light, and then put out the light" (5.1.7) and "Of one that loved not wisely but too well" (5.1.361). Vogel specifies that *Desdemona*, which "was written in thirty cinematic 'takes'" (176), should be performed in "jump cuts," with "no blackouts between scenes" (176). Mansbridge reports that the 1993 Circle Repertory production used flashes of bulbs and frozen tableaux (37), to offer simultaneously—"a museum diorama"—and "a film still" (38). The lack of blackouts negates Shakespeare's "Put out the light."

Near the end, Desdemona poignantly defamiliarizes, through negation, "one who loved not wisely but too well." Realizing, the directions state, that "*Othello's been smelling the sheets for traces of a lover*," she wails, "That isn't love. It isn't love" (223). Desdemona's ensuing comment, "Surely he'll not

... harm a sleeping woman" then rings hollow not just because we know her canonical end but also because she subconsciously realizes the lengths to which her jealous husband is being driven. Emilia brushes Desdemona's hair, preparing her for what we know will be her death scene, giving exactly "ninety-nine" (224) strokes before the play ends one stroke away from impending death. When Vogel finally gives the stage direction "*Blackout*" (224), we realize the sad finality of the moment. Vogel's powerful use of "put out the light" and "that loved not wisely" from *Othello* is all the more remarkable given that she told a 2012 audience that she "didn't re-read it on purpose" (Herren 12) while writing *Desdemona*.

Desdemona did not attract attention outside Ithaca, New York, and possibly Louisville, Kentucky, until the success of *The Baltimore Waltz* helped prompt New York's Circle Repertory Company 1993 production. Mixed reviews lauded Vogel's "extended bit of intellectual vaudeville" that offered "a certain shocked gratification" (Brantley "Iago's Subterfuge") and saw a "biting diversion" (Gerard) in its premises. For Ben Brantley, however, "the novelty of the joke wears thin," while Jeremy Gerard deemed the entire play "woefully underwritten." Both critics compared *Desdemona* unfavorably with Stoppard's *Rosencrantz and Guildenstern Are Dead*.[4] Comments on the actors were kinder, especially for Cherry Jones. Brantley wrote that she "finds a moving, wounded quality in Bianca that transcends the lines she has been given to speak."

The passage of two decades and the emergence of new critics would see *Desdemona* receive more favorable reviews. Keith Glab opened his review of a 2013 production at Chicago's Sea Change Theatre with a neutral comparison between the play and Stoppard's. After a cautionary note about "bastardizing a Shakespearean masterpiece," he concluded by saying the production "lands enough interesting moments in this ambitious undertaking to make the show worth a view." One year later, Camilla Gurtler, in reviewing a Park Theatre production in London, gushed. She called the play "a hilarious and incredibly imaginative other side to the lives of the women." She considered the production "incredibly funny and touching, and a female tour-de-force." It offered, Gurtler concluded, some "secret voices of Shakespeare's women." Perhaps more importantly, although Desdemona is neither as original nor as unique as Vogel's work would soon become, it offers what Mansbridge has called a drama in which "we can hear Vogel defining her own authorial voice" (47).

In *The Oldest Profession*, that voice has addressed topics closer to home and has matured, even though Vogel had not yet turned thirty. As in *Desdemona*, *The Oldest Profession* engages in dialogue with an existing text, but this time the author is American David Mamet and the text contemporary, *Duck Variations*. *Duck Variations* (1972) has only two characters, a pair of elderly men who tell stories about ducks that are, in reality, meditations on their fear of aging and dying. In *The Oldest Profession*, Vogel expands the cast to five women in their seventies and eighties who are "*sitting in the sun*" on a "*long bench on 72nd Street and Broadway, New York City*" (emphasis in original) (131). The play is set "shortly after the election of Ronald Reagan in 1980" (130). During a series of blackouts, the cast is reduced by one character at a time until, just before the final blackout, the sole remaining character sits "*plaintively quiet, at times watching the traffic*" from "*the middle of the bench*." She looks "*very frail, and a bit frightened*" during "*a slow fade-out*" (172).

The play is not so much about death, however, as it is about the memories the women cherish and the present they inhabit. They differ from almost any such group of five women presented onstage in that they are all geriatric practitioners of what is euphemistically called "the oldest profession," sex work. The word "oldest" in the play's title cleverly puns off this euphemism and the fact that an audience is probably not prepared for five working prostitutes of these ages. Seeing women who toil at what feminism generally regards as work demeaning to women also contrasts with the "sunny day" (130) on which the play commences. Although "morning in America" will not become President Reagan's campaign slogan for another four years, this play makes clear that the prosperity alluded to in the slogan has not taken these five women off the street.

In *The Oldest Profession*, Vogel defamiliarizes Mamet's work by making the characters women and increasing their number. However, this defamiliarization has little to no effect on an audience that is far less likely to be familiar with *Duck Variations* than with *Othello*. Vogel's more difficult task lies in defamiliarizing older women and sex work: society does not normally associate older women with prostitution nor prostitution with the elderly. Indeed, viewing senior citizens in any context involving sexuality was problematic in 1980 and, despite various productions and publications addressing the subject, may remain so today. Mansbridge notes here a "double defamiliarization" (94). As she points out, most people view elderly women as sexless, yet Vogel's characters are sexually vigorous. Moreover, Vogel transforms prostitution from an act of sex and disease into one of nurture, even love. As troubling as sexually active women may have been when *The Oldest Profession* was written, the play also addresses and defamiliarizes another subject that may be even more problematical. Ronald Reagan was and is associated with the robust presentation of capitalism, but a valid question is whether the women in *The Oldest Profession* are engaging in capitalist activity or the survival sex more generally associated with at-risk teens who are often LGBT runaways.

Understanding *The Oldest Profession* requires balancing the political and economic issues the play raises with the individual personalities of the women involved. Bigsby defines them not by their means of income but rather, like Mamet's two old men, by stories. "Like Mamet's characters they, too, are storytellers," Bigsby writes. "Their meaning lies in part in their stories, as in their sense of social utility and shared circumstances" (*Modern* 412). Deaths silence these storytellers until "the play ends with a Beckett-like moment of silent stasis" (412).

We must ask ourselves what to make of these individual women and the stories they tell. For Vogel, the individual women and their stories are extremely important. As she has told Bigsby, "I named the youngest prostitute after my grandmother," who "suffered a heart attack that fall before I wrote [the play] and she was the youngest of five." Vogel adds, "All of the prostitutes are based on *stories and characters* of my older aunts and they died in the order that they died in the play" (in Bigsby, *Contemporary* 300, emphasis mine). Vogel's choices here came as a shock to some, none more than Jon Jory of the Actors Theatre of Louisville who had "commissioned this as a one-act." Jory's horror "that I would have my grandmother as a prostitute and that I would use the women in my family in that way" was so great that it "ruptured forever [Vogel's] relationship" (*Contemporary* 300)[5] with him.

Of the five characters, 83-year-old Mae is the oldest and has the oldest stories. She even discusses "[t]he depression of '97" (most probably the year of her birth), when her father's patronage of a brothel in Storeyville[6] ensures that Madam "Miss Sophie saved our lives" and "couldn't let us starve," so she "came and put groceries on our back step" (139). Mae, by 1980, has retired from sex work and become a madam, or management, herself. Still, she nostalgically recalls how after her father became solvent again, her mother became pregnant with a boy, and "Miss Sophie said she'd be real pleased if they named that boy after her gentleman protector" (140). This story is quite familiar to the other four women, who chant in unison "Radcliffe" when Mae starts, "So they named my brother" (140).

"Germanic" (130) Ursula, at seventy-nine, is the oldest practicing prostitute. Her stories recall both the Roaring Twenties and the Great

Depression of 1929. "I was making a pretty penny in 1927," she recalls of the Prohibition era, "until someone—one of you!—snitched on me" (140). Although Ursula acknowledges the effects of the Great Depression with her "I learned that the hard way in '29" (136) attack on banks, she nevertheless denounces "the whole Keynesian economy claptrap" and eschews the notion of an old age pension, proclaiming, "Subsidized begging—Medicare. Social Security has no place in a free market" (135). Ursula proclaims the value of advertising, which she calls "the soul of the modern marketplace" and recommends that the women "place pithy personals in the *Village Voice*" (141). She also suggests a niche market such as "a *Harold and Maude* situation" (142), citing the 1971 Hal Ashby film about Harold (Bud Cort), a young man in love with death, who consummates a relationship with Maude (Ruth Gordon), an old woman in love with life.

Lillian, a 75-year-old to whom "[a]ge has been gentle" (130), "wouldn't mind being eligible for a government subsidy each month in recognition of all my years of public service" (135). Hampered by failing eyesight and bad knees, she has gone from being "Miss Mae's Wild Irish Rose" and "the prettiest of us all" with her "loveliest skin" (153) to reduced circumstances that leave her "blowing half of Jefferson Square" (154). She also services a Mr. Loman, the father of "[t]wo good-for-nothing sons who are God-knows-where" (146), who pays with "*long silk stockings circa 1945*" (145) until Lillian dies and we learn he has "gone to the Presbyterian Home" (155).

Edna, a "good time girl," is seventy-four but still "[l]oves her work" (130). She is also Vera's best friend. Edna's "willing to die trying" (147), cheerful approach to her work helps make her financially productive, as when she brags, "Fourteen AND two dollars and fifty cents in tips" (144) about her haul in the first scene. Still, Edna seems to speak derisively when she says, "[Ursula's] been reading the *Wall Street Journal* again" (142), and she voices no concern about Mae's egalitarian attitude of dividing the funds equally. Ursula takes over after Mae's death and, her Depression-era distrust of banks notwithstanding, puts part of the group's funds into a certificate of deposit, which Edna calls "an account where we can't touch it" (160). Ursula's business approach inevitably contrasts with Edna's good time aesthetic, resulting in an "I quit" and "You can't quit. You're fired" exchange (164). Shepard and Lamb point out that "Edna . . . wants nothing to do with Ursula's promotion of such late-capitalist virtues as hyper-efficient worker productivity and profit maximization" (201). Edna finally reveals a secret she has held for more than four decades: "The money thing has always gone to your head. The same thing happened when you were bootlegging liquor;

you turned strange. I couldn't stand it. That's why I turned you in" (164). A few tense moments later, Edna returns from the third blackout with "I thought she'd never die" (167).

Vera, the character named for Vogel's grandmother, is, as noted earlier, the youngest at seventy-two. Her character "[l]oves the sun" (130). Vera clings to a dream of leaving the Life, telling her four companions that a "Mr. Simon has asked for my hand in marriage" (149). Mae takes the offer seriously, telling Vera, "Mr. Simon has a pension. And money in the bank. It's security" (150). Ursula attempts to dash Vera's hopes, however, with "Vera's not just a Woman with a Past; she's a Woman with an Epic" (150). Although Vera occupies herself with quotidian matters one might expect of a woman who desires a marriage, such as her opening speech on lemon sole, her meditation on a "cake for my birthday" that is "made with Grand Marnier" (134), and her concern for the price of brie at Mr. Zabar's (135), she nevertheless indicates loyalty to the group, telling them, "I can't do this to you. I'll just thank Mr. Simon for the honor but—" (151). The entire discussion is rendered moot when we learn that Mr. Simon's "kids have kidnapped him to New Jersey" (155), perhaps indicating their horror at the idea of a sexually active elderly father, particularly one who, seriously or not, proposes marriage to a prostitute.

The play's final scene contains no dialogue but offers a *"frail"* and *"frightened"* Vera *"sitting alone in the middle of the bench."* Together, the five elderly sex workers have eked out an existence; alone, Vera finds herself in a world where she must fend for herself without the benefit of a social safety net. The earlier discussion of Social Security and Medicare has been pointless, for not one of these five women qualifies for either. As Mansbridge points out, they derive from an "alienated labor force" (96) that is part of an underground economy. Vera's brief dream of a marriage also seems a chimera, especially in a society where children may overrule the wishes of parents simply because the parents have grown old and perhaps expressed a desire to behave contrary to the way that society defines "appropriate" behavior for people of that age. Vera may "like Donnie and Marie" (134), but the wholesome Osmonds would undoubtedly recoil in horror at the way Vera has lived her life. They may even be unable to fathom her.

Two sets of allusions in *The Oldest Profession* may help us see what Vogel is doing in the play. The aforementioned Mr. Loman is part of an extended homage to *Death of a Salesman*, Arthur Miller's searing indictment of the American Dream. Not only does the play refer to Mr. Loman's silk stockings and good-for-nothing sons, but it even contains an ersatz *"requiem for Mr.*

Loman" (146) that recalls Miller's final scene. Mansbridge asserts that Lillian's relationship with Mr. Loman transfers sex workers from the darkest "shadows" of Loman's existence to the "spotlight" (101).

For all their realization that "*Mr. Loman has lost his marbles*" (145), the women actually sound like Arthur Miller's character at such moments as Ursula's recalling her "pretty penny in 1927" (140) and their description of the defunct brothel at Storeyville. Edna recalls, "I liked Storeyville when it was legal,"[7] to which Ursula adds, "The working girls loved Storeyville" (140). Mae waxes nostalgic about "the House where we all first met" and a time when "[t]here was honor in the trade" (139). Ursula even ironically echoes Willy's parting speech about loyalty to Howard when she says, "Men who treated their wives and mothers right treated their mistresses right, too" (139).

The name Storeyville gives a mythic quality to the place the characters in *The Oldest Profession* describe, just as their reminiscences suggest a Golden Age of prostitution that recalls Willy's mythologizing his brother Ben and the early years of his own career. Other characters challenge Willy's inflated claims about the past, and we may do well to wonder whether a brothel really existed where the workers "knew them all; knew their wives and kids, too" (139). Shepard and Lamb argue that the women's "art of taking each other and us on tours of their rich lives in Storeyville . . . necessarily demands narrative selection and suppression" (201). Both Willy and the women of *The Oldest Profession* want to believe in a past and a set of possibilities, but legitimate questions persist about the extent to which their desires coincide with the realities available to them. Like Willy Loman, they reflect what James Truslow Adams identified in his 1931 book *The Epic of America*. Adams coined the term "American Dream" and defined it as:

> that dream of a land in which life should be better and richer and fuller for every man, with opportunity for each according to his ability or achievement. It is a difficult dream for the European upper classes to interpret adequately, and too many of us ourselves have grown weary and mistrustful of it. It is not a dream of motor cars and high wages merely, but a dream of a social order in which each man and each woman shall be able to attain to the fullest stature of which they are innately capable, and be recognized by others for what they are, regardless of the fortuitous circumstances of birth or position. (404)

Both Willy's and the women's recollections intimate a time when they lived the American Dream; both sets of reminiscences, however, are highly suspect.

Another possible allusion more subtly detailed in *The Oldest Profession* is to Tennessee Williams's *The Glass Menagerie*, particularly to Amanda Wingfield. Vogel has long been an admirer of Williams, telling Elizabeth Farnsworth of "the remarkable women characters written by Tennessee Williams" ("Prize-Winning"). Amanda Wingfield qualifies as one of Williams's great mature female characters. Born in the late nineteenth century in a minimally Reconstructed South, Amanda has not pursued nor does she expect for her daughter Laura an American Dream based on "ability or achievement" in any profession. Amanda tells Laura, "All women are a trap, a pretty trap, and men expect them to be!" This trap can even include the bra stuffers Amanda calls "Gay Deceivers" (1404). Although Amanda has failed to keep her own husband at home after he "fell in love with long distances" (1382), she nevertheless hopes her daughter can both trap and keep Jim O'Connor, the "gentleman caller" Tom invites unawares into the Wingfield home.

Amanda Wingfield does not cast the same long shadow over *The Oldest Profession* as Willy Loman, yet she is present. Ursula, the least nostalgic of the women, refers to "a dying breed" of "gentlemen callers" (141). Mae's "menfolk bathed, their hair combed back and dressed in their Sunday best, waiting downstairs happy and shy" (139) at the House in Storeyville call to mind Amanda's "Sunday afternoon in Blue Mountain" when she "received *seventeen!*—gentleman callers" (1384). We may see Storeyville representing to the women of *The Oldest Profession* what Blue Mountain does to Amanda Wingfield. Similarly, the clients Mae, Ursula, Lillian, Edna, and Vera have serviced become analogous (down to the choice of terms) to Amanda's "gentleman callers." Last, and perhaps most importantly, the artful seduction a prostitute would have learned in a more reputable brothel seems eerily similar to the "pretty trap" Amanda thinks it a woman's duty to set for a man. Perhaps Bigsby had Amanda Wingfield in mind when he wrote that *Profession*, "like Tennessee Williams's drama, places time and its ironies at the centre of attention, which dramatises the losing battle between love, or perhaps more patently, fiction, and the deconstructive logic of time" (*Contemporary* 303).

The characters in *The Oldest Profession* never address whether they entered the Life as an entrepreneurial choice, as an economic necessity, or for another reason. The cross purposes they have reached during their decades of sex work hint at multiple motives that would explain why Ursula speaks in late-capitalist terms against which Edna pushes back. Savran argues they look back to and thus have emerged from "a time when there was a palpable connection between people and both the work they performed and the things they consumed" ("Screws" xv). Mansbridge, on the other hand, situates the women in both the times of their youth and of their present, calling the play "[e]qual parts Beckett, Vaudeville, and *The Golden Girls*" (92) and also referencing the 1980s film *Cocoon*, another work that contains older women who continue to enjoy sexual activity.

Whatever their motivations and perhaps despite their origins, *Profession*'s quintet give a take on the American Dream. Mansbridge attributes the play with connecting sex work and the American Dream itself when Mae critiques prostitutes whose purview is the streets, not a brothel (95). Mae demands, "Where the hell is their pride? Where the hell is their ambition? This is America, where any girl can start in the alley and work her way up to Madam."[8] But is Mae correct? Vogel writes during an era following free love and in a city where Mayor Ed Koch has already begun and subsequent Mayor Giuliani will intensify what Mansbridge calls "the hypercommercialization of midtown Manhattan" that will banish prostitutes and sexually oriented businesses from the most desirable real estate. (94). Are the madams there, like their erstwhile clients, a dying breed?

Mae has done a remarkable job of holding her band together, rightfully boasting, "Well, I'll tell you what—this has been our beat for over forty-five years, and listen, baby, we still tick!" (137). The women, even as they occupy themselves with stories of days gone by, have also made attempts at keeping up with the times, rather than completely giving themselves over to the past. Ursula's free market advocacy and Mae's reminder that "President Reagan has called on all Americans to reduce the deficit, and to balance the budget" (148) reflect their efforts at self-reliance and ongoing relevance.

Still, even as they have persevered, the women have begun enduring hardships they lack the power to overcome. Ursula's rant against Social Security, a program already in place for more than forty years by 1980, seems untimely and certainly contrary to her own best interests. Worse, Vera's concerns about food prices are justified, for after Mae counts a day's take, she tells the women, "[W]e are depleting our savings account to the tune of fifty dollars per month" (148). None of the suggestions for additional work and income seems feasible.

The women have also fallen behind culturally. Shepard and Lamb point out that *Harold and Maude* is "Ursula's referent film" (201). "Edna's last movie," they add, was *The Sound of Music*, the 1965 musical that "romanticizes the pleasure of foiling fascism, [and] makes risk somewhat glamorous" (201). It is a dated film set in an even more distant past rendered ahistorical to the point that pluck and excellent show tunes provide everything one needs to escape even Nazis. Neither it nor anything else prepares Vera for the final scene, when, a forlorn figure, she sits alone in a world she no longer recognizes. She may occupy the middle of the bench, but she has symbolically come to the end of her road.

Like *Desdemona*, *The Oldest Profession* found only miniscule audiences for at least the first decade of its existence. The first published edition records only a New York City Hudson Guild production before 1988. In 1990, Vogel directed a reading of the play at Brown, with a cast that featured three professors, Susanne Woods, Anne Shaver, and Coppelia Kahn.[9] Finally, in 2004, the Off-Broadway Signature Theater Company, in a season devoted to Vogel's plays, staged a production that featured Marylouise Burke as Vera, Joyce Van Patten as Ursula, Carlin Glynn as Lillian, Katherine Helmond as Mae, and Priscilla Lopez as Edna.[10]

Reviews of this production and of the play itself were mixed. Ben Brantley of the *New York Times* found "some of [Vogel's] distinctive talent" in the play, which he called "Vogel's most Brechtian play," reflecting what "is not an approach that comes easily to her." He added that "Vogel gives the impression that she is leading with her heart instead of her head." David Rooney, writing for *Variety*, all but dismissed the play as "a distinctly minor early work" that was, in seemingly equal parts, "cryptofeminist sitcom," "poignant drama about the economic realities of aging women in a phallocentric world," "Lifetime movie," and "afterlife musical." Rooney praised the director, David Esbjornson, who he wrote "elevates the work" and all five performers, especially "the marvelous Burke, who invests slightly befuddled, tirelessly optimistic Vera with enormous heart." Brantley thought that "a more surreal, exaggerated style than Mr. Esbjornson has chosen" might have led to a stronger production, but he shared Rooney's appreciation of "the delightful Marylouise Burke."

Both Brantley and Rooney recorded noteworthy elements of the production not present in Vogel's printed text, which simply has characters disappear when they "die" during blackouts. Brantley writes that "they fall off the street-side bench where they assemble and into their graves—or, to be exact, into a bordello heaven of a red velvet piano parlor, where they sing lustily in the styles of Bessie Smith and Mae West." The result is a "mix of social instruction" (much of it, Brantley notes, about supply-side economics) "and stylized musical interludes." Rooney adds, "As each of the women expires she sheds her outer garments, revealing vampy bordello-wear underneath, and launches into a bawdy, innuendo-laden number." He specifically mentions one song, Edna's (Priscilla Lopez, a late replacement for Anita Gillette) "Sugar in My Bowl," which he deems "the show's musical highlight." The vampy music and upbeat "bordello in the sky" tone probably diminished the audience's appreciation of Vera's loneliness and isolation at play's end, a change that enhanced the spectacle yet detracted from the original script's pathos.

Granted, the director tried to retain at least part of that feeling. Vera is seen, Mansbridge writes, ultimately protecting herself from the outdoors with a "worn-out trench coat and newspaper" that constituted an "image of poverty" (103). Since Vera has previously spoken of more prosperous times with boyfriends and good food, Mansbridge finds the contrast "jarring" (103). All the same, with the four deceased prostitutes singing "The Sunny Side of the Street" from the security of the brothel, it is at least plausible that the audience would have felt Vera's temporal plight less keenly. Vera, even as she roots for food in the trash, is less a portrait of destitution than a presentation of traditional Christianity: paradise awaits.

Over the next few years, productions of *The Oldest Profession* remained sporadic and continued to receive mixed reviews, with a 2015 production at the Washington, D.C., Rainbow Theatre Project constituting a noteworthy exception. Writing for *DC Metro Theatre Arts*, Michael Poandl questioned the choice of the play for an LGBTQ theatre but nevertheless awarded *Profession* four out of five stars and called the "vibrant and usual" characters written for older actresses "so satisfying to watch." Poandl found the play's central concept "borderline dangerous," for "no one should be fooled into thinking this is anything like what the sex trade was ever like, in 1980 or otherwise." He allowed a "theatre is fantasy to an extent" spirit to prevail, however, and praised the show as "warm and funny," with "cabaret-style numbers [that] are a blast."

DC Theatre Scene critic Jeffrey Walker awarded the production a "Highly Recommended" rating. With Emily Morrison as Mae, Tricia McCauley as Ursula, Diana Haberstick as Lillian, Desiré Dubose as Edna, and Charlotte Akin as Vera, Walker deemed the cast "uniformly excellent in portraying the delicious individuality of each character." He also appreciated director Elizabeth Pringle's allowing "the simplicity of the play and its metaphysical atmosphere to intermingle," as well as "fine work by Maureen Codelka as the resident honky-tonk piano player," who took on the (new?) role of "narrator throughout the play."

This production also presented another stylistic change beyond the narrator. To incorporate the "paradise waiting . . . beyond the grave" (Walker), Pringle and set designer Greg Stevens divided the space into an upstage and downstage. Downstage consisted of "nothing more than a park bench, upon which the entire two hours traffic takes place" (Poandl). Poandl found the upstage part far more interesting, describing it as a "luscious harem-style quarter that can only be described as 'Whore Heaven.'" This staging resulted, Poandl added, "in the speaking actors getting upstaged quite a bit." Here, as in the Signature production, the tone may well have been greatly altered from the published version.

For all the difficulties Vogel faced reaching an audience with *Desdemona* and *The Oldest Profession*, she regards her 1984 work *And Baby Makes Seven* as her "Scottish play" ("Screws" xiv). This designation derives, in part, from the "Out, d-damned Spot!!" *Macbeth* reference in Orphan's "death" scene that concludes Scene Six. More significant, however, is what happened to the play early on at LA Theatre Works, a happening not cited in the published version of the play. There, Vogel recalled in an email to Mansbridge, an artistic director and a play director who both thought poorly of the play, set up a situation with "homophobia expressed in the room" (cited in Mansbridge 64). The production, predictably, "was disastrous" (Mansbridge 64).

This early treatment of *And Baby Makes Seven* contrasts tremendously with a note director Marc Stuart Weitz felt obliged to write when New York's Ohio Theatre staged a revival in 2014. Carey Purcell quotes Weitz as saying, "Paula imagined this particular non-conventional family amidst a very different cultural landscape." Weitz continued, "Modern families are becoming more visible on television, in movies, and on-stage." This word choice is almost certainly a nod to the commercially and critically successful ABC television series *Modern Family*, which includes a gay male couple bringing up a family in suburban Los Angeles. Despite advertised Wednesday night "Baby Talk" conversations that promised to "include Tony Award winner Pam MacKinnon, [MacArthur 'Genius Grant' winner and Vogel student] Sarah Ruhl and [veteran Vogel director] Mark Brokaw" (Purcell), this production also failed. *The New York Times* critic Eric Grode acknowledged that Vogel had "broached the topic of gay parenting a generation ahead of the curve" but then dismissed the play itself as "reductive, repetitive and extremely off-putting." Grode asserted that "the sight and sound of grown-ups mimicking high-pitched children will never *not* get old," indicating a likely predisposition against the play.

Developing a Unique Voice

Understanding why two productions more than a generation apart would fare so poorly requires a close look at both the environment in which Vogel wrote *And Baby Makes Seven* and the ambitious goals she undertakes dramaturgically as well as sociologically in the play. *And Baby Makes Seven* emerged from a time when a march toward legal equality for gay and lesbian Americans was far from certain. Stonewall was only fifteen years behind, and, following successful bans on gay teachers in Oklahoma and Arkansas, a coalition that included President Jimmy Carter, future President Ronald Reagan, Governor Jerry Brown, and San Francisco Supervisor Harvey Milk had beaten back California Proposition 6, aka The Briggs Initiative, only six years earlier. This initiative would have gone so far as to ban anyone who supported gay rights. Despite his opposition to Proposition 6, Ronald Reagan had then won the White House with enthusiastic support from the virulently anti-gay "Moral Majority." What is more, the United States Supreme Court decision, *Bowers v. Hardwick*, which upheld the constitutionality of state laws criminalizing private, consensual oral and anal sex still lay three years ahead. Finally, and frighteningly, the United States was just learning of the AIDS pandemic, which despite HIV's relative rarity among lesbians, was provoking yet another panic against LGBT Americans.

Into this climate Vogel presented a play that engaged with the Edward Albee classic *Who's Afraid of Virginia Woolf?*. This time, however, George and Martha gave way to Anna Epstein and Ruth Abrams, a lesbian couple. The imaginary child in Albee's play was replaced by Anna's very real pregnancy, plus three imaginary children: Cecil Bartholomew, a nine-year-old "genius" (63) played by Anna; Henri Dumont, an eight-year-old inspired by the 1956 Albert Lamorisse French short *The Red Balloon* and played by Ruth; and Orphan McDermott, a feral seven-year-old rescued from stray dogs at the Port Authority Bus Terminal, and (like Henri) played by Ruth. Anna has not conceived by artificial insemination, proclaiming, "No turkey baster for little Emma" (73), who later turns out to be a son, Nathan. Instead, she has had heterosexual coitus with gay friend Peter Leven, complete with such "little plots" as a "Nubian boy spread on a Persian rug," an "English school boy being disciplined," and a "young Greek sailor, swabbing the deck on his knees in the hot Mediterranean sun" (73).

This brief synopsis demonstrates that in *And Baby Makes Seven*, Vogel is defamiliarizing Albee, the notion of a settled couple, the idea of family, and a larger sense of what constitutes play. Mansbridge observes how the play treats the domestic sphere, employs broad humor, and emphasizes role-play, arguing that "*Baby* can be read as a burlesque of *Woolf*" (50). What Vogel burlesques deserves mention. *Woolf* has earned canonical status, and the play's longstanding influence plus its run of 664 performances that began on October 13, 1962, a time when, as Matthew Roudané writes, "Broadway had reached a low point" (33), may obscure the shock value it initially held for the American theatrical audiences Albee infamously called "placid cows." Roudané notes that *Woolf* "earned Albee the reputation of being a nihilist, social protestor, moralist, allegorist, parodist, dramatic innovator, affirmative existentialist, charlatan, and absurdist" (33). George and Martha's *Walpurgisnacht* subjects Nick and Honey to an experience which, at minimum, borders on sadism before the play's "Joycean affirmative texture" hints at "more than a reconciliation of man and wife; it further suggests that they can now accept their life, with its cajoling ambiguity and terrifying flux, without illusion" (Roudané 38). To any audience approaching *Who's Afraid of Virginia Woolf?* for the first time, even today, Albee's drama likely defamiliarizes both the idea of play and the notion of what *a play* can do.

Coming shortly after *The American Dream* (1961), *Woolf* comes with Albee's "assurance that George and Martha derive their names from the first president and his wife[11] and that he sees the play as an examination of the fate of American values" (Bigsby *Modern* 131). Such an examination is reflected in George's career as a professor at the college where Martha's father is president. George is at mid-career stasis. George and Martha's marriage also merits a close look as a commentary upon the American nuclear family, replete with picket fence and children. The elaborate fiction George and Martha have constructed around an imaginary child leads to what Bigsby calls "apocalyptic implications of this betrayal of the real as he and Martha are forced by the logic of their own myth to surrender the child" (131). Roudané posits this apocalyptic potential as giving way to possible redemption, stating, "For O'Neill illusions help; for Albee they destroy" (36), and calling *Woolf* Albee's "most affirmative work" (35). The play's ending itself contains potential affirmation, for the last two words, Martha's "I am," function not only as an answer to the titular question but also as an existential declaration of her own existence.

In the combination of "real" and "imaginary" characters in *And Baby Makes Seven*, Vogel refuses, as Pellegrini says, to "offer us a cozy homosexual version of the idealized heterosexual family unit (mother, father, and baby makes three)" (480). "[I]nstead," Pellegrini continues, Vogel "blows the lid off the fantasy that *any* family structure is normal" (480). Mansbridge characterizes *Baby* as "intent on defamiliarizing moral responses to sexuality—which categorize it as either good or bad—presenting it, instead, as something positive, playful, and open to revision," with it and gender being "merely fictions, 'cultural conceits,' albeit with real, material effects" (59). For Pellegrini, such work is part of the way Vogel uses negative empathy "to shock audiences out of their complacencies in order to challenge our accustomed ways of seeing the world, even, sometimes, our accustomed *feminist* ways" (480). Vogel's refusal to "add same-sex couples and stir" thus "ultimately offers something far richer and more complex than mirror images" (480). As a result, *And Baby Makes Seven* transcends being a burlesque of *Woolf* and stands as an independent work.

Bigsby notes that "in some respects *And Baby Makes Seven* begins where *Who's Afraid of Virginia Woolf?* ends—with the killing of the fantasy children" (*Contemporary* 305). Bigsby even quotes Vogel joking about Albee's play, "[W]hat a shame they killed off their son. They could have had another wonderful ten years of marriage!" (303). One way Vogel goes well beyond Albee is in resurrecting the fantasy children after ostensibly "killing" them first and, as Bigsby writes, in that "Vogel's definition of reality incorporates fantasy, which is merely located at another point on the spectrum" (303). To some, "the romantic symbol or animal force" Orphan McDermott represents the id, Henri the libido, and "the effete intellectual," Cecil, the superego (Bigsby 303). As such, they may be temporarily repressed at Peter's insistence, but they cannot or will not ultimately disappear from the play. Peter behaves as he does, contends Mansbridge, because he lacks Anna and Ruth's commitment to fantasy, feeling instead "extraneous to pregnancy, or as Ruth and Anna jokingly call it, 'Woman Creating'"[12] (55).

The rich, dense texture of allusions to literature and film woven throughout *And Baby Makes Seven* makes for a play Bigsby deems "almost perversely metafictional" (*Contemporary* 306), with a "metatheatrical element" which possibly "extends to Vogel's own fantasy child, namely the play itself" (*Modern* 413). Jill Dolan identifies here a "curious, absurdist environment" that "exemplifies the range of Vogel's theatricality and her social imagination" (498). At times, characters speak in allusions in the scenes dominated by the "imaginary" characters and then speak about the allusions and metatheatrical moments in the scenes where the "real" characters prevail, but this distinction breaks down, particularly toward the end. Such important signifiers as props or set pieces help us identify which "world" the play inhabits at certain moments. For example, in the Prologue to Act One, Prologue to Act Two, and Epilogue, the stage directions call for a "*clown night-light*" to provide the only light onstage. This child's light immediately signifies that we are in the realm of Henri, Cecil, and the Orphan. Similarly, at the end of Scene Eleven, when "*Ruth holds out a deflated red balloon*" (109), this stage property tells us Henri has (temporarily, it turns out) left the play even as it recalls the Lamorisse short.

The first Prologue consists of a discussion of how babies are made. When Peter provides the semi-pornographic description that a "man rams his hot throbbing[13] member into a woman and humps so hard that he explodes just as she's screaming: 'Don't stop, don't stop!'" (65), Cecil replies, "Uncle Peter . . . you're not a well man" (65). Then, in the first line of Act One Scene One, Peter tells Anna and Ruth, "I think they have to go" (67). He has noticed, he says, the women "[g]oing into character" (67) so much that the "'kids' are always with us" (67) at home. He adds that "the line between reality and you know . . . well, it's getting dangerously thin around here" (70). Ruth's assurance, "We never do it out of the house" (70), the domestic sphere where this family that is unusual on so many levels enjoys a safe space, gives way to Ruth/Orphan biting Peter "*savagely*" (70), a moment that acquires new significance in Scene Fourteen. Peter leaves the home, mouthing, "I'll . . . I'll see you later" (71), in an echoing of Sam Nash's farewell, "I'll . . . I'll see you" in Neil Simon's *Plaza Suite*. Nash leaves his wife Karen alone in a hotel room allegedly to attend to business but almost certainly to continue his affair with Miss McCormack. Peter's needs are different, for he returns in the next scene to the question, "Did you have a good time with the boys?" and the admonition, "Promise me you're being careful" (72). These words all but declare that like Nash in Simon's play, Peter goes out for sex, but his preference is an anonymous gay hookup. In 1984, the caution to be careful carried special meaning and connoted great concern for Peter's health, but it did not pose an immediate existential threat to Peter's relationship with the women. He lives under sexual mores different from those of the middle-aged Second World War generation portrayed by Simon[14].

Anna and Ruth eventually agree to dispense with the imaginary children but not before, Ruth says, she gets her "last inch of fantasy out of them" (84). Already, a scene that has begun with Ruth/Henri making a peanut butter and jelly sandwich has turned into a metatheatrical (or metacinematic) "*Dr. Strangelovian battle*" between the Ruth/Henri hand and the Ruth/Orphan hand. Ruth agrees, however, "We're going to tidy up the plots. No loose ends dangling." "We're going to kill them," she adds, "One by one. First Orphan. Then Henri. Cecil will be the last to go" (84). True to her word, Ruth shrugs off Anna's lament, "I can't go through with this. This is just too awful" (88)

Developing a Unique Voice

by giving Orphan a death that befits his having been raised by stray dogs, a fatal case of rabies. In what is most likely the play's most metatheatrical scene, Orphan's death recalls "*the many voices of Mercedes McCambridge in* The Exorcist" (88), alluding (in order) to the William Friedkin film, Shakespeare's *Romeo and Juliet,* Tennessee Williams's *A Streetcar Named Desire,* Shakespeare's *Othello,* Henrik Ibsen's *Ghosts,* the 1940s swing tune "Chattanooga Choo Choo," Shakespeare's *Hamlet,* Shakespeare's *Macbeth,* and the 1950s television show *Lassie*—all "badly quoted," as Anna later notes (95).

Once Orphan has died, the play hints at his possible return when Anna/Cecil points out that "matter can't be destroyed, but only changed" (91). Before the destruction proceeds, however, Anna reacts peculiarly when she discovers Ruth wearing Peter's shirt. After querying Ruth, "Did you ask if you could wear it?" (96), Anna escalates the situation until she exclaims, "I'm supposed to give up coffee, smoking, drinking, fucking, spicy foods, and I'm expected to be understanding of what Ruth wants, what Peter needs.—Who the fuck am I, some kind of knocked-up Miss Manners?" (97). Anna vehemently denies that her anger derives at all from her late-stage pregnancy, shouting from offstage, "AND DON'T YOU DARE TELL ME IT'S HORMONES!" (97). Especially in light of Shepard and Lamb's observation "that Ruth, who is not pregnant, feels threatened by the biological bond between Anna and Peter" (202), as simple a gender-bending gesture as Ruth wearing a man's shirt would seem innocuous, but it is worth noting that Mansbridge characterizes Ruth/Henri's declaration to Peter, "I want to have your baby!!" (*Baby* 66), as an attempt on Ruth's part "to seduce Peter" (59) by which "any attempt to view sexuality as a fixed identity is comically subverted" (59). What appears to have happened here is a blurring of the lines between the "real" world of the play and the "play" world of the play, with Anna unexpectedly jealous of the way Ruth and Peter interact. Ruth's being able to wear Peter's shirt while a pregnant Anna cannot becomes a metonym of all the activities open to Ruth but temporarily closed off to Anna. It is also Vogel's way of showing how even in the nontraditional household of *Baby,* one woman's resentment of a non-pregnant woman, even if that woman is her partner, can arise. Vogel simply won't let us have a happy nuclear family—however defined—living in domestic bliss.

In the next scene, Scene Nine, Peter, Ruth/Henri, and Anna/Cecil leave their apartment for the first and only time. While at a zoo, "Henri" and "Cecil" never break character, with Henri making juvenile comments about a monkey "pulling his pudding" (99), and Cecil quoting Darwin's "one general law—namely, Multiply, Let the Strongest Live, and the Weakest Die . . . ." Having the play's only scene outside the domestic sphere take place in a zoo, at minimum, suggests an analogue to Albee's 1959 play *The Zoo Story*, in which one of the two characters is also named Peter. Filled, like this moment in *Baby*, with what Henri discerns in Cecil as "angst" (100), which Peter characterizes as a "German sadness" (100), *The Zoo Story* is "a classic fable of anxiety and identity" (Roudané 28). Anna/Cecil quotes Shakespeare's *Julius Caesar*, "'runs' on the 'sword'" (114), and so dies a noble Roman, killing off the superego just as the death of Orphan has killed the id and that of Henri, the libido.

Something, however, has gone awry. By Scene Ten, Ruth challenges the agreement to eliminate the imaginary children, telling Anna, "I don't see why we can't change the . . . the narrative at this point" (105). Anna is dismissive here, responding, "We can't stop now. Not in the middle of the story" (105). Ruth's suggestion gains impetus, though, in Scene Twelve, when Peter suggests to Cecil, "Look—do you think maybe we could . . . change the ending? Deus ex machina? I'd really like it if you could stick around" (113). Anna, speaking as Cecil, again declines, having Cecil say, "I don't think so. Not without Henri" (113) and then "die" within a few lines.

Any doubts the audience may have about the rationale for dispensing with the imaginary children seem dispelled after Nathan is born, and we see Ruth and Peter at the "*end of a very long day*" in Scene Thirteen. Here, Ruth and Peter, truly alone together for the only time in the play, have the sort of conversation that likely has occurred in one of the offstage moments that have provoked Anna's jealousy back in Scene Eight. Ruth speaks at great length, giving Peter a history of her and Anna's desire to have a child and telling why Ruth has ceded the actual childbirth to Anna. Ruth tells Peter, "I can always see my own face anytime I want in the mirror." Through a baby, however, Ruth can appreciate "Anna's face at birth, Anna in diapers, a little Anna coming home from school." In perhaps a surprising development, Ruth confides that a boy child would be "even better" because he would give her a glimpse of "his Adam's apple beneath her chin" and "that awkward moment right before puberty, before his voice changes, when I mistake his hello on the phone for hers" (116). This last image hints at the fluidity of gender and even sex itself as well as letting us see why the presence of someone with a y chromosome does not threaten the home or relationship Ruth and Anna have built. Although abandoned by his own father, Peter may freely "make it up on [his] own, this father thing" (113).

This agency granted Peter helps explain what Shepard and Lamb call the "magical realism" (204) of Scene Fourteen and the Epilogue. Scene Fourteen begins with Anna "*sitting in profile to the audience, nursing Nathan*" (118) and then presents Anna, Ruth, and Peter sitting down to dinner while the baby rests nearby. During a conversation about "dishes," "diapers," and "the life" that "[m]ost men dream of" (120), Peter's behavior grows ever stranger until he exclaims, "Orphan! Revenge! Oorrrppphannnn..." (121). Ruth's "Orphan?!" and Anna's "What does he..." (121) reflect an initial amazement that quickly gives way to a joint "Rabies!!" (122) that indicates the game is on again. Cecil, Henri, Orphan, Anna, Ruth, and Peter all speak in the Epilogue, and the baby coos along. The last spoken line is Peter's "I'm eating you up, yummyyummyyummyyummy-yummmm—Nathan's all gone!" (125) before the apartment, per the stage directions, becomes "*one apartment among hundreds of their neighbors*" and "*Nathan's giggles and squeals*" (125) take the play to blackout.

If we acknowledge Orphan, Henri, and Cecil representing id, libido, and superego respectively, their return is necessary on the most basic of psychological bases: they are essential to human psychology. Dismissing their reemergence as nothing more than that undermines their dramaturgical importance; to wit, Bigsby quotes Vogel as saying their representing the id, libido, and superego "was not that tidy" (*Contemporary* 304), suggesting we do her characters a disservice by viewing them purely in Freudian terms. Bigsby explains, "Life, like this play, is interlaced with fiction and, indeed, having killed off their fantasies, Peter, Ruth and Anna reinvent them rather than settle for a life untransformed by the imagination" (*Contemporary* 306). Bigsby moreover believes that the "reverse zoom" after the dialogue ends makes the audience "become aware that this 'family' is in essence like all those which surround them in the city just beyond their apartment" (306). Mansbridge adds that *Baby* "undermines traditional psychological paradigms of sexual development and family structures," and suggests instead an alternative to the "Oedipal mother-father-child triad." In addition, Mansbridge asserts, the play proves as well "the Lacanian Imaginary-Real-Symbolic... to be an inadequate framework" (57).

Although, as noted earlier, Vogel has dubbed *And Baby Makes Seven* her "Scottish play" and some theatre critics have been, at best, unkind, the play has found some receptive viewers. Even in a generally negative 1993 *Variety* review of "a small play" with a "small punch," Jeremy Gerard discerned that Anna and Ruth "seem to believe that preparation for parenthood must include putting out the child within us, and of course the opposite is the case, as Vogel's coda makes clear." Mel Gussow, another critic generally unsympathetic to the play, still credited the same 1993 production with an intermittent "responsive note, especially at those moments when the characters jettison their invented friends," and praised the "intuitive charm and intelligence" of Cherry Jones as Anna, adding, "The fact that she can be so lightsome while playing a pregnant woman pretending to be a schoolboy is testimony to her theatrical alchemy."[15]

Sophia Polin, writing in 2014 for *Stage Buddy*, noted that the New Ohio Theater production found "the emotional core of the play" in "the murders—and subsequent resurrections" of the imaginary children. Finding Anna and Ruth "intentionally underdeveloped," Polin praised Constance Zaytoun and Susan Bott less for their portrayals of Anna and Ruth than for their presenting the children, writing, "Witnessing a grown woman playing a feral child dying in a rabid fit with all the verbal frills of a Shakespearean suicide should intrigue you." According to Polin, Bott's performance here was "clever enough to keep you wondering about the true source of the scene's power," which "isn't obvious." Zachary Stewart's 2014 *Theater Mania* review concurred with Polin about Bott's performance of Orphan's death scene, which he called "a tour de force." Stewart also wrote sensitively about Peter (Ken Barnett), describing him as "a gay(ish) man" and commenting on this "pansexual threesome" by quoting Vogel's recollection, "I wrote this play in the twentieth century, when I still had the energy to envision a sexual utopia." Stewart even went so far as to eschew easy comparisons with *Modern Family* and *The New Normal*, considering *Baby* "a reminder of a time when gay people weren't so obsessed with the desire to fit in." Stewart concludes by observing that even as we recall how "LGBT rights have made huge gains in the last three decades," *Baby* insists that "we should also stop and ask ourselves, 'What has been lost?'"

Whether reviews such as Stewart's indicate that *And Baby Makes Seven* will ultimately be consigned as a period piece or will take its place in the canon is a matter that only time will tell. I am more sanguine about *Desdemona* and even more so about *The Oldest Profession*, with two caveats: artistic directors of theatres large and small need to produce these plays more frequently, and scholars and critics of theatre need to assign and study them. As the 1990s dawned, these happenings would have seemed highly improbable. Then came *The Baltimore Waltz* and, with it, an upward arc to Vogel's career that has seen her reputation climb, at times in fits and starts, for more than three decades.

CHAPTER 3
BUILDING AN INTERNATIONAL REPUTATION

In 1986 Carl Vogel invited younger sister Paula to travel with him to Europe. Thinking herself short on money but, in her mid-thirties, long on time, she declined. Paula Vogel could not have been more wrong about time. Unbeknownst to her, Carl had been diagnosed with HIV, the virus that causes AIDS. Carl Vogel died on January 9, 1988, but even during what Vogel decades later called "that final watch," he said, with "a twinkle in his eye," from his deathbed, "You're going to write about this, aren't you?" ("Paula Vogel on *The Baltimore Waltz*"). "BECAUSE," she wrote, "I CANNOT SEW" (*Baltimore Waltz* 3), Vogel did not opt to memorialize her brother through the NAMES Project AIDS Memorial Quilt conceived by Cleve Jones. Instead, during a summer 1989 stay at the MacDowell Colony in New Hampshire, she treated Carl's words as "a deathbed wish that I had to do." In "completely unplanned" fashion, Vogel went into what she later called "this state" and "didn't sleep for two weeks" ("Paula Vogel on"). Simultaneously grief-stricken and inspired, Vogel called upon her skill as a dramatist and crafted *The Baltimore Waltz*, a play about "a journey with Carl to a Europe that exists only in the imagination" (*Baltimore Waltz* 2).

Of all the Vogel plays printed and published over her first seventy years, *The Baltimore Waltz* is the one best known, at the time, to have been the most directly inspired by her own biography. Because the trauma behind the play was so great, Vogel of necessity drew upon all her dramaturgical resources. Vogel told David Savran,

> If I had sat down and said, "I'm going to write a play about my brother's death from AIDS," I never would have written a play, I would [have] simply curled up in a little ball and wept. But if I say I'm going to write a play on language lessons, knowing full well it's about my brother's death, you allow yourself to forget ("Driving").

As a result, David Krasner notes that even in its exploration of Elizabeth Kubler-Ross's "stages of grief," *The Baltimore Waltz* "provides a refreshing perspective on AIDS" (151–2), functioning "[i]n contrast to the powerful but overwrought AIDS 'rage' dramas of the 1980s such as *Normal Heart* and *As Is*" (*American* 152). Vogel apparently looks back less in anger—or sorrow—than with an odd sense of mirth.

The Baltimore Waltz defamiliarizes AIDS into Acquired Toilet Disease, scourge of elementary school teachers. The play also employs dramatically the narrative structure of Ambrose Bierce's 1890 short story "An Occurrence at Owl Creek Bridge," a surreal (before the term "Surrealism" was invented) tale which takes place entirely in the mind of Confederate sympathizer Peyton Farquhar during the moment he is executed by hanging. Vogel sets *The Baltimore Waltz* entirely in the moment Anna's brother Carl dies from AIDS-related complications, but Vogel conceals this fact through the first twenty-nine scenes of the play. As Mansbridge writes, "We watch the play believing that Anna has just been diagnosed with Acquired Toilet Disease (ATD), while Carl is the healthy brother who accompanies his sister on a European adventure" (149). Along the way, a stuffed rabbit, fantastical urine-drinking Dr. Todesrocheln,[1] the "little Dutch boy who put his thumb in the dyke" (33) at age fifty, and other characters—all of them played by the same actor—appear. The 1949 Carol Reed film noir *The Third Man*, based on a Graham Greene script, and its mysterious Harry Lime, portrayed cinematically by Orson Welles, also loom prominently.

In Elisabeth Kubler-Ross's stages of grief, the first stage is denial, and as Krasner, also referencing "An Occurrence at Owl Creek Bridge," points out, "Denial is the force which drives both Bierce's and Vogel's characters" (151). So, too, does music. The "Playwright's Note" reproduces verbatim the letter Carl Vogel wrote to his sister "after his first bout with pneumonia at Johns Hopkins Hospital in Baltimore, Maryland" (2), the city where Anna has her vision. Carl writes, "I would like really good music," such as Fauré, Gluck, and Verdi, as well as "I Dream of Jeannie," a spiritual such as "Steal Away," perhaps "Nearer My God to Thee," and maybe even one of the Jeannette MacDonald tunes from *San Francisco* (3). Add what Bigsby calls the "mysterious images, oblique symbols," and "lush lighting," and "a kaleidoscope of scenes (thirty in all) which reflect a mind flicking restlessly through a distorted memory bank" (*Modern* 413) ensues.

The first words in this play that deals intensely with recollection and loss are Anna's "Help me please," followed soon after by "There's nothing I can do" and "I have no memory" (7). Ostensibly, Anna refers to her failure at translating her ideas into passable Dutch and French, but in reality, both she and Vogel attempt to translate a loss into something each may process. Bigsby states that "the writing of the play was a therapeutic gesture, a way of discharging a mixture of anger, regret, obligation, a means of coming to terms with the finality of death" for Vogel (*Contemporary* 307). The same applies to Anna. In Scene Thirty, the audience hears the Doctor tell Anna, "I'm sorry. There was nothing we could do" (56), a declaration of finality faintly foreshadowed in Anna's opening speech. At the beginning, however, the power of denial is too strong for the audience to predict or understand what will come.

Turning AIDS into ATD defamiliarizes the syndrome that during the 1980s became all too familiar, especially to the LGBT community and its allies, "through the parodic humor and displacement," writes Mansbridge, of the factors we typically associate with AIDS. (149). Anna quickly dispels any possibility that ATD may be a sexually transmitted disease, asking the Doctor, "So there's no danger to anyone by . . . what I mean, Doctor, is that I can't infect anyone by—" (11), to which the Doctor assures her that if she will "use precautions" (12) such as "wash your hands" and "never lick paper money or coins" (11), "she can fuck her brains out" (12). Anna, who has contracted ATD as what Bigsby calls "a virginal school teacher" (310), resolves therefore upon the sexual conquest of "every Thomas, Deiter und Heinrich" (42) she likes in Europe.

Vogel's decision not to make ATD sexually transmitted has more than one result. Peter Dickinson states, "Indeed, one of the things that was so refreshing about Vogel's play when it first appeared was how exuberantly 'unchaste' it was in its AIDS dramaturgy" (201). This distinction, or lack of chastity, matters because of the stigma attached to AIDS, which many powerful individuals and groups in the United States saw as a disease of marginalized people based on risky sexual behaviors and intravenous drug use. Writing against the "innocent victim" trope, Vogel reversed what is innocent and what is deviant in *Waltz*, Mansbridge writes, and so "defamiliarizes" the conservative view of AIDS, one of retribution (151). Dickinson adds that "Anna's potty mouth, speaking from and to the pathogenesis *and* the pathologisation of her disease, expresses what Kubler-Ross has no room for in her strictly delimited five stages of grief, namely the *eros* of loss" (201).

Mansbridge and Bigsby, among others, do note that the play hints obliquely at AIDS and public indifference or antipathy toward it when an "*Agitated*" Carl remarks, "If just one grandchild of George Bush caught this thing . . . that would be the last we'd hear about the space program. Why isn't someone doing something?!" (12). Otherwise, however, AIDS is far in the background and sexuality in the foreground. After racing through the five stages in the Kubler-Ross model, the Third Man mentions a sixth not usually included, Hope, followed by something unique to Vogel. The Third Man tells the audience, "Unbeknownst to Elizabeth Kubler-Ross, there is a Seventh Stage for the dying" which he calls "a growing urge to fight the sickness of the body with the health of the body" (29). In keeping with Dickinson's comment about eros, the Third Man adds "The Seventh Stage: Lust" (29). Fittingly, then, sexual activity is salutary, not life threatening, and as the Radical Student Activist tells Anna, "Fucking is a revolutionary act" (45). Anna's reply, "Your hovel or my hotel?" (45), connotes both humor and concurrence. Mansbridge comments that only sex is "literal" in *The Baltimore Waltz*, neither more nor less than "bodily" (156).

In addition to the Kubler-Ross model, *The Baltimore Waltz* also offers a series of lessons, all of them about language. Lesson Number One deals with the "Subject Position," expressed as "I. Je. Ich. Ik" (9), first-person singular in four different languages. From there, the lessons move to "Basic Dialogue," specifically the phone call (13), followed by "Pronouns and the Possessive Case" (14), "Present Tense of Faire" [French, "to do"] (14), a "Basic Dialogue" for the airport (15), "Direct Pronouns" (17), and finally "Basic Vocabulary. Parts of the Body" (23). Seven language lessons, when combined with the play's unique seven stages of dying or grief, call to mind the biblical connotations of seven, especially since the final stage, lust, is also one of Christianity's seven deadly sins. In the Revelation of John, the opening of Seven Seals brings forth the Second Coming, indirectly hinting at a connection with another apocalyptic AIDS-related play, Tony Kushner's *Angels in America*, which was concurrent with *The Baltimore Waltz*.

The last language lesson is a bawdy discussion of body parts between Anna and the Garcon that seems directly inspired by Shakespeare's *Henry V* Act Four, Scene Three. Shakespeare's Alice gives Princess Katherine of France, the future wife of English King Henry V, a course in English vocabulary until Katherine becomes exasperated by "foot" and "count." These words sound enough like the French words "*foutre*" and "*con*," vulgar French terms that refer to having sex and the female genitalia, respectively, that Katherine denounces them but not without uttering them three times. Much the same goes on between Anna and the Garcon except that this time, the French speaker enthusiastically participates in the lesson. Anna has already told Carl that the Eiffel Tower "looks so . . . phallic" (19). The

Garcon reinforces this Freudian interpretation when he refers to his penis as "Ma Tour Eiffel" and "Charles de Gaulle" while also recalling that his grandfather "called his Napoléon" (25). In response to Anna admiring "I guess it runs in your family," the Garcon goes on to discuss his "Grand-mère" and her "con," pausing to ask if Anna can tell "what I am meaning?" (25). Anna replies, "You're making yourself completely clear." In response, the Garcon adds, "We called hers the Waterloo de mon grand-père" (25). The scene ends not in anger but, rather, after Anna "[d]igs under the sheets more," with the Garcon cryptically answering, "Only the Germans have a word for that" (25) just before Carl enters and disrupts the discussion.

Before the language lessons even begin, however, Anna hints at something deeper than merely translating English into other languages spoken in Europe and having some bawdy fun while doing so. Anna reflects a true horror at and an ultimate need to fuse what Swiss linguist and semiotician Ferdinand de Saussure famously termed the *langue* and the *parole*, the signified and the signifier. When Anna says, "It's the language that terrifies me" (10), unbeknownst to her audience, she is recoiling against words like "AIDS" and "death," and she enters the fugue state where Carl says, "I'm here, darling. Right here." Then, Carl gives Anna her first language lesson, which fittingly details first-person pronouns and statements of regret, and he accompanies her on this imaginary voyage that ultimately results in her unconscious processing what she already consciously knows.

Not only is the truth about the language Anna hears withheld from her conscious, but by hiding it behind a flurry of jargon, Vogel keeps it from the audience as well. Consider, for example, one of the Doctor's speeches when he is asked to "explain it very slowly" (9): "Also known as Löffler's Syndrome, i.e., eosinophilia, resulting in fibroblastic thickening, persistent tachycardia, hepatomegaly, splenomegaly, serious effusions into the pleural cavity with edema. It may be *Brugia malayi* or *Wuchereria bencofti*— also known as Weingarten's Syndrome. Often seen with effusions, either exudate or transudate" (9). Each term in this speech has a literal meaning, but together the result is an effusion of words that only a medical doctor (and most likely one with multiple specialities, at that) or researcher could understand. Anna and Carl's confusion in response to the doctor duplicates what AIDS patients and their supporters felt when first encountering such terms as Kaposi's sarcoma or cryptococcal meningitis, maladies once little known that became commonly understood as the AIDS pandemic spread.

As Anna moves from the Baltimore hospital to her remaining language lessons and her European adventure, she will be reminded of her "first sense of loss" and how "[i]t's not a crime. It's an illness" (17). Such recollections serve toward Anna's exorcizing herself of any internalized homophobia (what Vogel finds so objectionable about the "innocent victim" notion). Lesson Number Two introduces *The Third Man*'s Harry Lime to the play. Later, the focus of Lesson Four on verb tense is rendered all the more poignant in the final scene, when the Doctor hands her the "brochures for Europe" and Anna says, "I've never been abroad. We're going to go when he gets—" (57). Here, she pauses for a moment before resuming, "I must learn to use the past tense. We would have gone had he gotten better" (57).

The play is set, with the exception of the end, in the liminal time when Anna cannot yet use the past tense to talk or think about her brother, and so she resurrects him, just as Harry Lime is resurrected in *The Third Man*. Since, as Bigsby notes, the "fact of death must be countered by evidence of life" (*Contemporary* 310), Harry Lime, an American in Vienna, illicitly delivered or denied the new life-saving drug penicillin and also faked his death only to reappear. Thus, he serves as a useful, possibly ideal foil. An important difference lies in the fact that penicillin has, in fact, saved millions of lives since it was introduced to common usage as the Second World War wound down in 1945. The expensive "new drug" available only via the "[b]lack market" (13) is likely azidothymidine (AZT), which, from the mid-1980s on, provided medical relief and a measure of hope to some patients until better medication became available a decade later. Lime plays upon the idea that his drug serves *his* purposes when he tells Carl, "Listen, old man, if you want to be a millionaire, you go into real estate. If you want to be a billionaire, you sell hope" (50). Those upon whom Lime preys remind us of how, Shepard and Lamb note, "America feeds on disenfranchisement" (205), just as Lime reinforces the play's "analogy between Cold War-era anxieties about subversive infiltration and Reagan-era anxieties about the risks posed by those infected with HIV" (205).

The Vogel version of Harry Lime offers no more hope than the man he calls the "Yellow Queen of Vienna" (50), Dr. Todesrocheln, who reenacts the *And Baby Makes Seven* Strangelovian scene, this time replacing the peanut butter and jelly sandwich with a flask of Anna's urine, from which he drinks. At the conclusion of the Todesrocheln scene, the stage directions call for "*the stage lights* [to] *become, for the first time, harsh, stark and white*" (54). The odd slides from Scene Nineteen, which were all (three Disneyland slides excluded) purportedly from Carl's experiences in Europe but in reality a series of depressing photographs of Baltimore, now at last come into only too clear a focus. The audience realizes that the slides have depicted Baltimore not because Carl has been deceived but, rather, because Anna has deceived herself while she struggles to process what she, who has "never been abroad—unless you count Baltimore, Maryland" (7), has just experienced and witnessed.

Finally, the instant in which *The Baltimore Waltz* takes place constitutes, on the part of both Anna and Vogel, a first step in what Jacques Derrida has called "ethical mourning." As Meyda Yeğenoğlu explains, "According to Derrida, mourning, or rather the ethical mourning implies an unending dialogue with the dead other" (27). This "understanding of mourning is based on the question of how to be responsible to the other/friend one mourns for and enables its voice to be heard" (27). Through the play, Anna and, in a much larger sense, Vogel allow both the dramatic Carl and the actual Carl Vogel to speak and, moreover, to do so in a manner Carl Vogel's 1987 letter to his sister very much suggests he would avow. The many ways the play burlesques other works of literature and film is consistent with the "full drag" (*Baltimore* 5) Carl teasingly (?) mentions. Yeğenoğlu adds that "what Derrida calls *ethical mourning* is about not repressing, eliminating, burying or discarding the dead or non-present other" (26). Rather, "memory [of the deceased] is not simply about the past but is a future oriented one" (27). "Derrida," Yeğenoğlu adds, "suggests that the dead other is part of us and . . . because the other is infiltrated to us, it speaks through us; it resists all kinds of annexation" (27).

This definition of mourning contrasts greatly with the Freudian psychoanalytic notion that "the mourner must relive and consequently renounce his/her attachment to the other" and that the mourner "must slowly detach its libido from a loved object and has to put to death the loved one" (Yeğenoğlu 26). Derrida's model of mourning acknowledges what Vogel accomplishes in *The Baltimore Waltz*. Neither she nor Anna denies the "otherness" of Carl, going all the way back to what the Third Man calls the "first separation—your first sense of loss." This occurred when Anna was five, Carl was seven, and their "parents would not let [them] sleep in the same bed anymore" (17). Anna does acknowledge the need to use the past tense going forward, but each time the play is enacted, Carl exists for its first twenty-nine scenes in the present tense and retains a voice. Carl Vogel is deceased, and yet both his memory and even his presence live on in an ongoing dialogue between Anna and her Carl.

The Baltimore Waltz prompted two major critical responses that enhanced Vogel's career. Told by her committee at Brown University, where she was up for tenure, "You're a wonderful teacher. We want to keep you here, but you haven't written a play since *And Baby Makes Seven*," Vogel interrupted her research for *Hot 'N' Throbbing* to write *The Baltimore Waltz* and earned tenure ("Paula Vogel on *The Baltimore Waltz*"). More famously, the play also received the 1992 Obie Award for Best New American Play as well as an acting Obie for Cherry Jones and a directing Obie for Anne Bogart. It was widely, but not universally, praised. Frank Rich, writing for *The New York Times*, wrote that it is a "brittle play" that the Circle Repertory production "handled... sensitively." Rich found Cherry Jones, "that wonderful actress," an "irresistible human guide through the heady wordplay of Ms. Vogel's text." He deemed Richard Thompson "likable in the role of Carl" but was more impressed by director Bogart's "principal accomplice" Joe Mantello (the Third Man and other roles), "who winningly performs a potpourri of burlesque turns in cameo roles of several nationalities and sexual dispositions" (Rich, "Play About AIDS").

Malcolm L. Johnson, *Hartford Courant* Theater Critic, also reviewed the Circle Rep production and countered Rich's claim that "[w]ho Carl is we can only imagine," identifying *The Baltimore Waltz* as "Vogel's reflection on the life and death of her brother Carl."[2] Johnson conceded that the play "sounds like one of those cutesy, self-indulgent, even tasteless new plays that can make theater-going a dreaded experience" but then quickly added that despite, "no, rather in large part because of" such odd touches as the rabbit, the sex scenes, and the ATD jokes, "Vogel's uproarious, searching and finally devastating creation adds up to the very best of theater." Johnson wrote that Vogel "can do as she wishes with an audience" and that Anne Bogart's direction was "finely calibrated, yet free and easy." Jones, she wrote, was "winsome" and "appealingly off-kilter," while Mantello played the "showiest roles." It was Thompson, however, whom Johnson called "the most watchable and charming of actors."

J. Wynn Rousuck, the Theater Critic for *The Baltimore Sun*, was unstinting in her praise for a Baltimore Center Stage production that ran just after the Circle Rep production ended, "[o]pening the same day that former tennis star Arthur Ashe announced he has AIDS." Rousuck called *Waltz* a "landmark play" which "is perhaps the most glowing and creative theatrical effort yet to demystify this dreadful disease." While Rousuck praised the way director Michael Greif "manipulates the play's delicate tone shifts" and also noted much humor in Robert Dorfman's "performance in a dozen different roles," she found as much, if not more, to like in Kristine Nielsen (Anna) and Jonathan Fried (Carl), who conveyed "palpable sibling affection." Rousuck added that "Vogel has said she envisioned [Fried] when she wrote the role of Carl" (Rousuck *Baltimore*). Unlike Rich, who noted that the play's lack of an intermission "did not prevent several Circle Rep subscribers from walking out at a critics' preview," Rousuck found "no question audiences will view [AIDS] differently by the end of this 90-minute production."

One potentially problematic scene with transgressive possibilities is Scene Twenty, in which Anna seduces the *"very young"* (40) Munich Virgin. The lad is a "bellhop" (40) in a hotel owned by his "vater" (41), where he hopes to work his way up to "the responsibility of the front desk" (41). Anna tells the Munich Virgin that she is "very honored" at being his first, for "[y]ou always remember your first time" (41). Anna adds, "I'm a schoolteacher" and offers a "little lesson" (41). Mansbridge notes that this youth's age is "ambiguously described" (158), but the way she chooses to characterize Anna's seduction and concomitant lesson is "tender, almost maternal" (158). Indeed, Mansbridge notes how Anna here perhaps anticipates L'il Bit and the high school student in *How I Learned to Drive* (158). At a minimum, both the seduction in *Waltz* and that in *Drive* require that we consider how we feel about sex between a woman who is approximately thirty years old and a male who is almost certainly a teen. We must also keep in mind that both females are teachers who seduce the much younger male. In light of these considerations, we must contemplate whether such "almost maternal" behavior is predatory.

In addition to the award of tenure and the Obie Award, another direct consequence of *The Baltimore Waltz* and its success is that theatre companies began to perform Vogel's previously neglected plays. Cherry Jones, coming off her own Obie win for *Waltz*, appeared as Anna in a 1993 Circle Rep production of *And Baby Makes Seven* and, later that same year, as Bianca in the same company's production of *Desdemona*.[3] Critics applauded Jones, as noted in Chapter 2, even as they varied in their opinions of these two plays. Anne Bogart facilitated the meeting between Vogel and Jones, encouraging each of them to work with the other. In a joint 1998 interview, Vogel recalled Bogart saying, "There's this great woman. You've got to meet her," and Jones remembered, "There's this great playwright and this great play. Will you do it?" Although Jones, who described herself as "thick when it comes to reading plays," did not argue with Vogel's later assessment that she "didn't understand a word" ("Role") of the play at first, Jones accepted the role, and a productive collaboration between playwright and actor began.

Vogel and Jones experienced professional highs and lows together. Their Obie Awards for *The Baltimore Waltz* were a major high. After the success of *Waltz*, Jones later recalled, her partner "Mary and I would get postcards from Paula and Anne [Fausto-Sterling, Vogel's partner] from exciting locales like Italy or Brazil--and all because productions of the play were being put on there. Suddenly Paula Vogel, this little girl from Maryland, was traveling the world because of this play she had written for the love of her brother" ("Role"). A significant low soon followed in each woman's experience with *And Baby Makes Seven*. Jones received some favorable reviews for her performance, but her recollection was that "it was the biggest disaster I ever had in my career. I had a nervous breakdown." Vogel concurred:

> I was close to a nervous breakdown. As a matter of fact, I was sitting in the back of the theater the week before we opened. [A friend of mine] came because she knew I was in trouble. I held her hand and wept, and I said to her, "I'm so glad that this is happening after my brother died, because I know that that's real tragedy and this is just going to be a show that flops." ("Role")

Neither Vogel nor Jones blamed the other for this production of *Baby* failing. Jones recalled, "There were marvelous people involved all across the board. It just was not the time, and maybe that's all we should say." Vogel offered an assessment of the play itself when she added, "I actually think it's a very sweet little play. It seems to work well as long as it's done on no budget somewhere and if I'm not ever involved" ("Role"). Hence, the two worked together again on *Desdemona*. Moreover, a further collaboration was in mind a few years later when Vogel told Rosemarie Tichler and Barry Jay Kaplan, "I was going to write a play about a castrato for Cherry Jones . . . I was going to write her a 'breeches' role about the greatest castrato of all time, Farinelli, as a young man." Vogel said that she had "the whole thing worked out" (121) until fate intervened via a phone call from Jones, who told Vogel, "I got the role in *The Heiress*. My first Broadway lead" (121). Vogel simply said, "You've got to take that" (121), and moved onto another idea, which became *How I Learned to Drive*.[4]

Just as *The Heiress* took Cherry Jones to Broadway, *The Baltimore Waltz* launched Vogel's career as a national (even international, according to Jones) playwright. In *Waltz*, Vogel, like her protagonist, engages in an act of ethical mourning that any person who has lost a loved one too soon may understand. That the AIDS pandemic, at least in the first world, has largely subsided thanks to protease inhibitors and Truvada (PrEP) in no way minimizes the effect *The Baltimore Waltz* may have upon one who mourns someone taken away by a pandemic,[5] accident, war, or any other death that comes far too early.

David Savran writes that Vogel's plays are about "a return to the scene of the crime, as it were, that signals that everything has remained the same and, simultaneously, changed radically" ("Loose Screws" xiii). In no case is this statement more true than of *Hot 'N' Throbbing*, the play that followed *The Baltimore Waltz* (1995). Vogel recalls that "the play's ending came upon [her] with a terrible clarity" (*Baltimore* 229) while she drove around Provincetown, Rhode Island, late at night, in 1985. Her research took a more formal turn in 1990, "after [her] brother's illness and *Baltimore Waltz*," when Vogel "began reading about domestic violence" after she overheard a violent incident in a car, "drove behind the car at a fast pace until [she] could flag down a police car to pursue the chase," and recoiled in horror when the female victim "declined to press charges" (229). Less than one year later, Vogel writes, she had accumulated a file "crammed two inches thick" (230) of newspaper clippings that reported domestic violence in the city of Provincetown alone.

The 1990 plight of the "NEA Four" (Karen Finley, Tim Miller, John Fleck, and Holly Hughes), who lost their proposed grants because National Endowment for the Arts chairman John Frohnmayer deemed their works obscene, struck Vogel as akin to domestic violence. Learning that "'obscene' came from the Greek, for 'offstage'" (231), Vogel responded to the obscenity pledge required of all NEA fellows when she "applied for an NEA grant, received one and wrote *Hot 'N' Throbbing* to see just what would be perceived as pornographic, eager to test the censorship of the NEA pledge" (230).[6] By 1995, however, Vogel would write that she sensed less of a threat to the artistic community from "Jesse Helms and the fundamentalist Right" than from a reliance on "seasonal offerings and often vacuous theatre" as "theatres have been choosing their seasons from fear rather than conviction" (230). Her own agent, Peter Franklin, whom Vogel characterized as "a man of both literary discrimination and marketing savvy," responded to the first draft of *Hot 'N' Throbbing* by telling Vogel, "I think we may get two productions of this play—one here and one abroad" (230). Vogel expressed her fear that "a benign censorship, a censorship within" could signal "that there is no longer a place for audiences to come to a civic space—the theatre—to confront the disturbing questions of our time" (230). In *Hot 'N' Throbbing*, she both fearfully (because the play may not be performed) and fearlessly (because she moved the obscenity onstage) sought to shine "a communal light in the darkness of our theatres" (231).

Years earlier, in *Desdemona*, Vogel had contemplated the moment before Othello "put out the light" (*Othello* 5.2.7) of Desdemona's life. In *The Oldest Profession*, death takes away Lillian, Mae, Ursula, and Edna, one by one. *And Baby Makes Seven* "kills" Cecil, Henri, and Orphan (albeit temporarily). Finally, *The Baltimore Waltz* has Carl succumb to AIDS. In each case, however, the violence is either at least an instant away in time and/or place or farcical. *Desdemona* ends one brushstroke before Desdemona goes to her deathbed. The women in *The Oldest Profession* all die between scenes, of natural causes, and in a timely fashion. The imaginary children's "deaths" in *Baby* inflict no real pain. Even Carl's death in *The Baltimore Waltz*, which occurs because of the devastation wrought by a horrible illness, occurs out of view and is defamiliarized to the point that when Anna finally confronts it, she does so in the sterile light of a hospital corridor. The violence is literally "obscene," offstage.

Hot 'N' Throbbing is Vogel's first play to enact what the audience should regard as an actual death onstage. What is more, in what Shepard and Lamb call "Vogel's grimmest play" (205), she opts to put out the light in a gruesome manner, the "lust murder" (286), or "snuff film" (235). The masculine Voice, through Claude Dwyers, strangles Charlene with his bare hands, "reenacting Othello's murder of Desdemona" (Shepard and Lamb 206). This act destroys not only the life but also the willed fiction of Charlene, who has thought she was "in control" of "her body," "her thoughts," and "of . . . him" (235). A battered wife who has taken out a restraining order against her husband, Charlene lives in what the directions call "a townhouse that cost $79,900 five years ago, on a 9 ½% mortgage, no deposit down" (233) with "wall-to-wall shag" (234). There, she strives to support her fifteen-year-old daughter, Leslie Ann (who prefers Layla, a name meaning "night" and connoting intoxication and desirability), and fourteen-year-old son, Calvin, by writing women's erotica for Gyno Productions. Like the Voice Over and Gyno Productions, Charlene tries "to create women as protagonists in their own dramas, rather than objects. And we try to appreciate the male body as an object of desire" (262).[7]

From the beginning, *Hot 'N' Throbbing* raises compelling questions of control, not only in the immediate environment of Charlene Dwyers's home but also in the larger sense of who maintains control in what some view as erotica, others as pornography, and still others as obscenity. Bigsby sees this play as a particular instance where Vogel has created "her Yoknapatawpha County" in "work [that] is deliberately sexualized," including a drama "which is simultaneously aware of the degree to which sexual imagery has a history that is predominantly, if not exclusively, male" (*Modern* 415). Although Charlene, at her typewriter, strives to write in her own voice, she also, Mansbridge notes, must negotiate between competing traditions. She strives "to become an author of female pleasure and desire within a history that persistently positions women as object and spectacle" (68). The traditions are represented by two characters, The Voice and the Voice Over (V.O.) Mansbridge describes The Voice as "embodied" and "male" as he speaks from the canon, including Joyce's *Ulysses*, Nabokov's *Lolita*, and Shakespeare's *Othello*. These allusions "both pervade and interrupt Charlene's own narrative voice" (Mansbridge 68). The female V.O., on the other hand, "enacts—more particularly, overacts—and directs," notes Mansbridge, Charlene's script (68). This female V.O. enacts women as the "commodified" and "hypersexualized" onstage "stripper," Mansbridge observes. The Voice eventually turns out to be not only omniscient but also omnipotent, telling V.O., "Cut! Listen, there's been a change in the script" (287). Over the V.O.'s protest, "That's not what we rehearsed," The Voice retorts, "Since when are movies made by screenwriters? Directors make the movies. Not some broad sitting on her ass" (287). Over the course of the play, Charlene has gone from the illusion that she is in control to her diminution into a female object that will soon be destroyed.

That this destructive process would ensnare Charlene results from an ever-increasing need for more exotic and violent sex fare on the part of Clyde and the masculine impulses he represents. Several times, Vogel employs the words of "William Acton, nineteenth-century sexologist" (296) and author of what today's reader would recognize as the pseudoscientific and pseudo psychological text *The Functions and Disorders of the Reproductive Organs in Childhood, Youth, Adult Age and Advanced Life Considered in Their Physiological, Social and Moral Relations*, which she notes came out in its third edition in 1871. She then attributes quotations from Acton's book on male sexuality, especially masturbation, to Richard von Krafft-Ebing, another sexologist who attributed what he called "cerebral neuroses" involving sexuality to masturbation among boys.

At other times, Vogel states in a footnote she has "fabricated . . . quotes in the style of Krafft-Ebing's *Psychopathia Sexualis*" (296) and used them to describe Clyde's "case." The Voice, in a Krafft-Ebing tone, narrates how Clyde, "as a schoolboy, faced disciplinary action due to hyperesthesia sexualis—Masturbatio Coram Discipulis in Schola" (254). The V.O., at first, "*is impressed*" and responds "*[e]rotically*" (254) to this apparent show of erudition. Despite this "self-abuse," we learn, Clyde "fulfilled his marital duties in a typical if somewhat energetic manner, not yet exhibiting the traits of hysteria virilis that led to the breakdown of said marriage" (255). Moments later, The Voice (as Krafft-Ebing) ominously continues, "However, in time the constant excitation of hysteria virilis leads in turn to paresthesia sexualis. The subject became convinced in his mind that only violence done to his fetishized obsession could restore him to his former virility" (263). We see such violence enacted in a flashback to three years ago, when The Voice tells us, "Subject increasingly resorted to violence against wife as an erotic stimulus for erec—" (274). Stage directions state, "*The Man strikes The Woman hard on the face; in slow motion, it almost looks like a caress*" (274). Perhaps a degree of apparent confusion between love and violence helps explain why Charlene waits before leaving Clyde and, eventually, seeking legal remedy against him.

The next time the subject of Clyde's increasing need for violent stimulation comes up, it does so in his own words. He tells Charlene, "I go into a corner bookstore, and it's packed. And I change a five into quarters, and slip into the booth. . .and I—" (283), leading her possibly to believe he satisfies his lust until he confesses, "All it does is get me even more agitated." Clyde goes on, "I'm like numb to that by now" (283), and so he searches his truck for the money to hire a prostitute. Clyde has wound up at Charlene's house because finding only "a lousy eighteen dollars and thirty-seven cents" (283) means he cannot afford a sex worker. Clyde's hopes for a satisfactory sexual experience with Charlene seem to be a chimera, however, for he admits that "lately nothing really seems to do it for me," and "all the usual . . . uh . . . escapes . . . turn me on but they don't work anymore" (284). He acknowledges that "it's building up into a big problem now" (284) and soon breaks into tears.

Charlene's decision in response is as shocking as it is unfortunate for her. She tells Clyde, "Okay—listen. I'm just a woman on a Friday night, okay? I've come down on my price for you—just one—just tonight—for $18.37" (285). Clyde, "*unable to believe his luck*," tells Charlene, "I don't have . . . anything on me . . . you know? In case" (285). Charlene laughingly replies that she has "got some protection in the house" (285), in response to which Clyde "*scowls*," and The Voice echoes, "She's got protection in the house" (285). Soon after, what The Voice calls "a change in the script" occurs, and the V.O. fruitlessly protests, "Hey, guys, wait, these restraints are awfully tight" (287). As the action returns to Charlene and Clyde, they exchange what at first seem tender embraces until Clyde, perhaps ritualistically, "*rubs her face with the blood*" (289) she drew earlier when she shot him in the buttock. During the ever more violent scene that follows, the Man (Clyde) lip syncs what The Voice says while the Woman (Charlene) and V.O. do likewise. The Voice asks if the female(s) can remember "the last time," an occasion "[w]hen I beat you to within an inch of your life," but even so, Charlene "didn't learn" (290).

The "heavily stylized" yet "raw and painful" (Shepard and Lamb 207) murder scene enacts many of the tragic clichés of domestic violence. The Voice calls V.O./Charlene a "Bitch" and demands, "What makes you think, with your big fat butt and your cow thighs, that you're worth eighteen bucks?" (292). When Clyde's voice takes over, he even cries as he claims, "You're the one making me do this, Charlene. You shoud of never—never gotten that restraining order" (293). "A man's house," he goes on, "is his Castle. His. Fucking. Castle. What we do here is our business" (293). The Voice, in a speech "*[w]hispered under/simultaneous with Voice-Over*," cites Molly Bloom's lines that conclude James Joyce's *Ulysses*, including a "yes." V.O., to the contrary, protests, "no" (293). Clyde ends Charlene's bid for freedom and her life when he "*strangles The Woman with his bare hands*" and "*leaves*" (294). Continuing to quote Joyce, The Voice concludes with Molly Bloom's final echoed "Yes" (294), perverted beyond anything besides rote recognition. The idea of Charlene possessing sexual agency that excludes him has rendered Clyde temporarily mad, as he indicates when telling her that she's "the one *making me* do this" (293, emphasis mine). Thus, Joyce, wrenched horribly from context or placed firmly within the context of what Bigsby calls "a male attempt to enter a female sensibility, to understand something of female sexuality" (*Contemporary* 314), fittingly narrates the events surrounding this ultimate confrontation of and combination between sex and violence.

Arguably even more than Voice and V.O. or Charlene and Clyde, the third set of two in *Hot 'N' Throbbing*—The Girl/Leslie Ann/Layla and The Boy/Calvin—constitute the most problematic pair in the play. The first two couples behave in a way that is both canonically and culturally overdetermined. Vogel's use of the canon shows, note Shepard and Lamb, "that it is a shorter distance than is usually acknowledged from *Ulysses*, *Plexus*, *Lolita*, or *Othello* . . . to its own final scene" (206). Charlene's agreement to prostitute herself for Clyde's benefit, Shepard and Lamb go on, "is a fantasy she has agreed to act out because her cultural training to please her man overrides both her memories of their relationship and her instincts" (207). Vogel reinforces the cultural component with her aforementioned file of local domestic violence articles and her reminder that the "premiere of *Hot 'N' Throbbing* occurred two months before the murder of Nicole Simpson" (230). Vogel also presents Leslie Ann and Calvin so as to reinforce that what they observe around them imprints itself upon their adolescent consciousness and consciences.

The play opens when, "*[i]n a growing* **blue light**, *we see The Girl dressed in very tight pants and a halter top, making suggestive stripper or vogueing movements*" (235), inappropriate attire and activities for a child of approximately fifteen. When she speaks soon after, although she remains "*dressed as before*," her words suit her age better. "MAAHM!" she screams. "WHERE'S YOUR EYELINER?" (235). Part of what follows echoes a scene repeated in families every weekend across America: Leslie Ann wants to go to her friend Lisa's for a sleepover, Charlene initially forbids her to go because she does not believe Lisa is properly supervised, Leslie Ann disobeys and flees to Lisa's car while Charlene is annoyed enough to say, "Oh, Jesus. I could use a cigarette" (241). Charlene's fears soon give way to the pressure of being "behind . . . schedule," for "I've got to get out forty pages by the first mail tomorrow morning, and I'm on page twenty-six" (237).

These words and actions may seem ordinary or "normal" enough until they are juxtaposed with other parts of the first scene. Granted, Vogel has told Bigsby, "I would not believe ANYTHING in *Hot 'N' Throbbing* that takes place under blue light . . . like Peter Shaffer's *Black Comedy*, the stage lights are a device to separate stage worlds: the blue lights signify a stage fantasy that is not literally true" (*Contemporary* 313). Nonetheless, what happens under both the blue light and the stage light can be disturbing. Before Calvin speaks, under blue light we see "*[e]xaggerated movements of Boy humping Girl from behind with clothes on*" (237). Under stage light, Calvin asks, "Are you going out in those tight pants?" (237), which he says are "so tight you can see your P.L.s" (237).[8] Leslie Ann calls Calvin a "creep" (237) and suggests, "Why don't you just go beat-off in your room, you little pervo . . ." (238). Over Calvin's denial, Leslie Ann insists, "You beat-off! In the catcher's mitt Daddy gave you for Christmas! I can feel the walls shaking!" (239). Rather than inquiring into her son's sexual habits, Charlene immediately eroticizes his possible fetish, "*making notes*" that include "Catcher's mitt. Open Window. Show Clipboard. Notes: Leather catcher's mitt" (239). Still under stage light and while Charlene is absorbed with her work, Leslie Ann tells Calvin, "I might just learn you something interesting" so that "you won't haveta hang in the bushes outside the house" (240). When Calvin "*is suddenly quiet, beet red*," Leslie Ann confirms her suspicion that "it was you. Watching me undressing" (240). Rather than becoming angry, however, she goes on, "Yeah. I might just let you learn" (240). A blue light scene with a quotation from *Lolita* follows, and soon after comes another scene where Calvin "*stands, like a somnambulist, with his catcher mitt, looking up, staring*" (244) and later, under stage light, "*fondling his catcher's mitt*" (245). This youth, "not yet old enough to shave" (244),[9] already possesses what Mansbridge calls a "burgeoning sexuality," and the references, both under blue light and stage light, to Calvin's masturbation reveal "the ubiquitous and intersecting ways we learn and perform our sexualities, both inside and outside the home" (75). That these performances can be intertwined with members of our biological families may hint at the greater dysfunction within the family of *Hot 'N' Throbbing*.

When Clyde breaks down the door to Charlene's house, violating both the restraining order and what should be the safe space in which Charlene, Leslie Ann, and Calvin live, Calvin interrupts his reverie of mindlessly feeding quarters into a peep show and tries to come to his mother's rescue. Charlene and Clyde begin to kiss, only to be interrupted when "*The Boy flies into the room*" and, assuming the role of Charlene's protector tells his father, "I AM. GONNA. *KILL* YOU!!" (266). Although Charlene interrupts, "CALVIN! NO! STOP!" (267), father and son wrestle, and "*The Boy, from behind, gets The Man in a lock*" and even begins "*choking him*" (267). In a moment which recalls August Wilson's *Fences*, Calvin echoes Cory's "You don't count around here no more" when he says, "*You* don't live here anymore. Get it?" (287). Clyde is no more receptive to his son's assertion of masculine power than is Troy Maxson in *Fences*, gaining the upper hand but, unlike Troy's banishment of Cory, inducing Calvin into a chorus of "I'm warmer than shit and tighter than mud" (269). After this moment fades, however, Calvin eventually exclaims, "I AM SO FUCKED UP!" (273) before he slams the door and leaves, not to reappear until, "*watching the action*," he "*cries*" during the eventual "snuff film" (288). Calvin, arguably in hopeless, repetitive fashion, exemplifies what Bigsby calls "the voyeurism which is [the play's] apparent subject but then led, by a seemingly inexorable logic, to the violence which provides its climax" (*Contemporary* 316). The oddity of Charlene's describing to Calvin, early on, her frustrating search for synonyms for "throbbing" (242 ff.) gives way to the horror of the youth viewing the action that results in his mother's body no longer throbbing or its heart beating at all. His final words are both true and prophetic.[10]

Leslie Ann is no less problematic than her brother. The attire she wears when we first see her, which seems inappropriate to her age, fits with initial movement under the blue light as well as with an elaborate fantasy life

Calvin constructs for her. Calvin describes a complicated trip into town and "this joint" where the bouncer "always pats Leslie Ann on the fanny" (246). Changing into "the scanty sequins and the two inch heels," the "jailbait" teens "wrap their legs around the poles" and eventually perform "full splits to scoop up the dollar bills that will pay for the midnight double feature at the Mall and the burgers afterward at Big Bob's" (247). This juxtaposition of the striptease and teens enjoying the Mall and burgers jars the audience's minds, most likely even after Calvin tries to calm his mother's worries with "Jesus, mom. Take a joke, will ya? She probably hangs out at Lisa's being dumb" (247). This more benign vision is, indeed, what Vogel has told Bigsby is the way she understands Leslie Ann, who she has said "is innocently with her girlfriends at a slumber party and driving around, and watching horror movies in someone's basement" (*Contemporary* 314). That may well be. A seed has been sown, nevertheless, that blooms into Calvin's eroticizing and fetishizing his sister's body. Clyde joins in, telling Calvin, "You gotta watch her, son" because "That body of hers . . . your sister should be *licensed*" (269). Calvin's "I watch her all the time" (269) reveals more than he intends. Even Charlene participates in the heightened sexuality within her own nuclear family, for driven by her need to earn a living through her words, she draws erotic material not only from Calvin and his catcher's mitt but also from what may be a fantasy of her stripper daughter.

When Leslie Ann finally discusses sexuality while apart from her nuclear family, she does so while addressing "*her best friend Lisa*" (276) but in reality hearing replies from V.O. Leslie Ann opens with an unsurprising question: "Do you . . . do you . . . think of boys a lot?" (277). V.O./Lisa replies that she does, and then Lisa greatly intensifies the discussion. "[D]o you think of them, like, 'hurting' you?" (278) she demands. Then, she adds, "Well, I don't mean like hurting you, but like, you're tied down and you can't stop them." She qualifies her comments by claiming that "it makes you get hot only it's 'cause it's not for real" (278). The notion that Leslie Ann's fantasies draw influence and inspiration from her mother's writing makes perfect sense and renders Charlene's next line, "Leslie Ann is still a child. And I want her to have every second of childhood that she can get" (278), all the more hollow. This wish comes too late, as Leslie Ann hammers home when she concludes the play by sitting at her mother's chair and retyping the first words of the play, down to Vogel's tag, "VOICE-OVER: She was hot. She was throbbing. But she was in control. Control of her body. Control of her thoughts" (295).

Shepard and Lamb despair in the conclusion. They note that Leslie Ann "seems unmoved by Woman's [aka her mother's] cooling body on stage as she enters and picks up where Charlene had stopped in the first scene" (206). From this and other evidence in the last scene, they lament that "the hint that Woman may have died in vain is difficult to ignore" (208). Bigsby finds more ambiguity in the conclusion, writing, "In one sense [Leslie Ann] deliberately de-feminises herself . . . avoiding the male gaze, refusing to be looked at, but also replicating her mother's actions, apparently learning nothing" (315). Bigsby does grant, "In another sense, she becomes the manipulator rather than the manipulated" but then blasts any hopefulness by noting "that in this play the two roles hardly seem to differ" (315).

Mansbridge discerns Vogel's own trouble extricating the play from the "cycles of violence" (86) represented in *Hot 'N' Throbbing* in a discussion of three different stagings of the end that were put onstage between 1994 and 2005. In one of these productions, Molly Smith overruled Vogel's desire to present Leslie Ann as a university professor lecturing about violence and sexuality (Mansbridge 87) and, instead, had Leslie freeze upon encountering her mother's corpse and then relax upon hearing, "It's okay. It's all right" (Mansbridge 87) from V.O.[11] Finally, in the 2005 Signature Theatre production, Les Waters directed a version that offered what Mansbridge calls "Vogel's preferred ending," to show Leslie Ann as a literature professor and Calvin, ten years on, teaching while he works as a Hollywood screenwriter (87). Ending the play this way, Mansbridge writes, calls particular attention to what can result from an "intellectual engagement," a "critical questioning," and a "revision" of the past and of works that still "inform our bodies and imaginations" (87–8). This brief history illustrates a willingness on Vogel's part to revise, even after a work has appeared in print (as *Hot* did in 1996). The play, not the text, is the thing.

Reviewer Markland Taylor wrote that the 1994 American Repertory Theatre production, directed by Anne Bogart, was "finding it hard to live up to [major financial supporters'] faith in it" and "may have more impact if it were simplified or if it were turned into a film script." Taylor did grant that "Vogel poses numerous questions, including what differences there are between pornography, erotica and adult entertainment and what, if anything, they contribute to sexual abuse" and, moreover, that it "is a legitimate reaction to the current rash of sexual revelations on the sleaze-talkshow [sic] circuit." Ultimately, however, Taylor found the play "just another reworking of the dysfunctional family cliché."

Baltimore Sun critic J. Wynn Rousuck thought better of the 1999 Molly Smith-directed production. Calling the play "a theatrical 911 call that no serious theatergoer can afford to ignore," Rousuck found in the Arena Stage production "an ending that now contains the slightest vestige of hope for the next generation" while, at the same time, *Hot* "still seems uncompromisingly honest, and it is performed with searing intensity—and occasional flashes of humor—by Smith's closely attuned cast."[12]

The 2005 Signature Theatre production, directed by Les Waters, concluded a Signature season devoted to Vogel's works. Dan Bacalzo, writing for *Theater Mania*, deemed it "a nice way to wrap up the company's season." Bacalzo acknowledged the production as "not perfect," particularly the performance of Matthew Stadelmann as Calvin, whom he called "never believable" and whose "awkward mannerisms take the viewer out of the production." Among the "few plot holes that are hard to swallow," Bacalzo did not discuss the ending, and he praised the rest of the performances as "absolutely terrific" and singled out the set design, light design, costuming, and sound as all praiseworthy.

New York Times reviewer Jason Zinoman wrote as if he had seen a different play and production. Zinoman sarcastically wrote of Vogel's preferred ending, "The play concludes, appropriately enough, in a lecture hall" and added that the play was neither "hot" nor "throbbing." Zinoman granted that Vogel's "kind of daring has resulted in some triumphs," but he added that "it also has potential pitfalls, some of which are prominently on display in Les Waters's off-key production." While "[c]elebrities like Paris Hilton and the porn star Jenna Jameson have helped put pornography increasingly into the homes of mainstream American families, making this play seem as relevant as ever," Zinoman went on to say, "the play still feels as if it could use one more round of editing." This statement, Zinoman understood, applied to the third different version of the play.

These varying responses to the multiple versions of *Hot 'N' Throbbing* seem to make it what Shakespeare scholars would call a problem play. Vogel appears to have written a harsh critique (or three harsh critiques if we view each ending as producing a separate play) of the masculine gaze, even when a woman attempts to be "in control" of it. This message has not impressed itself upon many reviewers, who often do not know what to make of the stage business that is not performed by the central characters onstage. Nor do reviewers like Zinoman understand the didactic nature of a grown-up Leslie Ann as a professor, for they pass the lecture hall off as yet another place of dull speeches. The central conceit in *Hot 'N' Throbbing* remains elusive, at least for now.

To a lesser extent, the Munich Virgin in *The Baltimore Waltz* and, to a far greater extent, the Girl/Leslie Ann of "[a]bout fifteen" and the Boy/Calvin of "[a]bout fourteen" (*Hot* 232) in *Hot 'N' Throbbing* demonstrate how, by the 1990s, Vogel was coming to terms dramatically with characters who are physically mature yet still legally children. The multiple endings of *Hot 'N' Throbbing*, the first of which imagines the Girl maturing, dressing, and becoming "*protected from our gaze*" (294) until she takes her mother's place at the keyboard, and the last of which presents her as a university professor who has achieved "an intellectual engagement with the past" (Mansbridge 87–8) which liberates her from writing pornography and puts her under a gaze stereotypically addressed toward male authority figures, strongly suggest the playwright's own struggles to reconcile these issues for herself. In *How I Learned to Drive* (1997), Vogel confronted the issue of adolescent sexuality directly and achieved her greatest success to date.

How I Learned to Drive, like Vogel's earlier works, both engages canonical texts and incorporates autobiographical elements. Vogel sets the play in Beltsville, Maryland, in the 1960s, approximately the place and time of her youth, and she invokes her own grandparents, including the Grandfather L'il Bit identifies as the source of her "cracker background" and who "[v]oted for George Wallace" (21). L'il Bit also mentions Grandmother believing in "all the sacraments of the church, to the day she died" (42) and has her mother ask, "What does an eighty-year-old priest know about love-making with girls" (49), positing an unusual identity of a Catholic "Cracker" that seems consistent with what we know of Phyllis Rita Bremerman Vogel's family. Grandfather's voracious sexual appetite dates back to his having sex thrice daily with Grandma when she was a "child bride" who still "believed in Santa Claus and the Easter Bunny" (42), and functions, at least somewhat, to problematize the audience's attitude toward the only comparatively recent illegality of Peck's behavior toward L'il Bit.

Vogel's engagement with other literary texts is less pervasive than when *Desdemona* goes behind the scenes of *Othello* or *And Baby Makes Seven* elaborates upon unusual families as presented in Albee's *Who's Afraid of Virginia Woolf?* The engagement is sometimes subtle, as in when C. W. E. Bigsby writes that *Drive* "was inspired, or perhaps provoked, by Mamet's *Oleanna*" (*Modern* 415), a play Bigsby describes as "purported to create a balance between its two characters, one male, one female" (*Contemporary* 318). Mansbridge challenges Bigsby's characterization of *Oleanna*, noting that the play's ending seems "inevitable," given the work's "linear naturalism" (123). The recursive *Drive*, on the other hand, is both reminiscent of such earlier plays as *Waltz* and a way for Vogel to disclose information precisely as she wishes.

The more obvious influence on *Drive* comes from Nabokov's *Lolita*; indeed, Vogel described the play to Elizabeth Farnsworth as "*Lolita* from Lolita's point of view" ("A Prize-Winning"). This statement requires considering *Lolita* from Vogel's point of view. In her interview with Farnsworth, Vogel calls *Drive* "in many ways a love story between Little [*sic*] Bit and her uncle, Uncle Peck" (Vogel "Prize-Winning"). While interviewing Vogel, Arthur Holmberg stated, "*Drive* dramatizes in a disturbing way how we receive great harm from the people who love us." Vogel demurred. Instead, she said, "I would reverse that. I would say that we can receive great love from the people who harm us." She tells Holmberg this reversal comes as a denial of the "culture of victimization," where "great harm can be inflicted by well-intentioned therapists, social workers, and talk show hosts who encourage people to dwell in their identity as victim." Despite the pain we may endure from others, Vogel argues that "great gifts . . . can also be inside that box of abuse" (Holmberg "Through the Eyes"). We may infer, then, that Vogel feels at least a modicum of sympathy—or even negative empathy—for Nabokov's Humbert Humbert.

This understanding of *Lolita* is controversial and hotly debated. Lisa Zunshine calls *Lolita* "another novel that challenged its readers' metarepresentational capacity with its figure of the unreliable narrator" (101). In Zunshine's view, Humbert is nothing more than a liar and a "sexual predator" (101), and she cites none other than Nabokov himself as an author who "felt compelled to correct his readers' misperception" (102) and called Humbert "a vain and cruel wretch who manages to appear touching" (Nabokov 94). Deborah Hull points out that *Lolita* and *Drive* both rely upon the automobile, which Humbert Humbert utilizes as "a confined space in which Humbert can forge a closer relationship with his step-daughter" (49), even though, it must be noted, Lolita is trapped in the vehicle while L'il Bit is literally at the wheel. Hull echoes Zunshine (and, in fact, Nabokov) in her declaration "that Nabokov never intended for his audience to sympathize with Humbert Humbert, as Vogel does with Uncle Peck" (4). To readers who agree with Zunshine and Hull, Vogel's sympathy for Humbert (and, similarly, perhaps for Uncle Peck) will be discomfiting.

This is not to say, however, that Vogel wishes the audience to sympathize entirely or even primarily with Uncle Peck. Peck's name, Vogel has said repeatedly, was inspired by the actor Gregory Peck, who portrayed Atticus Finch in the 1962 Robert Mulligan filmed version of Harper Lee's *To Kill a Mockingbird*. The name also has another source, which the adult L'il Bit reveals: "In my family, folks tend to get nicknamed for their genitalia. Uncle Peck, for example" (16). Peck, then, derives from the crude slang term "pecker" and is not even Uncle Peck's real name, an appellation we never learn. Uncle Peck's being identified and driven by his genitals clearly lessens both sympathy and empathy directed toward him. Still, in keeping with Vogel's telling Holmberg that "it takes a whole village to molest a child" (Vogel "Through the Eyes"), Vogel has Peck behave very differently from Humbert in that he agrees to clear boundaries with L'il Bit, telling her, "Nothing is going to happen until you want it to" (37), and Uncle Peck repeatedly brings L'il Bit home to her family, where he is accepted and even loved. His wife Mary suspects something amiss but does not blame her husband. Mary tells the audience, "And I want to say this about my niece. She's a sly one, that one is. She knows exactly what she's doing." Mary also defends Peck: "My husband was such a good man—is. Is such a good man" (76).

Peck tells L'il Bit, "I'm just a very ordinary man" (34), but he is unordinary both in the ways he inflicts and reflects trauma. Vogel withholds the full extent of L'il Bit's trauma until the final two scenes, the first of which reveals that Uncle Peck began molesting L'il Bit when she was only eleven years old. Her response was one of denial and possibly disassociation: "This isn't happening," she says, "*[t]rying not to cry*" (103). The last scene then begins with L'il Bit recalling, "That day was the last day I lived in my body. I retreated above the neck, and I've lived inside the 'fire' in my head ever since" (103). Alan Shepard and Mary Lamb discuss this disjunction of mind and body, discovering in the entirety of Vogel's plays "that memory is recorded and recalled through sensory experiences, that the human body is an archive of its past, that the past is sometimes known to the body generally but not to the mind itself" (208). Hence, the adult L'il Bit calls to mind "A Walk Down Mammary Lane" (59).

Shepard and Lamb also assert a theory that is less persuasive, in light of the way L'il Bit seems to perpetuate the cycle of violation in the carefully choreographed scene, all the way down to her using "dramaturgically speaking" (47), with the youth who claims to be a high school senior at Walt Whitman High School. According to Shepard and Lamb, "L'il Bit's recovery from the abuse does not depend on her telling her story as a kind of therapy," but rather the story "emerges in a controlled, distanced way," neither as "unmediated recollection" nor "the return of the repressed" (208). The play undercuts this notion at least three times. One comes in L'il Bit's plaintive query, "Who did it to you, Uncle Peck? How old were you? Were you eleven?" (98). Furthermore, she describes how she was "kicked out of that fancy school in 1970" because of her "constant companion," the alcoholic beverage "Canadian V.O. A fifth a day" (25). Then, in a moment that echoes Uncle Peck's having missed Thanksgiving of 1964 because "there were . . . 'things' going on" (80), L'il Bit tells the audience, "I stayed away from Christmas and Thanksgiving for years after" (97).

In the most obvious sense, the "it" that L'il Bit believes happens to Uncle Peck is sexual violation like that which he perpetrates upon her and, by inference, Cousin Bobby in South Carolina. Bigsby notes that the scene with Bobby "had not featured in [Vogel's] own outline for the play," but nevertheless, "[w]hen she was invited to delete the scene she insisted on retaining it" because she saw Peck's "equal attraction to young girls and boys as a necessary counterbalance to assumptions that paedophiles are gay" (*Contemporary* 322) and as a way of defending Carl Vogel posthumously against gay slurs. The very inclusion of this scene requires a willing suspension of disbelief by the audience, for it is the only scene which L'il Bit, the narrator of the play, has no means of witnessing.

This "it" may also extend beyond sexual exploitation. We learn that Uncle Peck is a Second World War veteran who, when L'il Bit inquires about his service, becomes "*[s]uddenly taciturn*" and stutters, "I . . . I did just this and that. Nothing heroic or spectacular" (31). Although Uncle Peck's Second World War service comes long after he is eleven, the experiences he had while fighting may well have had the same traumatizing influence upon him as one or more sexual molestations. Aunt Mary refers to his "troubles" and says, "I wonder, sometimes, what happened to him during the war," a time when soldiers "didn't have 'rap sessions' to talk about their feelings" (77). She believes this trouble dating to the 1940s "has burrowed deeper than the scar tissue" and, with unspecified frequency, leads to his "having a bad spell" that renders him passive "until it passes" (77). Bigsby describes the man as "plainly lonely and disturbed, driven by demons he can neither name nor defeat" (326). Nor may L'il Bit or Aunt Mary name what afflicts Uncle Peck, other than to offer cogent guesses about its origins.

A twenty-first-century audience may identify what we call post-traumatic stress disorder (PTSD) as the source of Uncle Peck's problems. As Hull points out, however, "it was not until 1980 that post-traumatic stress disorder (PTSD) was coined in the third edition of the Diagnostic and Statistical Manual of Mental Disorders (DSM)" (17–18). "Terms," Hull adds, "such as 'soldier's heart' or 'irritable heart,' 'shell-shocked,' and 'combat fatigue' dominate the rhetoric of war history" (17) and literature prior to the identification and naming of PTSD. This is not to say that pre-1980 war literature lacked examples and a language to describe what we would eventually see as PTSD. Ernest Hemingway's 1925 story "Soldier's Home," for example, introduces the character Harold Krebs, who "came back much too late" (41) to his Oklahoma home town from the Great War, or what we now call the First World War. Krebs experiences a time when he "did not want to talk about the war at all" (41), and when he does, he tells lies twice and then "had a reaction against the war and against talking about it" (41). Krebs lives in an ennui, most likely depression, which seems an ongoing version of Uncle Peck's "spells." Krebs only minimally experiences sexual desire: "Vaguely he wanted a girl but he did not want to have to work to get her" (42). "You did not need a girl" (43), he tells himself. After an extended period, Krebs's worried and confused parents finally intervene, with his mother delivering the message that he needs to stir from home and the library. When Harold shows no real interest in "mak[ing] a start at something" (46), his mother implores, "Don't you love your mother, dear boy?" (46). The heartrending answer is, "No." (46). An ensuing lie that he "didn't mean it" (46) seems to bring the mother some comfort, but it leaves Krebs still numb, for "none of it had touched him" (47). A "sick and vaguely nauseated" Krebs does not self-medicate with alcohol, as does Uncle Peck, but his method of coping, in the short period the story covers, seems scarcely more effective than Uncle Peck's.

Hull "cannot say with authority that Uncle Peck satisfies the two criteria necessary to be diagnosed with PTSD" (19); nevertheless, she believes the evidence "shows Uncle Peck has deep and lasting psychic alterations caused by the war" (19–20). For both Uncle Peck and Harold Krebs, however, an attempt to psychoanalyze thoroughly and to render a diagnosis may result in a futile struggle with semantics. David Morse, the actor who originated the role of Uncle Peck, states simply, "He's a guy who's been through World War II and suffered terrible things over there . . . which are only hinted at in the play" (Morse). We don't need to know the exact nature of what either Krebs or Uncle Peck has experienced during a world war to understand how each man is traumatized to the point of dissociation and dysfunction such as that which has Uncle Peck finally drink himself to death circa 1976. Uncle Peck's having been, in L'il Bit's mind, almost certainly the victim of molestation only renders his life more complicated and sad. L'il Bit says,

"Sometimes I think of my uncle as a kind of Flying Dutchman." Forever "in his Chevy '56, a spirit driving up and down the back roads of Carolina," this Uncle Peck seeks but cannot find "a young girl who, of her own free will, will love him. Release him" (98).

L'il Bit refuses to view Uncle Peck entirely as a monster. Bigsby, too, discerns an "attempt to create a character with negative empathy, to find ways of engaging audiences with a character to whom they would feel instinctively hostile" (*Modern* 415). The pastiche of attitudes toward adolescent sexuality presented in the play draws attention away from what we may, at first, call perversion on Uncle Peck's part. His behavior, while transgressive, is not dissimilar to that of Grandfather. Back when, Grandmother recalls, "[i]t was legal, what Daddy and I did" and "fourteen was a grown-up woman" (43), Grandfather singled her out as "the baby of the family" (43) with an entire "herd of [older] sisters" (43) and began imposing his sexual will upon her immediately. Grandfather also objectifies and embarrasses a seventeen-year-old L'il Bit when he says, "She's got all the credentials she'll need on her chest" (20). He mocks Grandmother's wish that "maybe someone in this family will finish high school" (50). When L'il Bit speaks enthusiastically about a college Shakespeare course, Grandfather snorts, "How is Shakespeare going to help her lie on her back in the dark?" (21). Even so, while misogynistic Grandfather disgustingly gazes upon his own granddaughter, he never crosses a line toward pedophilia and seems to have his desires still sated by the young girl, now grown old, whom he married.

Neither Grandmother's early history nor *Lolita* readings by such critics as Zunshine suggest any agency on the part of L'il Bit that would further mitigate our attitudes toward Uncle Peck, but other factors do. Not the least is Vogel's own attitude toward *Lolita*. Bigsby quotes Vogel in the Century Theatre *Playbill* as calling Nabokov's novel "fascinating to me because it was so even handed and so neutral" (*Contemporary* 319). Viewing *Lolita* may require granting Lolita some agency. Bigsby takes the next logical step, saying that *How I Learned to Drive* is, in fact, "a genuine love story in which love finds its apotheosis not in consummation but sacrifice" (*Contemporary* 319). The play's only mention of pedophilia is in a neologism, "pedophilish (?)" (6), which comes in a stage direction describing period music.

Music in *Drive* helps portray a zeitgeist where dismissing the possibility of L'il Bit having agency solely on the basis of her age is difficult. Dipa Janardanan raises the issue of how music problematizes our understanding of L'il Bit, writing, "Or, is there something larger going on? What should we think? ... stage directions state that any Sam Cooke will do" [31] (9). Vogel's directions also say that "sixties music is rife with [such] references" as "the 'You're Sixteen' genre hits" like the Beach Boys' "Little Surfer Girl" (9). L'il Bit develops a woman's body early, and Vogel repeatedly calls attention to her breasts, packaging the play with *The Minneola Twins* in a volume titled *The Mammary Plays*, and in the shower scene, when two girls confirm that L'il Bit's large breasts are not the result of padding her brassiere. One girl exults, "Told you it's not foam rubber!" (62).

The legal system may lay one claim about whether a young teen bears any responsibility for what happens to her sexually, but Bigsby writes, "as L'il Bit's grandmother reminds her, the law and biology are not the same" (*Contemporary* 326). Granted, Mother's telling eleven-year-old L'il Bit, "I'm warning you—if anything happens, I'm holding you responsible" (100) is a cruel echo of what Grandmother told L'il Bit's unwed, pregnant mother, and the timing could not be worse: it immediately precedes the first molestation. However, the ongoing sessions between the two are presented as L'il Bit's idea. While Uncle Peck washes the Christmas dishes in 1964, a thirteen-year-old L'il Bit suggests, "We could meet and talk—once a week" (81). The secrecy surrounding these meetings also comes from L'il Bit, who says, "I don't think I'd want Mom to know. Or Aunt Mary" (82). L'il Bit further indicates agency when, at seventeen, she says, "That's right" after Uncle Peck assures her, "I'm not gonna do anything you don't want me to do." She grants him permission to "undo" her bra as long as he will "be quick about it" (13). This scene, which is presented at the beginning of the play so as to build sympathy for Uncle Peck before darker revelations come, illustrates what Bigsby calls "the arbitrariness of the lines drawn by society" (*Contemporary* 322) between statutory rape and legal sex.

Adolescent L'il Bit can hardly control the way society genders her mature body or the early attention it receives, any more than the automobile can choose how it will be gendered. The audience actually witnesses the moment when L'il Bit genders Uncle Peck's automobile. "It doesn't have to be a 'she,'" Uncle Peck says, recommending that L'il Bit "close your eyes and think of someone who responds to your touch—someone who performs just for you and gives you what you ask for" (58). Having been taught "to drive like a man," meaning "with confidence—with aggression" (58), L'il Bit recalls, "I closed my eyes—and decided not to change the gender" (59). This particular lesson seems to Mansbridge part of L'il Bit's effort "to find the ontological middle road between active subject and passive object, masculine and feminine, power and powerlessness" (132). Although Uncle

Peck sees himself as subject and L'il Bit as object, his insistence that she learn the "control" that "[m]anual gives you" (56) allows her to view herself as a subject and the car as an object. Uncle Peck's teaching L'il Bit to drive ultimately gives her a power he almost certainly cannot anticipate, the power the (barely) adult L'il Bit has to drive him away when her response to his marriage proposal is "You should go home to Aunt Mary. Go home now, Uncle Peck" (97). Her never seeing him again is proof that these are not idle words. It might even be argued that L'il Bit, without both the positive and negative influences of Uncle Peck, never could have moved into an independent adulthood with an identity not fully determined by her unsympathetic family. This potentiality is lost, to be certain, on an audience that focuses entirely on both age and gender, however. Graley Herren points out that "L'il Bit angers some audience members by not being sufficiently angry at Peck" (112). Even Mary-Louise Parker noted the occasional outrage, telling Vogel, "They walked out of *How I Learned to Drive* sometimes." An unfazed Vogel replied, "There's something wrong with the play if they don't" (Paula Vogel *Bomb*).

Both the text of *Drive* and the extant criticism emphasize the importance of gender and the controversial nature of age. Two comments by Bigsby are particularly illustrative. The first statement is "If the genders were reversed we would have *Tea and Sympathy*" (*Contemporary* 321), and the second is "Reverse the genders and you have *The Graduate*," in which Bigsby discerns "what appears to be a compassionate act of initiation into the adult world, an act not without its humor" (*Modern* 416). Depending upon the reader's point of view, the contrast between the play (later motion picture) and novella (far better known through its film adaptation) referenced by Bigsby may constitute a slight difference or a chasm. *The Graduate* and *Tea and Sympathy* both feature the seduction of a young male by a much older woman, but the circumstances are very different.[13] The Benjamin Braddock seduced by Mrs. Robinson in *The Graduate* is twenty-one years old and pondering graduation from college, an adult in every legal sense of the word. On the other hand, *Tea and Sympathy*'s Tom Lee, whom Laura Reynolds pursues sexually in part because he is taunted for perceived effeminacy and possible homosexuality, is a seventeen-year-old student at a private boarding school. Although posited as occupying the liminal space between adolescence and adulthood, he is legally, like L'il Bit at the opening of *Drive*, still a child. Bigsby's simply substituting one work for the other does not reflect upon the legal ramifications of one affair as opposed to the other because the genders *are* reversed from *How I Learned to Drive*.

In 1998, Andrew Kimbrough explained this double standard to Holmberg: "Leonardo DiCaprio enjoys cult status because he looks prepubescent" (Holmberg). Kimbrough notes that "it is acceptable and encouraged in American culture for boys to experiment sexually at a young age, but not girls" (58). Examples abound in popular culture of how this experimentation may involve adult women and juvenile males. One that particularly resonates with respect to *Drive* portrays Hermie, a character largely based on the real-life experience of screenwriter Herman Raucher, in the 1971 hit movie (and later novel) *Summer of '42*, who is only fifteen when he presumably has sex with the newly widowed Dorothy. Decades after this one night of comfort and passion, middle-aged Hermie wonders what has become of her. He evinces no sense of violation, nor did most of the millions of viewers who enjoyed the film or readers who bought the subsequent novel Raucher wrote during post-production.[14] Audiences simply ignored the legal status of sex between a fifteen-year-old and an adult and assumed Hermie possessed the agency to consent.[15]

Even when the relationship between a female adult and teen is a custodial one, such as teacher and student, society and the law have been willing to minimize the technical crime involved. For example, the 2006 case of Debra Lafave shows that even if the woman is a teacher, she may face a far less harsh sentence than a man guilty of the same crime with a student the same age, especially if her lawyer may plausibly argue she is "too pretty for prison." Lafave seduced a fourteen-year-old, having sex with him in a school classroom, a space where her physical custody over him was most strongly defined. Nevertheless, reporter Suzanne Goldenberg wrote for an English newspaper, "Her victim was turned into a running joke on late-night television. Didn't every teenage boy fantasise about having sex with his hot blond teacher?" This widespread attitude led the victim's mother to spare her son from having to testify in court, regardless of the consequences for the legal case.

Drive problematizes the way we understand Uncle Peck and, even more so, L'il Bit during the "long bus trip to Upstate New York" (46) in 1979, when L'il Bit is in her late twenties. Now a teacher, L'il Bit meets a youth with "that miserable equivalent of vocal acne, not quite falsetto and not tenor, either" (46). He "concentrate[s] on lowering his voice" and proclaims, "I'm a senior. Walt Whitman High" (47). L'il Bit recalls that "perhaps he was—with a very high voice" (47). Then, she shifts into the role of dramatist, telling us, "I could see the whole evening before me," when "dramaturgically speaking," there will be a "slightly comical 'first act,'" the "very briefest of intermissions, and an extremely capable and forceful and sustained second act," followed by "the second act climax and a gentle denouement"—and then a "post-play discussion" (47). L'il Bit tells us that between denouement and discussion, "I lay on my back in the dark and I thought about you, Uncle Peck" (47). Kimbrough explains, "At the age of twenty-eight, after Peck had been dead three years, and ten years since she saw him last, L'il Bit allows herself a liaison with a young man *whom she does not believe* when he claims to be a senior in high school (emphasis mine)" (58). "In essence," Kimbrough argues, "L'il Bit identifies herself as the transgressive other when she decides to engage in behavior identified with her pedophilic uncle—having sex with a minor, someone under the age of consent. However, it is unlikely that many in the audience would understand this particular implication of the scene" (58).

This scene calls to mind not only Uncle Peck but also Vogel's earlier *Baltimore Waltz* and the Munich Virgin scene. Anna, who is also a schoolteacher, seduces the Munich Virgin, telling him, "I'm very honored" (41) after she verifies that this is "[his] first time."[16] She asks if she may offer a "little lesson," and she tells him that if he will be "just a little bit nervous . . . like [he is] right now," "it will always be the first time" (41). L'il Bit describes her experience with the Walt Whitman High student as "Being older. Being the first. Being the translator, the teacher, the epicure, the already jaded" (47). Until the word "jaded," which likely reminds us of why L'il Bit thinks of Uncle Peck and recalls his own transgressions toward her, this speech sounds like something Anna may have told the Munich Virgin and hints, as do both the artistic and historical examples cited above, that something of the day when what Grandmother and Grandfather did was legal lingers.

Both *Drive*'s eventual revelation that Uncle Peck began molesting L'il Bit when she was only eleven and the Cousin Bobby scene take us back to the sad fact that Uncle Peck causes real harm. Indeed, L'il Bit presents a litany of symptoms: her drinking, her expulsion from school, her "string of dead-end jobs that didn't last very long" during the 1970 "Nixon recession" (25), and her recollection of Uncle Peck while she figuratively directs what a teen believes is his seduction of her. Together, these point toward the possibility that she has "retreated above the neck, and . . . lived inside the 'fire' in my head ever since" (103) the first day Uncle Peck violated her because she is experiencing dissociative PTSD. One of the questions she asks Uncle Peck posthumously, "Were you eleven?" (98), emphasizes the difference between what we finally learn and such other moments as the opening car scene and L'il Bit's time with the student. Just as *Summer of '42* and the real-life case of

Debra Lafave illustrate, we retain a jumble of feelings about certain sexual activity between adults and post-pubescent children.

Puberty ushers children into adolescence, when, strictly speaking, attraction toward them transforms from pedophilia to ephebophilia. Kimbrough notes, however, that the term "ephebophilia" was "not coined until 1955 because before then attraction to adolescents was not viewed as a problem" (64n). Most of us do not recognize or use this term because, according to Kimbrough, "ephebophilia is not considered as transgressive as pedophilia, and therefore not as attractive and useful to a public discourse that aims to inflame rather than dispel hysteria and misinformation" (51). As a result of such hysteria, "U.S. media no longer uses the term 'youths' in reference to teenagers, but instead employs 'children' to refer to everyone between infancy and seventeen, particularly in stories about child pornography" (64n). Kimbrough notes ephebophilia in L'il Bit's actions and thoughts on that 1979 bus trip, postulating, "In her quest to understand her uncle, she learns to recognize the ephebophile/pedophile within her" (59). We are unlikely to judge L'il Bit here at least in part because the student has gone through puberty and could present himself as an adult. Uncle Peck's behavior toward Cousin Bobby and eleven-year-old L'il Bit (even though her bust has begun to develop), however, is another matter.

L'il Bit, all the same, is not fully trapped in her traumatic past. She functions as the narrator of the play, and we see the events in an order she determines and from a perspective she employs. In this way, according to Herren, L'il Bit "breaks the stereotype of helpless victim by taking creative control over the staging of her memories" (112). L'il Bit "presides as the memory maestro of a highly selective, highly stylized rendition of her past," a "memory play [which] traces its descent through *The Glass Menagerie* line" (Herren 107). She recalls Tom Wingfield, who tells us in his first line, "I have tricks in my pocket, I have things up my sleeve." Carolyn Clay asked Vogel about the "arguably provocative appellation" *The Mammary Plays*, an obvious pun on Tom Wingfield's "memory play," which the reader encounters shortly after the direction that "memory is seated predominantly in the heart" (Clay "Drive"), Vogel explained, "All of my plays are concerned with the different ways it feels to be a woman in this world, to walk down the street as a woman. I don't know if there will ever be a way to solve the biological rupture, but the culture differences wrought by secondary sexual characteristics are great" (Clay "Drive").[17] Does *Drive*, then, hint that memory somehow resides in the mammary glands?[18] While a definite answer to this question seems elusive, Herren believes memory, which must be stored somewhere in the body, has given L'il Bit, just as it did Tom Wingfield, a conduit to freedom. L'il Bit and Tom Wingfield, he tells us, "already got it before we meet them; they cannot quite get over it, but they do get it, and they want to try to give it to us, too" (107).

L'il Bit's final memory and final gift to the audience contains Uncle Peck, this time as a "spirit" now "sitting in the back seat of the car" (104). When L'il Bit "sees him in the mirror," we learn, she "smiles," he "nods at her," and "[t]hey are happy to be going for a long drive together" (104). L'il Bit has not exorcized herself of Uncle Peck; rather, she has incorporated both the good and the bad and has settled in for a ride that may seem as endless as that of the Flying Dutchman but far more pleasant. Herren and Savran argue that we have witnessed healing and maturation. Savran calls this technique a "slyly subversive dramatization of how a girl—perhaps any girl—becomes an adult" ("Driving"). Herren adds that "under L'il Bit's able direction, the theatre becomes an ideal place for narrating, witnessing, and healing drama" (106). Herren goes on, "The theatre is perhaps second only to the courtroom as a forum for therapeutic testimony about previous trauma before a roomful of witnesses." Linking courtroom witnesses with a theatrical audience further, Herren adds, "The place she is at is the theatre, before an audience, and we are as necessary a catalyst for her healing as is her epiphany of forgiveness" (111). Savran concludes, "She learns how to use the theatre, and the act of self-preservation, to put herself quite literally in the driver's seat" ("Driving"). The performance ends when L'il Bit "floor[s] it" (105), signifying that she exercises control.

How I Learned to Drive, directed by Mark Brokaw and featuring Mary-Louise Parker as L'il Bit and David Morse as Uncle Peck, debuted at the Vineyard Theatre in March 1997. Vogel tells us, "The role of L'il Bit was originally written as a character who is forty-something" (*Drive* 7), but Parker was only thirty-two when the play opened. Vogel explained the effects of a younger actress to Clay: "With an older actress, the play becomes more contemplative, whereas when you cast it younger, there's more immediate danger. I had originally intended, in terms of the divided empathy, for L'il Bit to be becoming Peck's age" (Clay). When Vogel published the play, she granted "a great deal of flexibility in age" (7), cognizant of the different effects the age of the actor could have. Using a younger actor in New York did not perturb critics; Mansbridge writes that reviews were "almost unanimous" in praising Vogel's "keen sense of balance and the play's nuanced depiction of a delicate subject" (143).

New York Times reviewer Ben Brantley called David Morse "excellent" as Peck, whom he considered "surely the most engaging pedophile to walk across an American stage" ("Pedophile"). Brantley also credited "the captivating Mary-Louise Parker" as a L'il Bit who is "a lyrical, ambivalent narrator of her own memories in the tradition of Tom in *The Glass Menagerie*." Director Mark Brokaw was, according to Brantley, a "fast-rising star," and the performance constituted "a lovely, harrowing guide to the crippling persistence of one woman's memories." In Brantley's judgment, Vogel "couldn't be better served than she is by this production," including its minor characters and its skillful employment of music, which he considered "L'il Bit's main defense against the sound of her own feelings of guilt."

Variety reviewer Robert L. Daniels also praised the play highly, calling it "a potent and convincing comment on a taboo subject," with "its impact sneak[ing] up on its audience" ("Review"). Daniels saw Morse's Uncle Peck as "tragic, rather than chilling," and noted in Parker "an expressive range, from the cautious, manipulated teen to a mature but permanently scarred college student." Although Daniels did not comment on the music, he did praise Mark McCullough's lighting, Brokaw's "fluent staging," and supporting actor Johanna Day's characterizations, which included "offering an amusing dissertation on what drinks young ladies should shun to prevent the advances of older men." On the other hand, however, John Heilpern wrote a contrarian *New York Observer* review in 1997, and his attitude only hardened before he published *How Good Is David Mamet, Anyway? Writings on Theatre and Why It Matters* in 2000. In a chapter called "Safe Pedophilia," Heilpern blasted Vogel as "earnest" but not possessing "any humor" (134). "What's Ms. Vogel's Message?" he demanded. "Relax with incest? Pedophilia, the tragicomedy?" (134). Overall, he found *Drive* a "bland, ingratiatingly poor drama," (134) a work by a "timid" playwright who has "neutralized the issues" and rendered them "more or less harmless"[19] (136).

Jill Dolan's *Theatre Journal* review of the Vineyard Theatre production comes close to definitiveness. Dolan identifies Vogel as a playwright who "tends to select sensitive, difficult, fraught issues to theatricalize, and to spin them with a dramaturgy that's at once creative, highly imaginative, and brutally honest" (127). Dolan praises both of the lead actors, writing, "As played with affable gentility and gentleness by Morse, Peck is charming, kind, and sympathetic, a man driven toward children by his own demons but attentive to L'il Bit's adolescent needs in ways that are never violent, paternalistic, or condescending" (127). Similarly, "Parker's virtuosic performance illustrates the nuances of L'il Bit's desire and loathing for a man who taught her so much and could finally give her so little" (127). Dolan adds, "Through Parker's and Morse's multilayered performances, power and danger are always present, but so are moments of understanding and mutuality" (128). In sum, "Vogel's play is about forgiveness and family, about the instability of sexuality, about the unpredictable ways in which we learn who we are, how we desire, and how our growth is built on loss" (128).

Drive won several important awards, including Vogel's second Obie; Obie Awards for Brokaw, Morse, and Parker; Drama Desk Awards for Vogel, Brokaw, and Morse; the New York Drama Critics Award for Best Play; and the Outer Critics Circle Award for Outstanding Off-Broadway Play. More importantly, the play garnered the 1998 Pulitzer Prize for Drama, making Vogel only the tenth woman and the first out lesbian to win this award.[20] To emphasize the importance of this last accomplishment, Bigsby writes, "The woman whose first play about an immoral Desdemona was turned down by every theatre to which it was initially sent had won one of the country's major prizes without ever compromising on her determination to sail against the current, to challenge theatrical models and moral presumptions alike" (*Modern* 418). From *Desdemona* on, Vogel had both endured and now prevailed.

After *Drive* won the Pulitzer Prize, it became, according to *American Theatre*, the most produced play of the 1998–9 season, with twenty-six productions reported ("The Top Ten"). At this point, one could have been forgiven for thinking of Vogel as a Broadway playwright even though Broadway had not yet called. In a 2017 interview, Vogel noted that *How I Learned to Drive* "is being done all over the world. It's being done on large Broadway-sized stages in Iceland, for God's sake. So why is it not universal? Why are we not in that canon?" (Paulson). An answer finally came in the affirmative for *Drive* in 2022, when the play made its Broadway debut at the Samuel J. Friedman Theatre on March 29. This production was in key respects a reprise of the original Vineyard staging, with Mark Brokaw directing Mary-Louise Parker as L'il Bit and David Morse as Uncle Peck.[21] At nearly a quarter of a century old, *How I Learned to Drive* was at last a Broadway play. Both in the moral and temporal senses, of course, *Drive* should have gone to Broadway earlier. The play had long been a staple of textbooks and regional theatres when, in August 2019, *Playbill* reported that it would appear at the Manhattan Theatre club the following season. The Covid-19 pandemic intervened, delaying the opening by some two additional years.

Building an International Reputation

On the day that *How I Learned to Drive* opened at the Friedman, *The New York Times* ran a review that wryly termed its Broadway debut "overdue." Maya Phillips added that Parker and Morse "already had the play in their bones" in the best sense, inspiring an audience that "listened with rapt attention" and an "awed silence."[22] Not only that, but in Peck, Phillips wrote, "Vogel allows us to empathize with a despicable character without condoning his actions." Thus, Phillips tacitly acknowledged the negative empathy that characterizes many of Vogel's most memorable characters. Parker, too, came in for high praise, with Phillips attributing to her an "agelessness" and "astute choreography" that crucially made "every physicality a statement on her relationship to her body."

Writing for *Variety*, Marilyn Stasio deemed the production a "first-rate revival of a theater piece that never gets stale, not so long as there are sexual predators abroad in the land and girls with lovely minds who think they know it all, but haven't a clue about grown men with dirty minds" ("How").Vogel, Stasio continued, is a "genuine wordsmith" who employs "almost indecently seductive" language. "Indecently" seems derived from the Vogel and Taichman drama *Indecent*, which Stasio has also reviewed, and winks at Vogel's endless wordplay. Stasio praised "killer intensity" from Mark Brokaw, a "sturdy scene director" of what she called a "memory play," a reminder of Tennessee Williams's description of *The Glass Menagerie*. Parker and Morse came in for even higher praise, with Stasio declaring that David Morse "is one of those slow-burn actors who knows how to hold a pause until it hollers" while Mary-Louise Parker portrayed L'il Bit "to shattering perfection."

At least two reviewers reflected awareness of the play's history and sought to establish it as both timely and timeless even as they set it within a broader context. For example, writing for *The New York Daily News*, Chris Jones called the play "as unsettling now as when it broke ground" in the 1990s. Jones acknowledged changes within the society at large, adding that *How I Learned to Drive*, emerging before the "Me Too" movement, "helped expose abuse" and "probably saved some lives" by calling attention to what has come to be known as "grooming."

Christian Lewis echoed Jones's reference to L'il Bit "being sexually groomed" while having only "an illusion of agency." In a review drawing upon the Twitter meme "More Vogel Less Mamet," Lewis wrote of "a culture, a system, a situation, and an abusive relationship that" L'il Bit "was raised and stuck in." While, according to Lewis, *American Buffalo* played in "a lackluster revival," *Drive* offered a "masterpiece." Lewis posited that Parker performed "a masterclass in acting, skillfully capturing the contours of sexual trauma." Meanwhile, Morse gave "a similarly spot-on performance, finding the perfect balance between his creepiness and the alluring kindness of the character." In sum, Lewis found it "hard to have anything but praise for this piece." To support the "More Vogel" part of the mantra, Lewis assessed *How I Learned to Drive* as "one of those plays, like *Fefu and Her Friends* or *Cloud Nine*, that have been canonized, anthologized, and taught in so many drama classes, but are infrequently produced." The latter part of this description connotes a note of sadness, but the statement overall offered what to Vogel could have been only the highest praise. Placing *Drive* alongside plays by Fornés and Churchill put Vogel into a pantheon with the two women among her "gods." "I hope this Broadway [production] begins a trend of much more Vogel, indeed," Lewis concluded.

The Broadway version of *Drive* also offered something for scholars and dramaturges. In an interview, David Morse confirmed Jones's claim that the play exposed abuse by telling how, "when we did this originally, there would—after every performance, there'd be people on the street who had been abused, and they couldn't leave. They couldn't go anywhere. They just needed to talk to somebody, and you know, we'd go out, and they just had to say 'I'm one of them,' you know?" ("Mary-Louise"). One specific victim of childhood sexual abuse who came forward as a result of *How I Learned to Drive* in general and the Broadway production in particular was Paula Vogel herself. In response to a reviewer's question, Vogel explained, "I made a deal with my mother that I would not say it was autobiographical in her lifetime." Vogel added that the abuse began "at age eleven" and that when she took her mother to see the play, one year before Phyllis Vogel died, the daughter was able to "have her in the theatre and to have us holding hands and for her to feel my forgiveness and my love through the mouthpieces of the actors." This experience, Vogel said, was "such a gift" ("Mary-Louise").

Vogel's description of the way she, as a woman in her mid-forties, experienced *How I Learned to Drive* with her mother parallels the experience of countless others. As noted earlier, *Drive* was a "Me Too" text before that movement existed. Unlike most such declarations, however, Vogel maintains carefully crafted negative empathy and plays as an unexpected grace note. Even if the scourge of sexual exploitation vanished, moreover, the ongoing nature of trauma itself would keep *How I Learned to Drive* relevant. While the play is not for everyone, particularly those who are unwilling or perhaps not yet able to see trauma so portrayed, it remains an important text by a major playwright. While long familiarity may have made it no longer novel, it remains no less singular because of the way it insists on taking us not only into L'il Bit but also into Peck. In a word, it, like Vogel, is bold.

True, Vogel has accepted and even embraced certain compromises along the way to *How I Learned to Drive* and beyond. Bigsby writes of the shift from Reagan's America to that of George H. W. Bush and a time when, in response to pressures such as those exerted by Jesse Helms, "financial restraint gave further impetus to a conservative impulse by reducing the resources that theatre, and hence the playwright, could command." Vogel, he reports, "saw in this not only a challenge to be addressed but further validation of the free imagination pressed ever closer to the margin" (Contemporary 296). If conveying her message required few actors, simple sets, and minimal properties, Vogel made the necessary concessions to keep a Paula Vogel production inexpensive. The aftermath of Vogel's Pulitzer for *Drive* made public the compromises Vogel is willing to make when she collaborates with a director. One such compromise is substituting thirty-something Mary-Louise Parker for forty-something Cherry Jones, the actress Vogel originally hoped would play L'il Bit. Vogel's note in the script about a L'il Bit in her forties has gone unheeded, even though L'il Bit's line, "And before you know it, I'll be thirty-five. That's getting up there for a woman" (103), would better parallel Uncle Peck's "I'm forty-five. That's not old for a man" (96) if L'il Bit said "forty-five" rather than "thirty-five." To wit, Molly Ringwald (in New York and Los Angeles), Elizabeth Reaser (2012 Second Stage New York revival), and Olivia Poulet (2015 Southwark Playhouse London revival) have played L'il Bit while in their thirties. Even Molly Smith, who had commissioned *Drive* while serving as Artistic Director for Perseverance Theatre (Juneau, Alaska) either tacitly accepted the change in L'il Bit's age or bowed to commercial pressure when she cast thirty-six-year-old Deirdre Lovejoy as L'il Bit in the 1999 Washington, D.C., Arena Stage production.[23]

This compromise made to meet the needs of casting is only one example of the way Vogel manifests a flexible style. The working script powerfully demonstrates why. Despite a view of the play text as sacrosanct that drives the search for the "true" *Hamlet* to this day, Vogel told Parker, "Words are cheap. They are very cheap. If they don't work, drop them, cut them, change them, it doesn't matter. What matters is simply that I'm writing notes for you to play the violin, as an excuse to hear you playing the violin" (Vogel *Bomb*). Rather than a finished, fixed product, Vogel added, "Every script, every new play, is a theory."

The Theatre of Paula Vogel

To illustrate how Vogel sees at least the process that leads up to written publication as collaborative, she told Parker, "If I wanted everything to be exactly as it was in my head, exactly word for word, I should be writing novels. The play doesn't belong to the playwright." Vogel goes on to describe what she observed Parker and David Morse do: "You guys, and Mark Brokaw, the director, knew that sections were overwritten, and you very gently waited for me to catch up. You were already editing the script with your acting" (*Bomb*). In a comment that explains why she may find an ongoing string of thirty-something L'il Bits acceptable, Vogel also stated that she leaves opening night with a different vision from the one she had when she handed over the script, and also a different one from anyone who buys and reads the script. "I don't remember what L'il Bit was before I saw you," she tells Parker. "The same way that I don't remember what Peck was in my head before I saw David. They're gone now. They've been effaced by your interpretation. You're seeing something on the page I don't see any longer" (*Bomb*).

Vogel's many years of hard work lifted her from comparative obscurity to becoming one of America's best-respected playwrights, one whom Joanna Mansbridge, in her *Methuen Drama Guide to Contemporary American Playwrights* chapter on Vogel, calls "a playwright's playwright" (372). Vogel's decades of teaching playwrights how to write and the success many of them have enjoyed support Mansbridge's definition. While it is clearly intended as a compliment, however, this statement is not what Vogel or almost any playwright would like to have as the last word about her. Ultimately, a playwright will want to become an audience's playwright whose works can draw people to come see them. In 1998, as a new Pulitzer winner, Vogel could hardly know what direction that quest would take. David Savran asked Vogel about future plans, "I'm hoping I can finally do this full-time. That's my goal," she said. She also spoke of a desire to "try and figure out what my voice is cinematically." "I'm starting an adaptation of *How I Learned to Drive*, which I originally saw as a movie and not a play," she added. Then, she told Savran, "I want to start to write for musical theatre." She added, "I'm mostly burning up to write musicals and movies."

CHAPTER 4
THE HOUSE OF PAULA VOGEL

From 1977 through 1984, Vogel lived in New York City, where, Bigsby records, she "continued to write plays at the rate of one a year, though without any success and with no financial resources" (*Contemporary* 295). Then, in 1984, Brown University hired Vogel to teach playwriting, and she remained at Brown until 2008, enjoying "a base from which to work" (295) and her longest tenure ever in any single location. While at Brown, Vogel earned both her Obies and Pulitzer and was financially successful enough that in 1999 Megan Rosenfeld noted that she had "made enough money to buy a vacation home in Cape Cod." Vogel left Brown for Yale, becoming a faculty member, ironically, in the very program that had rejected her student application thirty-four years earlier.

When Vogel the playwright finally reached Broadway in April 2017, Mark Kennedy summarized some of the highlights of her teaching career, writing, "Don't ask where Paula Vogel is, ask where isn't she" (Kennedy). Noting that *Indecent* had just opened at the Cort Theatre, Kennedy wrote, "A few blocks away, former student Lynn Nottage has opened *Sweat*. A stone's throw from that," he continued, "Steven Levenson, another former Vogel apprentice, is enjoying success with *Dear Evan Hansen*." Not only that, but "Over at Lincoln Center, there's a new play [*How to Transcend a Happy Marriage*] by former Vogel pupil Sarah Ruhl.[1] And former protégé Gina Gionfriddo just opened her new work [*Can You Forgive Her?*] at the Vineyard Theatre," which had offered the New York premieres of both *How I Learned to Drive* and *Indecent*. This list alone justifies Kennedy's claim that "the modern theater landscape is rich with [Vogel's] DNA," but it was hardly an exhaustive list. Kennedy also mentioned "onetime Vogel collaborator Ayad Akhtar, whose play *Disgraced* won the 2013 Pulitzer Prize for Drama and was nominated for a Tony Award in 2015"; Pulitzer winners Nilo Cruz, Quiara Alegría Hudes, and Lynn Nottage; 2017 Pulitzer finalist Sarah DeLappa, whom Kennedy characterized as "also a former Vogel student"; "Oscar-winning *Moonlight* playwright Tarell Alvin McCraney"; "Pulitzer-nominee Rajiv Joseph, who wrote *Bengal Tiger at the Baghdad Zoo*"; and "[a]nother former student, Stephen Karam, [who] last year had two works on Broadway, including *The Humans*, the Tony-winning best play last season."

Vogel has hardly restricted herself to teaching Ivy League college students who frequently go on to write famous or highly regarded plays, however. Beginning in 1984 in "Gordon Edelstein's downtown loft on Chamber St. in New York City," where, Vogel claims, she, Mac Wellman, Connie Congdon, and Jeff Jones initiated "a 'kvetch' session" (paulavogelplaywright .com) that developed into a 48-hour drama bakeoff, Vogel has taken this concept around the country. She has also conducted what she terms drama "boot camps" to audiences as diverse as maximum-security prison inmates, juveniles in detention centers, and according to attendee and drama critic J. Wynn Rousuck, possibly "even another critic" (48). Vogel has stated, "I think everybody is a playwright regardless of whether or not you own it" (May 22, 2017 workshop); moreover, she has acted on this belief by taking the craft to the masses.

Indeed, Vogel has taught some of our most successful professional playwrights, including Nilo Cruz, Sarah Ruhl, Quiara Alegría Hudes, and Lynn Nottage. Nottage is the first woman ever to win two Pulitzer Prizes for Drama. Then, too, she has offered bakeoffs and boot camps, among them the May 22, 2017, one-day Vineyard Theatre boot camp, which Vogel called "her first workshop aimed at the general public in 13 years" (Chow). Together, these elements convey a sense of Vogel's influence and importance, both among the elites and as a democratizing figure among major American teachers of playwriting.

Nilo Cruz, the first of Vogel's students to win a Pulitzer Prize, with *Anna in the Tropics* in 2003, was a literal "gift" (Herren *Text* 14) from one of Vogel's gods, María Irene Fornés (who told Vogel, "I'm sending you my pearl" [14]), and a person whose life and career manifest the magical realism associated with Fornés or a fictional Gabriel García Marquez work. Born in Matanzas, Cuba, around 1960, and a 1970 refugee "legally—on an airplane, not on a raft" (Tichler and Kaplan 261) from Fidel Castro's nation, Cruz is also the first Latino playwright to win the Pulitzer. Cruz's life and career reflect the influence of what may be regarded as a series of fairy godmothers, including Fornés, Vogel, and Cruz's own mother. Cruz writes how, during his early years in Cuba, his mother "used to find escape through prayer, and used cigar smoke to send her supplications to the Divine" ("The Alphabet of Smoke" 6). In a scene that seems to come straight out of Marquez, Ms. Cruz "made her own incense by inhaling the burning end of the cigar into her mouth and exhaling her breath through it," creating "a surge of smoke that bathed all her sacred status in a blue cloud" (6). Already, the boy had experienced a profound moment at a cabaret that arguably contributed to his future in theatre.

Only a year or two before the Cruz family left Cuba, they found themselves at a resort where everyone wanted to attend the cabaret, leaving no one behind to watch young Nilo. Because the father knew the owner of the restaurant, the family snuck Nilo in through the kitchen and hid the lad under the table. "Oh, he can stay," the waiter said upon discovering Nilo, allowing him to witness a combination of "burlesque comedic sketches" (Tichler and Kaplan 260) and, Cruz has told interviewer Ben Hodges, "ballet too" (14). Cruz has described "a lot of flesh, but no stripping and really wonderful, electrifying Cuban music" (Tichler and Kaplan 260). He has also called himself "dazzled by the vibrant music, by the exuberant energy coming from the stage" (Hodges 14).

Upon arriving in Miami, Cruz dedicated himself to becoming Americanized as soon as possible. "I realized I had to get out of ESL," he recalls. "I really wanted to integrate, I wanted to be American" (Tichler and Kaplan 261). As a result, his teacher soon moved him out of ESL, and Cruz began reading more and more in English, including poetry. He says, "I had discovered a poem by Emily Dickinson at the library at the school. I was completely taken by her work" (Tichler and Kaplan 263). Although Cruz no longer remembers which Dickinson poem he encountered when "I must have been eleven years old," he clearly remembers saying, "Ah, this is what I want to do. I want to write. I want to write like this" (263). Toward that goal, one of Cruz's fairy godmothers, his mother, made an important contribution by buying teenaged Cruz his first typewriter (Gussow). Cruz's adult style may be something of an amalgam between Dickinson's precise diction and the lyricism of his Cuban forebears, for a later godmother, Vogel herself, recalls Cruz saying, "My ancestors, my family, have never before in the history of theatre, been articulating themselves on stage." Moreover, their language, Cruz told Vogel, was "original" (Vineyard Boot Camp).

Cruz's introduction to drama followed "an epiphany that I had to go to the theatre. That night I went to the regional theatre in Miami at that time, which was the Coconut Grove Playhouse, and I saw *The Dresser*," a Ronald Harwood play, later adapted into a film by the same name, about a dresser for a Shakespearean actor. Then, "the next day I decided to enroll at a drama school at Miami Dade [sic] College" (Hodges 15). Cruz soon immersed himself fully in college theatre. Even though his first class was not for credit, Cruz wrote scenes and cast classmates in them. Soon, the professor, Teresa María Rojas, whom Cruz has described as "magical" (Tichler and Kaplan 265), told him, "You're a writer. You need to continue writing" (264). While still a student, Cruz directed the world premiere of the play (also an autobiography and later a film) *Before Night Falls*, by another Cuban who escaped to America, noted gay author and political dissident Reinaldo Arenas.

While taking a class taught by Patricia Gross, founder of Miami's South End Alternative Theater (SEAT), Cruz gained the opportunity to direct Gross in *Mud*, by Fornés. Fornés came to Miami to conduct a workshop around the time of the production, and while she was there, Patricia Gross told her of Cruz's writing and showed samples of it. Fornés invited Cruz to come to New York and join her workshop at INTAR (International Arts Relations), one of the United States' oldest theatres producing Latino voices. Cruz recalls,

> I had to make my decision right away because the lab was starting on Monday, and I had met Irene on Friday. And I had to move to New York immediately. I didn't even have money to move to New York. Thank God I had a friend in New York. I called her up and asked her if I could crash in her living room, and she said yes. I got some money, I had a little bit of money, I think I probably asked my parents for some money, and I came to New York, and I started to study with María Irene Fornés. (Tichler and Kaplan 265)

Cruz adds, "I borrowed a winter coat from a friend—I didn't even have a heavy coat, because you don't need one in Florida." The outcome was dramatic: "I studied with [Fornés] for three years. And as a result, my life changed" (Hodges 16).

In his early years as a playwright, like Fornés, Cruz chose to write primarily in English and not restrict himself to one ethnic community or region. José Esteban Muñoz discerns the clear influence of Fornés in this decision, writing that Fornés's plays "appear mysterious to North American eyes because they represent a specifically Latina/o *manera de ser*" (458). He writes of *Mud* that although "Mae's plight is meant to be felt by anyone who is sensitized to the transnational gendering of poverty, . . . it speaks to a Latina/o cognoscenti in powerful and culturally specific ways. The mysteriousness of Fornés is akin to a mysteriousness that saturates Cruz's work" (458). Cruz has observed "something about the sensibility of

Mud that feels like it comes from my country" (Hodges 18). As a result, it seems fair to say that Cruz's dramaturgy and characterization, like his understanding of Fornés's dramaturgy and characterization, are such that a Cruz or Fornés character may *feel* Latinx to an audience without having to *be* Latinx because of the sensibility the playwright brings both to the character and to the work.²

The way a child from Matanzas, Cuba, came to study in New York with and be informed by María Irene Fornés contains hints both of Surrealism and magical realism. Other surprises were yet to come. After Cruz had been at INTAR for a time, "Paula Vogel, who was the head of the playwriting program at Brown University, asked Irene if she had any participants in the lab that were interested in going back to school." Cruz "wanted to continue studying, so [he] applied to the master's program at Brown and was accepted" (Hodges 18). Evidently, Cruz required some persuading, however, for Vogel has recalled him saying, "I don't want to go to university, I don't want to become academic, I don't want to write university American English" (Herren *Text* 14).

Vogel was better situated than many, if not all, playwriting professors to respond to the objections Cruz raised at a time when he valued developing his own voice over assimilating. "Why would you want to do that?" (Herren 14), Vogel asked, eliciting, "Okay, here's my play" (14). Vogel then more than adequately filled the role of fairy godmother to Cruz, for Brown "gave [him] two years to be in a safe environment" (McAuliffe 466). Cruz acknowledges Vogel as "very influential . . . more as far as structure is concerned" and describes her as "so supportive that there was no right and there was no wrong. And you can see that with her structures: watching slides from a trip the actors never take in *Baltimore Waltz*, and lessons on driving in *How I Learned to Drive*" (466). Perhaps Cruz did find a way to do something marginally wrong in one of Vogel's bakeoffs, however, for as Vogel recalled decades later, he produced 110 pages of *Dancing on My Knees* during only forty-eight hours.³ "We almost killed him," Vogel said with a chuckle (Vineyard Workshop).

After earning his MFA from Brown in 1994, Cruz enjoyed minor successes with such plays as *Night Train* and *Two Sisters and a Piano* and became the playwright-in-residence at the New Theatre in Coral Gables, Florida. While at New Theatre, Cruz wrote *Anna in the Tropics*, and the play premiered there on October 12, 2002, directed by Rafael de Ache and with set design by Michelle Cumming, music and sound by M. Anthony Reimer, and costume design by Estela Vrancovich. The show's modest four-week run was a most inauspicious beginning for a play soon to win the Pulitzer Prize for Drama. The original production seems not to have been reviewed, nor did any of the 2003 Pulitzer jurors see *Anna in the Tropics* before casting their votes. The play was a huge underdog to *The Goat, or Who Is Sylvia?* by Edward Albee, and *Take Me Out* by Richard Greenberg.

When *Anna in the Tropics* unexpectedly won the Pulitzer Prize for Drama in 2003, it established two historic firsts: the first play to win the award with the jurors having only read the script and not seen the play and the first Pulitzer-winning drama by a Latino playwright. Emily Mann, who had "been waiting for an opportunity to direct one of [Cruz's] plays," finally "took the leap" (Mann) and directed a production that debuted on September 18, 2003, at the new Roger S. Berlind Theater, Princeton, New Jersey (Gussow). This production, featuring Jimmy Smits as lector Juan Julian and Daphne Rubin-Vega as Conchita, then traveled to Broadway's Royale Theatre on November 16, making Cruz not only the first Vogel student to win a Pulitzer but also the first to have a play on Broadway.

Since writing *Anna in the Tropics*, Nilo Cruz has gone on to a significant career even though he has acknowledged that "the Pulitzer Prize is definitely a blessing, but it's also a curse" (Tichler and Kaplan 280). The blessing, Cruz explains, comes in having theatre companies not only perform the play that won the prize but also consider the playwright's other works as well. For example, Lawrenceville, Georgia's, Aurora Theatre staged a 2015 production of Cruz's *Sotto Voce*, a play performed in English with Spanish subtitles, followed by a 2017 production of *Pais de Bicicleta* ("Bicycle Country"), performed in Spanish with English subtitles. These productions reflected language choices consistent with what Cruz told interviewer Rebecca Sutton in 2016. Describing his projects at Miami's Arca Images theatre company, the playwright said, "We're doing plays in English and in Spanish. Sometimes when we have a play in English, we have an audio system in which non-English audience members can listen to the play in Spanish, and vice versa. We're trying to reach out to different kinds of communities by providing simultaneous translations" (Cruz "Art Talk").

Cruz has spoken more than once about the "curse" of winning the Pulitzer, noting that "people anticipate that you will write another play like *Anna and the Tropics*" (Tichler and Kaplan 280) even though he describes himself as "not interested in formulas" (280). During his years as the only Hispanic winner of the Pulitzer Prize for Drama, Cruz recalled being mentioned as, "Oh, well, he's the Hispanic writer?" (283). Even after Quiara Alegría Hudes and Lin-Manuel Miranda also won Pulitzers, Cruz told Sutton, "I think there's still some xenophobia in the field" (Cruz "Art"). He also said, "Because I am a Latino writer, theaters put a lot of pressure on reaching out to the Latino community to come see my work, which I think is great and they should do that. But at the same time, I write plays for the world." Cruz insisted, "I'm not just interested in reaching out to the Latino community; I'm interested in the Asian community; I'm interested in the Haitian community here in Miami. So how can we bring all these communities to see the work? It's a complicated question"[4] (Cruz "Art").

Always a lyrical playwright, Cruz eventually turned to writing actual lyrics set to music. He collaborated with Gabriela Lena Frank, producing the libretti for *The Conquest Requiem* and *The Santos Oratorio*. He has also adapted the 2001 Ann Patchett novel *Bel Canto* for the Lyric Opera of Chicago. In addition, perhaps reflecting the influence of both Fornés and Vogel, he spent the 2019–20 academic year at the UCLA School of Theater, Film, and Music, where he served as playwright-in-residence. Cruz is María Irene Fornés's gift to Paula Vogel and the rest of the theatrical world who goes on giving.

Vogel discovered Sarah Ruhl in a memorable way, in 1995, when Ruhl was a student in Vogel's class at Brown. "In 'Dog Play,' her first piece, a ten-minute exercise assigned by [Vogel]," John Lahr writes, "Ruhl synthesized Kabuki stage techniques with a suburban American environment to evoke her grief over her father's death" from cancer in 1994, when Ruhl was twenty years old. Vogel told Lahr, "I sat with this short play in my study and sobbed. She had an emotional maturity that no one else in the class had" (Lahr "Surreal"). The memory has remained vivid for Vogel, who in telling her May 22, 2017, Vineyard Theatre Playwriting Workshop audience about a ten-minute assignment to write a "short play that is impossible to stage," mentioned a variation that requires a dog protagonist. In response to this particular requirement, Vogel indicated she had collected and kept many very good examples, including one from Ruhl that led the professor to ask her student, "Do you want to be a playwright?" (Vogel Vineyard).

Since completing her MFA at Brown in 2001, Ruhl has enjoyed almost continuous success. Several of her plays had already run at respected theatres by 2005, when her 2004 play *The Clean House* was a Pulitzer Prize finalist. The MacArthur Foundation recognized her with its Fellowship, aka the "genius grant," in 2006. She also won the PEN/Laura Pels International Foundation for Theater Award in 2006. Then, in 2009, Ruhl made her Broadway debut with *In the Next Room or the Vibrator Play*, her second work to become a finalist for the Pulitzer Prize. *In the Next Room* quickly became both Ruhl's most famous and most infamous play.

Ruhl has acknowledged that *In the Next Room* responds to at least two sources, Rachel Maines's *The Technology of Orgasm* (1999) and Phyllis Rose's *Parallel Lives: Five Victorian Marriages* (1984).[5] Maines takes a topic at least as old as the argument between Zeus and Hera that produced the prophet Tieresias,[6] female sexual pleasure, and situates it around the time when electricity was adapted for indoor purposes, particularly through the electric vibrator. Maines writes of the "androcentric definition of sex," which "recognizes three essential steps: preparation for penetration ('foreplay'), penetration, and male orgasm" (5). The occurrence of a female orgasm, according to this definition, is an inessential detail that does not diminish "the legitimacy of the act as 'real sex,'" a significant point since "more than half of all women, possibly more than 70 percent, do not regularly reach orgasm by means of penetration alone" (5). Maines evinces no surprise that doctors defined innumerable women as "abnormal or 'frigid.'" So many frustrated women had doctors define them in terms of a malfunctioning or even dislocated womb rendering them "hysterics" that many nineteenth-century doctors claimed "hysteria was pandemic in their time" (5).

Thanks to the pioneering work Thomas Edison performed in the late 1800s, widespread commercial availability of a household electric current led to a short lived, if inaccurately recognized, revolution in female sexuality. The electric vibrator relieved medical professionals of the duty to induce manually what they called "paroxysms" in women diagnosed with hysteria. The vibrator became so popular that by 1918, the Sears, Roebuck and Company catalogue included a page of "Aids That Every Woman Appreciates." Along with electric fans and sewing machines, this icon of American mail-order selling offered a portable vibrator for $5.95 plus shipping and, for another $1.35 plus shipping, an attachment set to complement the vibrator (Maines 105). Edison's gift of readily and affordably available electric current allowed American women to please themselves with clinical detachment.[7]

As noted earlier, *In the Next Room* was the second Sarah Ruhl play to be a Pulitzer Prize finalist, losing the 2010 award to Tom Kitt and Brian Yorkey's rock musical *Next to Normal*. The Broadway production garnered three Tony Award nominations: Best Play, Best Featured Actress (Maria Dizzia as Mrs. Daldry), and Best Costume Design (David Zinn). With *The Oldest Boy* (2014) and *How to Transcend a Happy Marriage* (2017), both directed by Rebecca Taichman, Ruhl has seen her work performed at the Lincoln Center for the Performing Arts Mitzi E. Newhouse Theater.[8]

The House of Paula Vogel

Like Vogel, Quiara Alegría Hudes, born in 1977, is the daughter of a Jewish father and a Catholic mother. Henry Hudes, a carpenter, "sanded the curly maple of my writing desk" (Hudes 4), his daughter wrote in the Acknowledgments for *Water by the Spoonful*. Virginia Pérez is "a native of Arecibo, Puerto Rico who moved to Philadelphia when she was 12 years old" (Bryer and Hartig 152). Like the marriage of Vogel's parents, the Hudes's marriage ended while the playwright was a child, and Quiara grew up with her mother and stepfather, Sedo Sánchez. Hudes spent much of her childhood only a two- or three-hour drive from where Vogel spent most of her childhood, in what John Timpane calls "the rich, diverse neighborhood at 49th and [appropriately for a future Vogel student] Baltimore." Also like Vogel, Hudes comes from a family of storytellers; indeed, she has commented, "I felt there were incredible American stories in my family and in my community that deserved retelling, . . . funny, painful, wonderful stories" (Timpane). It is at least plausible that Hudes's own storytelling in her plays stems in part from what Vogel has called "Jewish genes" as well as the background of a mother born in the hemispheric South. Likewise, the fact that Victoria Sánchez is a composer, coupled with Bryer and Hartig's note that Hudes's "father's sister, a composer, taught her the importance of music" (152) shows how Hudes has inherited the dramatic use of music, something else she shares with Vogel, from both sides of her family.

"Hudes's mixed heritage," David Low writes, "has influenced and inspired her writing. Growing up, she observed educational and economic differences among her relatives." Hudes says, "I found myself in this strange situation of being at Thanksgiving dinner and to my left is a cousin who is on food stamps and struggling in severe poverty and on my right is an aunt who is a city councilwoman and across from me is another cousin who didn't finish middle school or is illiterate" (Low). The playwright, with two Ivy League degrees, has the most formal education of anyone at this Thanksgiving table, for Hudes holds an undergraduate degree from Yale and an MFA from Brown, where she studied under Vogel. This "crackling mixture of who we are and who we relate to in our family lives and communities," Hudes adds, "has found its way into my writing" (Low). Hudes has cautioned against using identity politics as a template for reading her work, telling Victoria Myers, "I think there's a danger whenever there's a slot for the 'outsider play,' whether it's aesthetically or the way we categorize human beings. It's just dangerous, and it leads to boring theatre and boring audiences. It's not healthy for anyone" (Hudes "An Interview"). Just as Vogel has recorded that Tom Stoppard does not face questions regarding his take on *Hamlet* that she does for hers on *Othello*, Hudes points out that Edward Albee "never gets asked, 'What does being a white male playwright mean?' He never gets asked that kind of stuff" (Hudes "An Interview").

Hudes's Elliot trilogy focuses on a Latinx man, Elliot Ortiz (based on Hudes's cousin) with an Anglo first name who serves the United States in the second Iraq War. Hudes began her first Elliot play, *Elliot, A Soldier's Fugue* (2006), while a student at Brown. Already a playwright of note, having won the Paula Vogel Award in Playwriting and other awards in 2003 for *Yemaya's Belly*, which received several productions, Hudes conceived of *Elliot, A Soldier's Fugue* as a play "that dramatized the effects of three wars (Korea, Vietnam, Iraq) on three generations of a Puerto Rican family" (Johnson) and that "was also inspired by Bach's music" (Low). Hudes, by her own reckoning, "had only written twenty pages" (Signature Season) when, during Vogel's Signature Theatre Residency 2004–5 season, Vogel arranged a series of readings by her students, including Hudes.

Hudes's 2004 Signature Theatre reading from *Elliot, A Soldier's Fugue* constitutes a moment of important theatre history. "Terrified of audience talkbacks" (Signature Season), Hudes agreed to be interviewed by Vogel in the talkback for her reading. "It just so happened," Hudes later recalled, "that in that audience were some young men who [sic] I had recently met named Tommy [Thomas] Kail and Lin-Manuel Miranda who had come to me when I moved to New York and said, 'Would you like to work on this musical with us?'" (Signature Season). The musical was *In the Heights*. Because Hudes was "dressed very professionally and [she] had on this button-down white shirt and a blazer" (Signature Season), Kail and Miranda told Hudes, "We are really intimidated to work with you now," an impression Hudes attributes to "Paula's very respectful framing of the . . . event" (Signature Series). Hudes adds, "That was a very nice way to start my collaboration with them, too, because they got to see who I was on my own terms, outside of this joint venture we were about to start" (Signature Series).

Both Hudes's collaboration with Kail and Miranda and her own work produced great success. The team won the 2008 Tony Award for Best Musical for In the Heights, and *Elliot, A Soldier's Fugue* was a finalist for the 2007 Pulitzer Prize for Drama. Hudes subsequently won the Pulitzer for *Water by the Spoonful* in 2012, becoming the first Latina to win the award. Miranda won the Pulitzer for *Hamilton* in 2016 on his way to becoming America's first celebrity playwright of the twenty-first century.

Water by the Spoonful is the second play in an Iraq War trilogy that Maurice Decaul has compared with David Rabe's Vietnam War trilogy *The Basic Training of Pavlo Hummel* (1971), *Sticks and Stones* (1971), and *Streamers* (1976). Born in 1940, Rabe drew upon his own 1960s Vietnam experience plus stories he had heard, while Hudes drew inspiration from the Iraq War without having gone to the country. Hudes's central character Elliot is based, Hudes told Decaul via email, on a "younger cousin [who] fled the fallout and snares of the war on drugs in Philadelphia by enlisting" (Decaul 22). This cousin saw the military as "his means to a paid salary, to an honored place in society" (22). After the cousin suffered a leg injury in Iraq, Hudes visited him at his California base and "registered an immediate but subtle change in his eyes" (22). *Elliot, A Soldier's Fugue* resulted from Hudes's need "to understand what had changed, how his selfhood and manhood had developed during his active military duty" (22).

According to critic Stuart Miller, the Elliot trilogy became a trilogy accidentally. "Hudes didn't set out to write a trilogy," Miller writes, "but she eventually felt compelled to return to Elliot's story" (87). *Water by the Spoonful*, the second play of the trilogy (followed, in 2013, by *The Happiest Song Plays Last*) marks this return. Twenty-four-year-old Elliot Ortiz, in *Water by the Spoonful*, has left the Marines by 2009 for his native Philadelphia and found work at a Subway Hoagies shop. Although this chain has a shop "around the corner" from where Elliot lives with his biological aunt Ginny, whom he calls Mom, he works "half an hour away" because he considers what he does a "[n]ot normal job. Shit job," dismissing himself as "a butler. A porter of sandwiches" (17). The only relative seemingly allowed to see Elliot in his Subway Hoagies polo shirt is his thirty-one-year-old cousin Yazmin, referred to as Yaz, who has made her family proud as an adjunct professor of music at Swarthmore and with what Elliot calls a *"Cosby Show"* (10) marriage to William. Yaz does not share this positive assessment of herself, telling Elliot that she had imagined herself "Waaay tenured, like by the age of twenty-four" and possessing such a reputation that "Carnegie Hall debuts Yazmin Ortiz's Oratorio for Electric Guitar and Children's Choir" (56). The younger Yaz wrote her professional goals as well as "[t]wo kids" and an "[e]qual housework marriage" on "a piece of paper and dug a hole in Fairmount Park and put it in the ground" (56), promising herself to return at thirty and "cross it all off," something she now says she will "never have the courage" (56) to do. Her marriage is also over but for a final "John Hancock" from a witness (10).

As Richard Zoglin has noted, *Water by the Spoonful* marked "the first time a play has snagged a Pulitzer without a New York staging since Nilo Cruz's *Anna in the Tropics* in 2003." In addition, just as Cruz was the first Latino playwright to win a Pulitzer Prize for Drama, Hudes was the first Latina. Zoglin considered it "no accident that both" of these two dramas to win the Pulitzer before playing New York "come from Hispanic-American playwrights," adding, "Plays that reflect America's ethnic diversity tend to get more attention in regional theaters than in the New York hothouse."[9] Reviewing *Water's* 2013 New York premiere at the Off-Broadway Second Stage Theater for *Time*, Zoglin noted that "we provincial New Yorkers can see what we missed," which he deemed "[q]uite a lot." He adjudged the writing "controlled and graceful," the fifteen scenes "perfectly balanced," and "the language both lyrical and lucid" without descending into "community-organizer didacticism or sentimentality."

Music would help bring Hudes the film career that has eluded Vogel, with her collaboration with Miranda, *In the Heights*, enjoying a long Broadway run and then becoming an HBO Max film in 2021.[10] In addition, Hudes collaborated with Manuel and others on the 2021 Netflix animated musical film *Vivo*. Hudes even enjoyed a moment on film, appearing in a cameo in the Manuel-directed 2021 version of Steven Levenson's *Tick, Tick . . . Boom!*[11]

In terms of major awards, Lynn Nottage, one of Vogel's earliest students at Brown University, is also easily her most successful. Nottage enrolled at Brown in 1982, two years before Vogel arrived, as a pre-med student, until "she gravitated toward her playwriting professor, George Bass, the executor of Langston Hughes's estate" (Schulman 32), who placed some of Hughes's ashes into Nottage's hands. After studying with Bass and Vogel, Nottage moved on to the Yale School of Drama, only to leave and pursue other interests because she "didn't think the school was invested in her as a playwright, and in turn she felt less invested in playwriting" (Schulman 32). Nottage has said, "I felt as though I had spent my entire life in school and I needed an alternative experience" (Nottage "Esteemed"), which she gained, along with social activism, as press person for Amnesty International. Once Nottage resumed writing plays, she recalls, "I cashed in my 401k, and I temped and I struggled for many years" ("Esteemed") before she enjoyed both commercial and critical success, starting perhaps most notably with *Intimate Apparel* (2003). Like Sarah Ruhl, Nottage has won a MacArthur "genius grant"; like Nilo Cruz and Quiara Alegría Hudes, Nottage has won a Pulitzer (for *Ruined*, 2010); unlike any other Vogel student or, indeed, any other woman to date, Nottage also won a second Pulitzer (for *Sweat*, 2017).

Born in 1964, Nottage is the daughter of Ruby and Wally Nottage, "what you'd call black bohemian folks" (Iqbal), who brought her up in the home where she resides today in Brooklyn, New York. Ruby Nottage, a school teacher, "gave her children an Afrocentric education, and filled in their picture books with a brown marker—the Little Prince became black" (Schulman 32). At the same time, Nottage also grew up as friends with author Jonathan Lethem, with whom she commuted to the High School of Music and Art in Manhattan. When Lethem later asked Nottage about what she remembered about the Boerum Hill neighborhood where they grew up, "She said, 'Every kid we grew up with either went to jail or into law enforcement.' [Lethem] replied, looking at her and [him]self, 'There was a third way—you could become a writer'" (in Schulman 32).

Intimate Apparel traces its genesis to the moment Nottage, while cleaning the house of her ailing grandmother, who was dying from complications of alcoholism, located the passport photograph of great-grandmother Ethel Armstrong. Lacking any living person with the capacity to tell her about Ethel, Nottage transformed Ethel into Esther. The past and the historical great-grandmother Ethel are present in *Intimate Apparel* not only in the abandonment but also in the nature of Esther's work and in her husband being an immigrant from the Caribbean. The present features in Esther's affection for Mr. Marks, which is inspired by Nottage's own marriage to a Jewish man, filmmaker Tony Gelber, with whom she has children Ruby and Melkamu. Living a century later than Esther and Mr. Marks, Nottage and Gerber enjoy the ability to share not only affections but a marriage and family such as scarcely could have occurred to Esther and the deeply religious Mr. Marks.

As both filmmaker and husband, Gerber joined Nottage in 2005 when she traveled to East Africa in 2004 with director Kate Whoriskey. The three were unable to enter the Congo then "because war was still raging in the Ituri Rainforest area and Congolese refugees kept flowing over the border into Uganda" (Gener "Defense" 118). Nevertheless, inspired by the Bertolt Brecht 1939 anti-war play *Mother Courage and Her Children*, Nottage had Gelber film while she interviewed refugees whose plights "provided a catalogue of routine brutality: conscription into prostitution, rape as an instrument of terror and, most harrowingly, the genital mutilation that [would give *Ruined*] its title" (Weinert-Kendt 35). Prompted at first by a belief frequently articulated by Vogel, her "gods," and her students that "I certainly don't want to write the same play again and again" (Zinoman), Nottage initially envisioned what she later described to Nilo Cruz as "a modern adaptation of *Mother Courage* set in the Congo" (Nottage "Nilo Cruz & Lynn Nottage" 24).[12] As a result, however, of "interviewing the women, traveling the landscape, absorbing the culture, eating the food, and listening to the music," Nottage came to realize she had found "a story that was so specific to Africa and the Congo, that suddenly Brecht's *Mother Courage* template was no longer applicable" (Nottage "Nilo" 24). While acknowledging that a debt to Brecht remained, Nottage focused so closely on "gender specific human rights abuses, and the way in which women are preyed upon during armed conflicts" that *Ruined* "is a departure from Mother Courage" (24).

Both music and film were integral parts of Nottage's writing process for *Ruined*. "Before Nottage starts a new play, she makes herself a soundtrack," notes Schulman (33). *Intimate Apparel* emerged from a soundtrack that included ragtime composer Scott Joplin. *Ruined* reflects the impact, both immediate and long lasting, of the music Nottage heard while onsite, conducting interviews and field research in East Africa. The films of interviews confirmed, after the fact, how much of the interviews went into the play's text. As Nottage told Cruz, she "didn't revisit them until many years later," for she "knew it would be difficult to revisit them because of the nature of the stories" (24). When she did return to these heartrending and graphic tales, Nottage discovered that "[o]ne woman was named Mama Nadi, another was Salim, and another's name was Sophie" (24). Since all three of these names appear in the play, "unconsciously [Nottage] had woven all of them into *Ruined*" (24).

Other than occasional hints, the play withholds exactly what "ruined" means. These include the fact that "*Sophie walks with some pain*" (9), a reference to how the "militia did ungodly things to the child, took her with . . . a bayonet and then left her for dead" (10), and the pamphlet Sophie produces when she tells Mama Nadi, "A woman that comes in here said she can help me. She said there is an operation for girls" (37). Perhaps Nottage withholds the details because they might overwhelm the audience, to the detriment of plot and character. Thus, Nottage draws the attention of some astute observers to the way "ruined," in this play world, starkly contrasts with the traditional understanding of a prostitute as "ruined" in such works as the Thomas Hardy poem "The Ruined Maid."

In its original performance, *Ruined* won not only the Pulitzer Prize but also numerous other awards as well. It gained the Obie for Best New

American Play and for actors, including Quincy Tyler Bernstine (Salima) and Saidah Arrika Ekulonia (Mama Nadi). *Ruined* also won Outstanding Play and, for Dominic Kanza, Outstanding Music in a Play at the Drama Desk Awards. The Louise Lortel Award for Outstanding Play and the Outer Critics Circle Award for Outstanding New Off-Broadway Play both went to Nottage. However, although Michael Schulman reports "talk of moving it to Broadway," Nottage told him, "repeatedly I heard, 'There are no black actresses who can open a Broadway play'" (31). Indeed, although Studio 54 transferred *Sweat* to Broadway in March 2017, not even Nottage's second Pulitzer Prize for Drama sustained *Sweat's* run, for it closed after 105 performances, shortly after it failed to win the Tony Award.[13]

Sweat's lack of success on Broadway notwithstanding, Nottage is unquestionably a major figure in early-twenty-first-century American drama. Already a staple Off-Broadway and in regional theatres, Nottage is now reaching larger audiences with *Sweat*, especially given the role played by Reading, Pennsylvania, where *Sweat* is set, and other "rust belt" towns in the 2016 election.[14]

As Broadway began to reopen following the Covid-19 pandemic, Nottage achieved new triumphs, "breaking barriers" and "making history" in New York, according to CBS New York. In January 2022, Nottage celebrated having three shows running simultaneously in New York. Two shows— *Clyde's* at the Hayes Theater and *MJ The Musical*, for which Nottage wrote the book, at the Neil Simon Theatre—ran on Broadway while the opera version of *Intimate Apparel* played at the Lincoln Center Theater.[15] Nottage told CBS that such an accomplishment was "something no other Black woman in the industry has done," with the network adding that it might even be said that "the Brooklyn native is taking over" ("Pulitzer Prize").

The many awards and positive reviews enjoyed by such Vogel students as Nilo Cruz, Sarah Ruhl, Quiara Alegría Hudes, Lynn Nottage, and others clearly show how she may call herself professor of some of America's most accomplished playwrights of the early twenty-first century. Vogel's ongoing relationships with her former students establish that they view her not only as a former professor but also as a teacher. Ruhl, for example, conducted talkbacks at the 2014 New Ohio Theatre production of *And Baby Makes Seven*. Rebecca Taichman, who had already directed several Sarah Ruhl plays, including *The Clean House* and *Stage Kiss*, co-created *Indecent* with Vogel before directing it at first Yale Rep and La Jolla, California, then Off-Broadway at the Vineyard (2016), and finally in Vogel's Broadway debut at the Cort Theatre (2017), for which Taichman won the Tony Award for

Best Direction. At the same time that Taichman was directing *Indecent* on Broadway, she was directing Ruhl's *How to Transcend a Happy Marriage* at the Lincoln Center. Vogel, moreover, interviewed Ruhl for *Bomb Magazine*.

Ruhl is hardly the only former student to maintain a professional relationship with or offer praise to Vogel. On opening night for *Indecent*, Hudes tweeted that this event, along with Nottage's second Pulitzer (for *Sweat*), marked a moment of "Broadway feminist joy" (@quiarahudes). With *Sweat* marking Nottage's Broadway debut, *The New Yorker* wrote a lengthy profile of Nottage, who acknowledged Vogel as a "teacher." According to Nottage, Vogel "introduced me to the notion that you can make a career as a playwright" (Schulman 32). On June 16, 2017, Nottage tweeted a nod to her teacher in the news that Vogel had won the Hull-Warriner Award for *Indecent* (@Lynnbrooklyn). Then, too, is the example of Steven Levenson, winner of the 2017 Tony Award for Best Book of a Musical for *Dear Evan Hansen*. Levenson stated, "Paula Vogel was my teacher in college and she has been a mentor to me" (Brunner).

Vogel has spoken of the importance that teaching and mentoring have played for her. In an interview called "The Urgency of Indecent Art," Vogel told Helen Eisenbach, "I always said I wanted people to enter [the classroom] as my students and leave as my peers and colleagues, and that I wanted them to make it in the field before I did." Then, Vogel added, "As a mentor and a godparent and a fan and a believer I've been [on Broadway] for Nilo Cruz, for Quiara Hudes, for Sarah Ruhl, and they've all honored me by sitting next to me to watch their play." Vogel characterized her life's work as "not about getting through the door alone; it's about forming circles. Circles rise faster than individuals can" (Vogel "Urgency"). These invitations from Cruz, Hudes, and Ruhl, all of whose work appeared on Broadway before Vogel's did, offer powerful testimony to the unbroken circles she has created as a professor who is truly a teacher.

The examples of successful Vogel students speak to her importance as a teacher, but they do not tell us about her teaching style. Fortunately, evidence abounds. Steven Levenson provides one good example, declaring that Vogel's "whole attitude is to teach fearlessness and just start writing. The hardest part about writing is writing. She urged us to just go. Don't judge, just start and finish" (Brunner). As evinced in the comment that "everybody's a writer, everybody's an artist, and everybody can write plays" (Rousuck 48), a statement Vogel has frequently voiced over the years, she believes that the writing itself is the thing, and she encourages her students to do it.

The House of Paula Vogel

For an Ivy League professor, Vogel has a broad definition of students. Although Vogel welcomes male students and has had them go on to success, perhaps most notably Cruz and Levenson, she has worked especially hard to expand opportunities available to lesbians in particular and women in general, responding, at least in part to a feeling for which she has said "[t]here should be a word—it's beyond homophobia and misogyny—for a bias against lesbians that's very particular" (Savran "Driving"). At the same time, Vogel has resisted universally condemning men, commenting, "To say that men are the enemy is patronizing. It makes me a victim, and I am not comfortable as a victim" (Holmberg). Vogel took a major step toward creating opportunities for women to write plays when, in 1984, she joined Mac Wellman, Connie Congdon, and Jeff Jones at "a 'kvetch' session that occurs between artists who cannot, as the saying goes, get arrested" (paulavogelplaywright.com/boot-camp). This meeting occurred at the New York loft of Gordon Edelstein, and from it emerged the idea of "the great American Play Bakeoff," inspired by the bakeoffs sponsored by Pillsbury since 1949. Vogel writes, "I loved the idea of creating plays as recipes, as a group responding to a staple in our diet and creating endless variations" (paulavogelplwright.com/boot-camp).

Along with her playwriting bakeoffs, Vogel has also created "boot camps," which she has offered beyond the walls of Brown and Yale, including such places as "juvenile detention centers, theatre boardrooms and maximum-security [women's] prisons" (Rousuck 48). Vogel has said of all her students, whether at Brown or a Provincetown detention center, "Anyone who writes in my class and puts their heart into it, I will support, encourage and love. Period" (Craig 223). These democratizing activities have occurred simultaneously with such financially necessary functions as what Randy Gener calls "daylong workshops for various species of theatrical creatures (producers, funders, subscribers, students)." Vogel gave Gener a picture of who, in her mind, should join these functions, saying, "I disagree with the stance of critics being objective journalists outside the theatre community," and adding, "Such an attitude is becoming destructive to our field, and I imagine it's hard for them to maintain their love of theatre as outsiders" (Gener 15).

Former *Baltimore Sun* critic J. Wynn Rousuck's experience offers an invaluable account of Vogel in the classroom. Rousuck writes that Vogel has a "perpetual sparkle in her eyes," and her "hair seems to bristle with energy" as she moves at "warp speed" (50). Carolyn Casey Craig adds that, in general, Vogel "gives the strong impression that she never thinks, talks, or writes in anything but high gear" (213). "'Impossible to teach' is what many would claim of playwriting," Rousuck notes, but "it's certainly not true in Vogel's classroom" (48). Her assignments speak to ambitious goals and her quirky personality: "'Write something in pure form,' 'write a five-act play,' 'write a farce,' 'use an older form to make it strange'" (Rousuck 50). A particularly intriguing assignment followed reading Lorca. Vogel told her students, "Go to a Providence truck diner; think of the truck as a puppet apparatus, and include the poet, the town bully, some description of Providence politics, and a vulgar ditty" (Rousuck 52). Rousuck reported, based on her own experience, that Vogel manifests "an uncanny knack for getting inside a student's head, understanding where the student is going, and helping guide the way" (51).

On May 14, 2017, *The New York Times* reporter Andrew R. Chow wrote that Vogel would "conduct a free playwriting workshop at the Vineyard Theatre on May 22." This opportunity would constitute what Vogel called "her first writing workshop aimed at the general public in 13 years," and the participants would be "the first 30 people who RSVP to indecentbootcamp @gmail.com starting at noon" on May 16 (Chow). Perceiving what may be a unique opportunity, I sent an RSVP almost immediately after noon and waited nervously. Shortly before 10:00 a.m. six days later, approximately thirty other people and I began arriving at the Vineyard, and I met Paula Vogel. Consistent with what Rousuck and Craig have written, the person who verified my registration observed the large cup of coffee in my hand and commented, "You're going to need that caffeine." The smiling playwright dressed in black who greeted several of us warmly and without apparent rush soon confirmed the observation. Vogel's "Stop me—stop me" offer to anyone who felt confused by her presentation proved necessary, not because she spoke particularly quickly but because even in a workshop organized so as to present multiple clear themes and ideas, Vogel mentioned offhandedly so many anecdotes and examples that the sheer volume was both impressive and at times overwhelming.

Indeed, a simple account of Vogel's presentation would read as a stream-of-consciousness Proustian rumination leavened with a great quantity of specific names and facts. I discerned, nonetheless, several topics that explicate, at least in part, Vogel's theories on drama and writing plays. Vogel acknowledged that what we were experiencing was "not per se a boot camp," which would normally consist of "an entire week . . . limited to ten or twelve" participants who, based on her having led many, would have a "bonding experience" that could result in participants keeping in touch for decades.[16] The overall impression, however, was not so much that Vogel felt forced to omit major topics from a typical workshop as from having to condense her presentation and give participants/students much less time to complete much briefer assignments. This workshop was hardly the first time Vogel had offered a shortened version of the boot camp, for she acknowledged that 2017 marked the third year she had done so at the Vineyard, with the previous two years' opportunities limited to playwrights and patrons of the Vineyard Theatre.

Since "the aim of each participant writing a short play by the end of the day" (Chow) was a stated goal of the workshop, Vogel told us something she has stated frequently, albeit in slightly different words, namely, "I think everybody is a playwright regardless of whether or not you own it." She then gave an overall theory of art, which she attributed to her former Cornell University professor and mentor Bert States. Vogel recommended a States book, *Great Reckonings in Little Rooms* (1985), a phenomenological volume which, according to Vogel, posits that all art moves through three stages: naïve, sophisticated, and decadent. Naïve art, she noted, can consist of artistic endeavors initiated at an informal gathering, such as dada. It is strange and defamiliarized, with the audience unaware of the rules. Sophisticated art ensues when someone with a general awareness says, "Let's go see dada or performance art." The sophisticated soon gives over to decadence as soon as the reaction is "Dada again?!" Form is developing, Vogel commented, faster than we can fix it, and "plays decay within a single performance" or as audiences become familiar with a work that is at first very strange. As an example of this latter phenomenon, Vogel cited Lin-Manuel Miranda's *Hamilton*. This play was in naïve form when audiences first encountered actors of color rapping the story of America's founders. Its popularity resulted in sophisticated form as the defamiliarization of style and performers fell away. Now, when audiences arrive prepared to sing along with the lyrics, *Hamilton* has moved on to decadent form. If Miranda wants to return to naïve form, he will have to create something very different from *Hamilton*, and the structure of naïve, sophisticated, and decadent form leaves a critic unable to predict what form this next work will need to take.

At the beginning of the workshop, Vogel had already written six types of dramas on the white board in front of the Vineyard stage. Her discussion filled in details about the six types: (1) Syllogistic i.e. linear i.e. Cause and Effect, (2) Qualitative i.e. Associative i.e. Shakespearean i.e. Epic, (3) Circle, (4) Pattern—repetitive, (5) Generic i.e. Conventional, and (6) Synthetic fragment. Understanding these types, Vogel stated, depends upon an awareness of the "engines" that drive dramatic creation. These engines fundamentally correspond with Aristotle's six essentials of drama: plot, character, thought or idea, language, spectacle, and music/harmony.[17] She suggested that playwrights consider switching their engine from play to play as one of several "ways not to write the same play over and over again."[18] While Vogel shared that she removes the Aristotelian essential (or engine) thought when writing, wishing to take a play through the naïve, sophisticated, and decadent stages by focusing on the *how* rather than the *what* (thought being the what), she also acknowledged having been "in love with spectacle or plasticity" for the past twenty years. She emphasized her own belief that spectacle is, indeed, plasticity, which she defined as every non-verbal element that fills the cube of space which is the play. Vogel's devotion to plasticity as an engine driving not only the writing of plays but also their performance is such that, she confided, she almost never uses the words "stage directions" because they interfere with the plasticity of the play world playwright, producer, director, and performers have created.

Referring to her own list on the white board, Vogel began explaining each type of play and providing examples as appropriate. The first, Syllogistic, she defined as quite rare, commenting, "There's no such thing as pure plot," or to put it another way, no one-to-one relationship between plot and our time, such as we experience when we cough or hear a fire alarm. Associative, however, she identified as quite common and the genre of Shakespeare, who she asserted writes plays that are very close to syllogistic except that he'll interrupt for an "Alas, poor Yorick" moment or a drunken porter in *Macbeth* scene that suspends time and gives the audience an opportunity to reflect. Strindberg, Vogel explained, invented the one-act play to stay in "real" time while presenting a drama. Vogel concluded her discussion of Associative drama by saying it is the default form in American drama.

Playwrights who do not opt for the default still have multiple dramatic forms available to them, starting with what Vogel called "Circle" plays. Examples of this form include the play version of *The Wizard of Oz*, Thornton Wilder's *Our Town*, Sartre's *No Exit*, and much of Beckett. Vogel described "Circle" plays as presenting "toc tic as opposed to tic toc," offering a vision of time without end.[19] Such plays have a cousin in "Pattern" plays. Chekhov's *Three Sisters* operates according to a type of pattern, according to Vogel, as does English playwright Nick Payne's 2012 drama *Constellations*, which has been performed to acclaim in London and New York and which is now a staple of regional theatres. For Vogel, the works of David Ives, in general, fall under the heading of "Pattern" plays. Vogel concluded her discussion of "Circle" and "Pattern" plays by discussing an 1897 play that was controversial a century ago and remains so (although largely forgotten) today, Arthur Schnitzler's *La Ronde*, originally titled *Reigen*, named for a dance accompanied by music called a "round," or circle.

"Generic," of course, is a loaded term that Vogel unpacked for the workshop. The audience already knows the form or genre and has expectations for a "Generic" play. It may contain syllogistic, qualitative, circular, or patterned elements, but they are presented in a ritualistic way. In hybrid form (e.g., "Generic" and "Circular"), these plays may be quite lucrative. As examples of "Generic" plays, Vogel provided the examples *Godspell* and *Jesus Christ, Superstar*, both of which have enjoyed regional, national, and international success for decades.

The final form Vogel discussed was what she describes as a "Synthetic Fragment," a postmodern form that may present all of time simultaneously. The most famous example of such a play Vogel cited was Tony Kushner's *Angels in America*, but she also referenced several other comparatively recent plays, including Heiner Muller's *Hamletmachine* (or *Die Hamletmaschine*), a 1977 take on Shakespeare's masterpiece. In addition, she included Lisa Loomer's 1996 play *The Waiting Room*, which was performed at the Vineyard Theatre among other places, and Katori Hall's 2009 account of Dr. Martin Luther King, Jr's, final night, *The Mountaintop*, which includes a collage of historical events between King's assassination and the moment the play is being performed. The "Synthetic Fragment," of course, may contain elements of the other dramatic forms, as Vogel indicated by stating that changing plot form among the six types she had listed allows a playwright to add variety, break up monotony, and as Ezra Pound discovered from his studies of Chinese culture, "make it new."

Almost as soon as Vogel finished her presentation on forms of drama, she interrupted the flow of the workshop by instructing the audience, "Please write a short play that is impossible to stage," adding, "I will see you at 11:30." Vogel returned to have several participants read their plays, stating that a variation on the assignment is a play with a dog protagonist. She went on to describe having collected many very good plays from such assignments, including the aforementioned composition that led her to recommend a playwriting career to a very young Sarah Ruhl.

Vogel described how she has developed her own categories for drama and characters that include the archetypal versus the individuated and the original versus the wounded, "borrowed," or "programmed." In her Vineyard

Theatre workshop, Vogel devoted more time to discussing archetypal versus individuated than toward original versus wounded, reflecting a concern she has with "realistic" drama. We use the term "realism," Vogel insisted, to describe dramas that are actually based on the well-made play, and playwrights or critics who are responsible for these "realistic" dramas are, according to Vogel, "reviving the patient" that should be dead. "Realism," she added, "is a way that we pretend that we are being objective" when, in fact, the plays most contemporary audiences see result in viewers being "conditioned" rather than defamiliarized, or shaken. Vogel does not find realism entirely objectionable, for in Ibsen's day it "was an avant-garde movement" that, over time and the conditioning she mentioned, has become bourgeois.[20] It has also led to some interpretations of plays that border on the bizarre. Indicting critics who insist upon seeing "realism" where the term has no place, Vogel quipped, "I actually wrote a realistic play called *How I Learned to Drive*." Readers and viewers influenced by this way of treating a defamiliarized play such as *Drive* have asked Vogel, many times, "What does Uncle Peck do for a living?" She answered, "I don't care," for Uncle Peck's profession is not part of the play world Vogel has created in the play.

Part of Vogel's objection to what she views as misapplications of the term "realism" stems from some of the assumptions in the current theatre. Without being too critical, Vogel suggested forgetting temporarily about Stanislavsky and the Method. She pointed out an assumption in today's drama that characters have full psychologies when not all do. Indeed, audiences generally assume characters are (or are based on) real people, what Vogel called "objective truth." Our dramatic ancestors who are archetypes lack such psychologies. Specifically, Oedipus and Everyman are archetypal, not three dimensional with psychologies. The same is true of Romeo and Juliet although they do provide movement toward the individuated Hamlet.[21] Archetypal characters have not ceased emerging from playwrights' imaginations to this day, for Vogel pointed out that from Shakespeare's day until today, female archetypes, such as Linda Loman, have stood on stages alongside individuated male characters, such as Willy. We can also encounter archetypal characters in places we might not expect to find characters at all: in particular, Vogel cited FBI profiles and obituaries as bad archetypal play writing, and she told us she sometimes asks her students to take a "Most Wanted" or deceased person and make that person a character in a scene that portrays an unexpected side of the character's now individuated psychology. Group company theatres, Vogel explained, are currently taking on the task of turning archetypal characters into individuated ones as are some television programs airing away from the traditional major networks. Asked for an example, Vogel cited the Netflix series *Stranger Things*.

In transitioning to her distinction between characters who are original versus those who are wounded (or borrowed or programmed), Vogel focused closely on dialogue. Playwrights craft wounded language when characters cannot express in the moment what is happening. The fractured syntax critics have labeled "Mamet speak" exemplifies wounded language familiar to today's audiences, as does the language characters use in Quentin Tarantino's films. The technique has a long history as well. King Lear, for example, uses wounded speech, perhaps most memorably in his "Howl" speech (5.3.270 ff.). Similarly, the playwrights of ancient Greece employ wounded speech.[22]

Vogel's comments on wounded speech segued into a discussion of plasticity. Vogel acknowledged that many levels of plasticity exist, but she chose to emphasize four, commenting that Tennessee Williams sometimes uses all of them at once.

1) Plasticity of the play world refers to emotional speech, how the space "feels." A line, which Vogel did not attribute, such as "The sky is the color of disappointment," helps create the plasticity of the play world. To design the plasticity of the play world for actors and the director (but not the audience), Vogel suggested that playwrights consider describing an action offstage.

2) Plasticity of the stage is a concept not intended to direct, but it does offer reminders. It tells us when we will see the color red, a pumpkin, an actor entering the audience, and so on.[23]

3) Plasticity of the page refers to the physical page specific to every play world a playwright creates. The physical layout, including spacing and font, can attract or repel a reader's attention. Vogel recommended that playwrights design their own manuscript pages.

4) Plasticity of the playwright is the playwright's own, perhaps unintentional, intrusion into the play. Vogel paraphrased her former professor Bert O. States describing this as virtually nonexistent, with most drama "the only form of writing where the playwright is not present." Vogel disagrees with States and sees the

young Tennessee Williams present in a certain line of a play like *The Glass Menagerie*. She also discerns this plasticity whenever a note includes such words as "My grandmother used to say."

The moment I had most been looking forward to came just before the lunch break when Vogel introduced the concept of the bakeoff that she and a group of her friends originally developed more than three decades ago. Before the writing began, Vogel discussed what she called "the maliciousness of objects," a concept she said her brother Carl had introduced to her and that we see reflected in works as seemingly disparate as *The Third Man*[24] and the "Chucky" films. She also described a notion familiar to readers of her plays, negative empathy, and stated that it is atypical in commercial theatres and studio films. As an example of negative empathy, Vogel described herself as a playgoer saying, "I'm not Othello. I'm not Othello. Oh, yes, I am," adding that if she as a woman may make such a statement manifesting negative empathy about Othello, anyone can. In the abbreviated bakeoff plays we were about to write, she emphasized, we would defy current entertainment's striving to make us feel good all the time and would therefore leave open the possibility for negative empathy.

Some of the "ingredients" for our bakeoff would result from a majority vote, but Vogel insisted upon two before the discussion began: Kellyanne Conway and Le Petomane.[25] Almost no one had heard of Le Petomane, the stage name of late-nineteenth-century and early-twentieth-century French performer Joseph Pujol (1857—1945), for whom the terms "fartiste" and "farteur" ("flatulist") were coined. Participants then offered approximately fifteen choices, among them an act of coitus interruptus, a tiny hand, and an alternative fact. The ingredients receiving the largest number of votes, however, were a malicious object, a tweet, and a moment of music. We were given the lunch hour to write a one-act play using Kellyanne Conway, Le Petomane, and the three ingredients selected by participants. As Vogel departed, suggesting that participants go elsewhere and write, she called out, "The thing about bakeoffs, they're supposed to end in the middle of a sentence."

Bakeoffs dominated the workshop after lunch. First, Vogel had several participants read their brief plays. In a longer workshop, she told us, participants would critique one another's work, but in this abbreviated version, we would not critique, and she would not collect any of the compositions. Once we heard three compositions involving the odd juxtaposition of ingredients required, Vogel described other types of bakeoffs she enjoys conducting. Ideally, she informed us, she likes to hold a bakeoff over a 48-hour period that follows a group of friends or other participants reading and viewing common works. For example, she described the "Possession" bakeoff, which she likes to begin with the film *Prelude to a Kiss*, the S. Ansky play *The Dybbuk*, and a barely known play that Vogel adores and highly recommends, Tom Cone's 1975 work *Herringbone*. As ingredients for this bakeoff, Vogel likes to use a trance, a prance, and a kiss; a betrothal; and, for extra credit, a child's toy.

Other bakeoff subjects include Don Juan, St. Joan, and Leda and the Swan. For the Don Juan bakeoff, Vogel recommends as ingredients a ghost, a statue, a master, a servant, swordplay, and a moment of *coitus interruptus*. The St. Joan bakeoff calls for a visitation of a girl in a field, convincing a higher authority, a defense of cross-dressing, and a match. Finally, the Leda and the Swan bakeoff could use two races, two species, the sky, a gust of wind, and a feather, with a plate glass window or electrical appliance suggested for extra credit. Vogel included recommended reading or viewing sources for this last bakeoff: Egloff paintings, Harold Bloom's writings on rape versus consent, and Yeats's "Leda and the Swan." Regardless of the subject, however, Vogel warns against treating the product of the bakeoff entirely as a play. Think of it, she admonished us, as a poker game with friends and a strict deadline. Very often, the friendly competition will lead to a complete play, one fueled, Vogel added, by alcohol, coffee, and food. In all cases, the encounter with the sources should occur at the beginning of the process.

Vogel concluded the bakeoff unit with a different kind of bakeoff, what she called a "Shakeoff," a homage to Shakespeare's plays. This concept, she acknowledged, has evolved beyond a competition among friends. She referenced her work with the Hudson Shakespeare Company in New York, where she has designed bakeoffs for works being performed and invited audiences to join in. She mentioned that she would like to see companies do these sorts of activities with each of Shakespeare's plays, and she added that the idea of bakeoffs specific to other playwrights appealed to her as well. Vogel's tone and enthusiasm hinted at unlimited possibilities for bakeoffs, ranging from the brief, informal session offered as part of her one-day workshop to far more intense and competitive experiences intended both to prompt a better understanding of an important extant work and possibly produce something new of significance as well. Decades after that day in Gordon Edelstein's New York loft apartment, Vogel continues to develop new variations on an idea.

The Theatre of Paula Vogel

Vogel concluded the Vineyard Theatre workshop at approximately 3:00. Not once had her energy flagged, nor did she ever mention that the same evening, she would receive a Lifetime Achievement Award at the 62nd annual Obies and would give an acceptance speech. During my brief time with Vogel, I developed an understanding of the way she has inspired and encouraged students over the years. Standing among the participants who were taking our leave of Vogel, I blurted out, "Now I want to write a play!" In the same tone of voice I had just used, Vogel immediately replied, "Do it!" I intuited that Vogel does not view other playwrights as competitors but rather, as she has all but told Craig in as many words (23), as colleagues. I also sensed that were I ever to spend a semester or longer with Vogel, as Cruz, Ruhl, Hudes, and Nottage have done, I would consider her a mentor and would want to maintain a relationship with her. She seemed a professor who would become a valued friend.

Vogel's enduring friendships with her former students who are professional playwrights illuminate her teaching effectiveness, but her relationships with her graduate students provide another perspective. Ruhl and Nottage, for instance, came to Vogel as undergraduates still in or barely out of their teens. Marc Silverstein (PhD 1989) is a professor at Auburn University on whose dissertation committee Vogel served in her early years at Brown.[26] According to Silverstein, "I owe Paula for being on [my committee]"[27] because Vogel did not know Silverstein when Silverstein, on the advice of dissertation director John Emigh, asked her to serve. Vogel's initial unfamiliarity with Silverstein did not prevent her from taking an active role. Silverstein recalls that Vogel, who was jointly appointed in English and theatre at Brown, "had in mind that I was chiefly writing for a dramatic literature audience" but was nonetheless able to tell him what theatre scholars would want to see in his dissertation about Harold Pinter. Vogel remained mindful of what Silverstein calls the "eighties old saw— theory and theatre come from the same root" even as she advised Silverstein when his dissertation dealt too heavily with theory and if he risked veering into the notion that playwright and theoretician perform the same work.

Silverstein speaks highly of Vogel not only as an academic advisor but also as a human being. He recalls that she never gave him dissertation feedback solely through written notes but invited him to her office, where she encouraged him to play backgammon on her office computer around sessions. Not only that, but Vogel invited Silverstein to her Providence home, where conversations about his dissertation continued over bagels and coffee. Both in her office and in her home, Vogel would speak to Silverstein on a combination of professional and human levels, especially whenever she commented, "Your argument makes sense to me."

Silverstein also attributes to Vogel one valuable piece of advice that he regrets not taking. Vogel encouraged Silverstein, before completing his dissertation, to direct a Pinter play and "engage it at some level performatively yourself" so as to understand it on a deeper level. Back in 1989, Silverstein's desire to complete his degree before moving to a tenure-track job waiting for him at Auburn prevented him from having time to direct a play, but he has grown to appreciate the insights such an experience could have yielded then or could yield yet. This sort of insight and, indeed, Silverstein's overall comments about Vogel confirm the vision of her as an engaged teacher and professor who counseled a developing and ultimately successful scholar.[28] Vogel, as described by Silverstein, comports with her playwright students' comments, the recorded reactions of her boot camp participants, and my own experience as her student for a few hours. I came to understand why Paula Vogel has enjoyed a significant career as a teacher of dramatists and a professor of drama.

CHAPTER 5
VOGEL IN THE TWENTY-FIRST CENTURY

In her 2008 play *A Civil War Christmas: An American Musical Celebration*, Vogel put live music on stage, performed by the actors themselves. Regarding Daryl Waters's adaptations of circa 1864 public domain songs, many of them Christmas carols, Vogel has written that "if the audience sings along on some of the carols, better still"[1] (8). *A Civil War Christmas* turns Vogel's attention to a topic she had earlier told David Savran ("Driving" 353) mattered immensely to her, musical theatre, as well as to a topic that would inform her Broadway debut several years hence, American history. The American Civil War has not yet become a time for musical celebration, however, and Charles Dickens's Tiny Tim, not Vogel's Abraham Lincoln, Decatur Bronson, or Moses Levy, remains the dramatic character most responsible, come Christmastime, for wishing that "God bless us, every one."

All the same, on Tuesday, music in theatre played a role when, on April 18, 2017, Quiara Alegría Hudes tweeted, "Pens out, historians!" (@quiarahudes). Prompting Hudes were two events: Lynn Nottage winning the 2017 Pulitzer (for *Sweat*, discussed in Chapter 4), making her the only woman twice awarded the Pulitzer Prize for Drama; and the official opening night of Paula Vogel's *Indecent* at Broadway's Cort Theatre.[2] After more than four decades as a playwright and university professor and with two Obie Awards, a Pulitzer, and induction into the American Theatre Hall of Fame, Vogel, at age sixty-five, was at last a Broadway playwright. Originally "commissioned by Oregon Shakespeare Festival's American Revolutions and Yale Repertory Theatre" ("Paula Vogel to Receive"), *Indecent* emerged in close collaboration with billed co-creator Rebecca Taichman (who directed the play multiple times, including on Broadway) and was produced at both Yale Repertory Theatre and California's La Jolla Playhouse in 2015 before it ran successfully Off-Broadway at the Vineyard Theatre, where *How I Learned to Drive* had appeared nearly two decades earlier, in the spring of

2016. Then, in October 2016, Robert Viagas reported that the play would move to the Cort Theatre in April 2017, as it did (Viagas).

Attendees at a performance of *Indecent* saw projected onstage that they were about to view "the true story of a little Jewish play." To Vogel, the "little Jewish play" referenced Polish writer Sholem Asch's 1906 drama *God of Vengeance*. Vogel first encountered *God of Vengeance* in 1974, when she was still coming to accept her identity as a lesbian. Already the teenaged Vogel had taken advantage of many forged sick notes from her mother and spent hours reading "out-of-print novels about lesbian life from the 1920s, 30s, and 50s." Vogel reports "a growing dismay" from reading these novels: "they ended with the protagonist crying to heaven: why can't I be normal? Or the girlfriend married a man who rescued her. Or worse yet, a la Lillian Hellman, there were a lot of suicides" ("A Note").

Cornell professor Bert States came to Vogel's rescue when he "gently said, 'I think you should read *God of Vengeance*.'" Vogel "raced to the library, found a yellowing copy of an out-of-print translation, and stood in the stacks" ("A Note"). When Asch wrote *God of Vengeance* in 1907, he was a recently married man in his mid-twenties. Having grown up in a traditional Jewish community, he almost certainly encountered little to no Sapphic literature during his education. Nevertheless, Vogel reports, "I was stunned." "To this day," she goes on, "I have not read so beautiful a scene between two women, one that accorded their love the pure desire of Romeo and Juliet on the balcony" ("A Note"). In Vogel's mind, *God of Vengeance* was "filled with a kind of feminism" or, to put it another way, represented "Arthur Miller before Arthur Miller's time in terms of what we are presenting onstage as tragedy" ("Livestreaming a Reading"). Why, Vogel and a few other fans of the play wondered, did such a work remain virtually forgotten? Not only did some of the few who knew the play find merit in it, including Pulitzer-winner Donald Margulies,[3] who brought out a 2004 adaptation, but the play also had a fascinating stage history. After touring Europe successfully and being translated into many languages, the play ran in New York's Bowery and was put on by the Provincetown Players before it was transferred to Broadway's Apollo Theatre. There, in response to the subject matter, the authorities halted the production, tried, and convicted the performers on charges of obscenity.[4]

The lesbian themes and the ensuing trials are landmarks in American theatrical history, yet they received very little attention from scholars. C. W. E. Bigsby barely elides by the event when his authoritative *A Critical Introduction to Twentieth-Century American Drama* states that the "Neighborhood Playhouse, established in 1912, . . . was an eclectic theatre, drawing on Noh drama and Hindu plays as well as work by Leonid Andreyev, Arnold Bennett, Harley Granville-Barker, George Bernhard Shaw and Sholem Asch" (vol. 1, 9). Nowhere else does Bigsby mention Asch, and never does he refer to the play. Perhaps one reason is that Asch himself eventually despaired of *God of Vengeance* and, upon learning of a planned 1946 Spanish-language production in Mexico City, "warned the Mexican theatre against producing the play and appealed to the cast to discontinue rehearsals" ("Sholem Asch Bans"). Asch even went so far as to announce his having "prohibited the production of his play . . . in any language in the United States and in other countries," explaining cryptically that "the situation described in the play is dated and exists no longer" ("Sholem Asch Bans").

All the same, while Vogel pondered *God of Vengeance* and how to write about it, Yale drama student Rebecca Taichman became fascinated by the obscenity trials and produced as her master's thesis the 2000 play *The People Vs. "The God of Vengeance,"* which the Yale Repertory Theatre performed from May 8 through 13 in conjunction with a May 13–15 "Sholem Asch Reconsidered" conference. Alvin Klein wrote that Asch's play and the trial had "aroused" Taichman "to reignite a once flourishing tradition of theater and to find parallels between the repressions of a silenced past and the ostensibly liberated attitudes of the [2000] present."[5] Klein discussed Donald Margulies's adaptation, then in progress, and quoted Taichman as saying that *God of Vengeance*'s "moment has come" as part of a "Yiddish renaissance." Taichman added, "This story has entered my soul. It seems to be my destiny."

Taichman's prophecy about the story behind *God of Vengeance* and the obscenity trials having become part of her destiny was proven true in her collaboration with Vogel on *Indecent*. What neither Vogel nor her co-creator anticipated, however, was how long the process would take. In fact, but for Taichman taking what she has described to Olivia Clement as "the longest shot that I could ever dream of" and placing a "hopeful cold call"[6] to Vogel, *Indecent* might never have appeared. Unbeknownst to Taichman, Vogel "had been tracking [Rebecca's] work and watching her productions, and just thinking what a remarkable gift this director has" (Clement "How"). "That hussy Sarah Ruhl," Vogel later jokingly recalled, had not only "started working with" Taichman ("Theatre Uncorked" podcast Episode 2), but the student had decided to give something back to her professor: "You really should work with Rebecca; you really should get to know each other" ("Uncorked"). "Within five minutes" of Vogel's accepting Taichman's phone call, Taichman remembers, "she said yes and we embarked on this extraordinary adventure together" (Clement "How"). Taichman credits Vogel with taking "this tiny little idea that I had and turn[ing] it into an extraordinary epic masterpiece" (Clement "How"). Vogel contradicts the modesty in Taichman's reference to a "tiny little idea," saying, "We have two minds as well as one. We have two visions and her vision always seems to open a door for me" (Clement "How").

By the time the play reached the Vineyard Theatre, this collaborative vision had seen many iterations: "I'm on my forty-first draft," Vogel told a 2016 *HowlRound* live streaming. More drafts would come before the play reached Broadway, and the sharing between the playwright and the woman who was her co-creator and eventual director would continue to occur in unusual, perhaps unexpected ways. During a June 2016 Drama Book Shop discussion, Vogel provided two examples of how close the collaboration was. While the play was being performed at Yale, Vogel recalled, she and Taichman stayed together, and then Vogel delved so deeply into her research that she would appear at breakfast and greet Taichman with a statement such as "Eugene O'Neill just appeared to me last night" (Vogel and Taichman). Not only that, but Vogel added that "as a woman playwright, when I take a bathroom break, I am sitting next to my director in the next stall," where, at times, "there'd be a little knock on the wall" (Vogel and Taichman), and one collaborator would promote her ideas to the other.

Taichman retrieved boxes of original, historical documents from the Beinecke Library, including her own dramatic account of the trial, and brought them to Vogel. Vogel realized early on that the eventual work should tell what she called "a bigger story" (Vogel and Taichman) than only that of the trial itself. Although Taichman had directly quoted the trial transcripts, she acknowledged, "I am really not a playwright, and don't have the capacity to write dialogue" (Vogel and Taichman). Often, Vogel and Taichman stated during a Drama Book Shop discussion that was live streamed over the internet, Taichman would produce an idea that Vogel translated into dialogue and action. Vogel attributed the ending to Taichman, telling the Drama Book Shop and online audiences that "she came in with the most fabulous bit of stage magic" (i.e., the final rendition of the rain scene). Vogel did report "one thing that was contentious, which was what was the title of the play" (Vogel and Taichman). Doug Wright of Sundance, himself a Pulitzer winner (*I Am My Own Wife*, 2004), suggested a short title in contrast with the title of Taichman's thesis. Both women agreed, but they rejected what Vogel describes as "six or seven single spaced pages of different titles," including other one-word options such as *Obscene* and *Immoral*, sometimes pondering the notion of a theatregoer requesting a ticket to *Obscene*. Wright, Vogel told David Noh, asked, "What about quoting the original obscenity indictment?" (Noh), and it was there that she and Taichman found and agreed upon *Indecent*.

Indecent both defamiliarizes and (re?)familiarizes. The defamiliarization occurs mainly in terms of what a 1923 district attorney and perhaps even some audience members today would regard as obscene, prurient, or primarily sexual. Vogel's technique of telling and showing bits of the rain scene repeatedly has the effect of taking such elements from the scene. Vogel has the actresses portraying Rivke and Manke in the 1923 production strenuously object to removing the rain scene, building sympathy for Asch's and stage manager Lemml's (a Vogel and Taichman creation) original version. Critic Ben Brantley describes these representations as "fuguelike variations, performed with grace," until the "dominant note of this erotic encounter isn't prurience, though; it's piety" (Brantley Review *Indecent*).[7]

Indecent must familiarize or refamiliarize its audience with "the true story" it presents. A metadramatic play by a frequently metadramatic playwright, it incorporates not only the love scene which initially drew Vogel to the play in 1974 but also Asch's concluding scene, in which the brothel owner responds to his daughter's love for one of his prostitutes by condemning her to the brothel downstairs and hoisting a Jewish Torah so as to hurl it to the floor (but not actually doing so in Vogel's retelling). This scene is played ever more melodramatically as the play is translated into multiple languages and moves from place to place, including Berlin and Bratislava. This melodrama serves an important dramatic function, keeping the audience entertained while also chronicling *God of Vengeance* throughout Europe. Rudolph Schildkraut, a performer in Max Reinhardt's theatre company and in German silent films, repeatedly portrayed Yekel, the brothel owner, husband, and father. When the play came to America in the late 1910s, Schildkraut resumed the role in the English-language Broadway production that created Broadway history and resulted in Schildkraut's arrest.

Indecent may play a role in (re?)familiarizing the audience with the zeitgeist in early-twentieth-century continental Europe. Around 1891 Frank Wedekind wrote and in 1906 Max Reinhardt directed *Frülings Erwchen*, the play depicting puberty, casual sex, abortion, and homosexuality that writer Steven Sater and composer/lyricist Duncan Sheik brought to Broadway as

Spring Awakening in 2006. *Spring Awakening* won eight Tony Awards and four Drama Desk Awards and garnered a Grammy Award for its cast recording while running for more than 800 performances. The play was a huge success for young audiences who were completely unaware they were viewing a show more than a century old that had been bowdlerized (e.g., a rape scene replaced by a more ambiguous loss of virginity) before being presented to them.

Asch and Wedekind were hardly alone in considering topics that would seem very new or even controversial a century later. As works that could shock an audience, *God of Vengeance* and the play that evolved into *Spring Awakening* offer mild fare when compared with Alfred Jarry's *Ubu Roi*. Jarry's infamous play, which ran for a single night in December 1896, began with a variation off the French word "*merde*" ("shit") and included what can best be described as vulgar, even scatological, homages to some of Shakespeare's plays. It sparked a riot and was outlawed. Nevertheless, *Ubu Roi* is considered an influential work, a text possibly influencing such movements as dada, futurism, and even modernism. A century later, in his 2001 polemic "How Sick Can We Get?," Richard Alleva acknowledged that "Jarry's writings influenced those of Apollinaire, André Breton, and Roger Vitrac, and eventually, at the end of a long chain of surrealists, those of Eugene Ionesco and Samuel Beckett" (17). Alleve added, "*King Ubu* has been surpassed but King Ubu still rules" (18). Jarry, for decades, has been far more influential than he ever was during his own lifetime.

Paula Vogel turned to *Ubu Roi* for inspiration in early 2018. As the American holiday President's Day drew near, Vogel sent out an appeal for a "National UBU ROI Bake-off." Adopting the motto "Fight Sh#*^ with Merdre," Vogel scheduled February 19, 2018, as a date when, according to her website, "People wrote plays and came together to share them all over the country" ("National UBU ROI Bake-off"). First, however, Vogel directed participants to read Alfred Jarry's play, Shakespeare's *Macbeth*, and any other Jarry materials. Prospective playwrights could click through to a "Resource Materials" link that led to French and English versions of *Ubu Roi*, *Macbeth*, a *Washington Post* article, the Wikipedia page for Le Petomane, a 2014 Dan Piepenbring *Paris Review* recounting of *Ubu Roi* titled "An Inglorious Slop-pail of a Play," and other sources (including YouTube videos).

As usual for a bakeoff, Vogel provided a list of "ingredients," which included "Covfefe," perhaps a misspelling of a famous misspelling, just as the extra character in "Fight Sh#*^" seems to follow Jarry's extra letter in "Merdre." She required authors to include the following:

- Pa Ubu 45 (supposedly 6'3", a trim 239 lbs, in "excellent health." And yes, the hair is his and real).
- Ma Ubu: strangely catatonic when in Pa Ubu's company.
- Angry Ambassadors from every country that Pa Ubu has insulted.
- A strange use of the English language. That is, it sounds like it is supposed to be English. i.e. words for Sh#t are prolonged like pshitte (in French Merdre!! see *covefe[8] below).
- *Covefe.
- A groveling, conniving, servile counselor who believes in conversion therapy for queers and trans & does not spend time in the company of women except his wife.
- A double-triple-quadruple-octahedral cheeseburger with special sauce. Freedom Fries on the side.
- A usurpation.[9]

Then, for "Extra Credit," participants could include "Enter a bear," "Protestors protesting Pa Ubu 45," "Posters protesting protestors of Pa Ubu 45," and "An unmentionable mop" that is a "pshit-stick." The title for Hayley Levitt's January 2018 Theatermania.com article, in a link Vogel's website provides, reported with considerable understatement that the event "Blends Playwriting with Activism" (Levitt).

Levitt characterizes *Ubu Roi* as "an 1896 revolutionary drama about a despot king awash in murder, genocide, a war with Russia, and the revolt of his own countrymen and women." She then reports the rules of this and numerous other Vogel bakeoffs: "participants will have 48 hours in advance of the Bake-Off day to create a short work—resembling a play, a poem, song, skit, stand-up, mini-opera, etc.—that they will be invited to perform for their peers." This time, participants had until precisely 7:00 p.m. on Saturday, February 16, to register, and then they wrote alongside approximately fifty peers. Each individual's final product ran about five minutes (Levitt).

Vogel provided essential commentary on her expectations here and for bakeoffs in general, stating, "It is my hope that across the U.S. and around the world, artists, theaters, and collectives will be writing in response to Alfred Jarry's text and performing it live on Presidents' Day in response to our global crisis." She then added, "There are no critiques. Bake-Offs are to theater what sketching is to oil paintings" (from Levitt). These statements spoke loudly to Vogel's Democratic leanings in politics as well as her democratic instincts regarding drama. Participants' autonomy to write their independent works prevailed even as Vogel, dogs leashed, looked out smilingly determined from a photograph at the bottom of her page. "IMPEACH PA UBU '45 NOW" read the poster she bore. She had created what she called, on her website, an exercise far "better than stewing at home."

The enduring influence of *Ubu Roi* and the popularity of the musical *Spring Awakening* suggest something in the American zeitgeist of the 2010s that anticipated Vogel's retelling of the story of Broadway's first lesbian relationship. Perhaps placing *Indecent* in this context helps explain why the graduate faculty of Cornell University selected this play (plus an introduction) as the dissertation for Vogel's PhD. Vogel received her Cornell PhD just before *Indecent* began its April 27 to June 19, 2016, run at the Vineyard Theatre. Taichman, who was listed alongside Vogel under "created by," directed. Reviews were enthusiastic, with *Variety* reviewer Marilyn Stasio praising the play as a "riveting backstage drama" such that "while we don't actually see the play performed, we're left with a vivid impression of the drama, beginning with its origins" ("Off Broadway Review"). Stasio particularly singled out for praise "Taichman's impressionistic direction and David Dorfman's stylized choreography" alongside Christopher Akerlind "for the eerie lighting design that has this phantom troupe suspended somewhere beyond time and space" ("Off").

Writing for *The Guardian*, Alexis Soloski called the backstory "a small flashpoint in Jewish and queer theatrical history" before favorably comparing *Indecent* with *Shuffle Along* as "a project of reclamation, an homage and a recuperation of a text that had its cultural moment and then vanished almost entirely." *Indecent*, unlike *Shuffle Along*, Soloski judged, "has tremendous affection for the whole of the [recovered] play and makes you long for the scenes—late arriving, but exquisite—when two of the women finally perform Asch's love scene." Soloski declared the restoration of the rain scene, which was cut from the 1923 Broadway production, "[o]ur great gain" ("Indecent review"). Similarly, Stasio called the scene "austerely beautiful" and "played in the rain with singular grace by the alluring Katrina Lenk and Adina Verson" ("Off Broadway").

The New York Times critic Charles Isherwood made *Indecent* a Critics' Pick, calling it "powerful" and "superbly realized" while, like Stasio and Soloski, he also noted the similarity to *Shuffle Along*, "another terrific show about a landmark Broadway production (almost) lost to history."[10]

Isherwood praised the songs, music, choreography, lighting (especially the use of projections), and "the forceful performance of its cast." He found a "tender poetry that clutches the heart more than a century later" in the rain scene and "gentle ardor" in country cousin Lemml's (Richard Topol) initial reaction to *God of Vengeance*, through to Lemml's taking on the job of stage manager across Europe, in New York, and finally and tragically, during the Holocaust in the Lodz ghetto. According to Isherwood, Vogel and Taichman provided "small doses" of Asch's play, yet "they retain a remarkable power." While Isherwood acknowledged the "necessary but still blunt expositional passages" and "occasional polemical touch," he believed that the "complex plot" was nonetheless "shaped by its creators with unusual finesse, using techniques associated with Brecht" (or, as Vogel might insist, Shklovsky). The question that began Isherwood's final paragraph ("What follows?") was intended to comment on the fact that "we never get to see a scene from the last act again" ("Review: *Indecent*"), but it might have been a musing upon what would next happen to Vogel and Taichman's reimaging of Asch.

Omnipresent social media facilitate knowledge about Vogel's interactions with her students and other playwrights. Vogel student Lynn Nottage tweeted on June 9, 2016, "Poetic & poignant. Gorgeously staged. Was totally taken" (@Lynnbrooklyn). An appreciative Vogel replied the same day, "Looking forward to seeing SWEAT. Xxp" (@VogelPaula). Vogel and Lin-Manuel Miranda (for *Hamilton*) both earned nominations for the Edward M Kennedy Prize for Drama Inspired by American History, an award won by Miranda. Vogel tweeted, "Congrats LMfor Kennedy Prize: Hope to see all nominationsin 2016. Honored to be in your midst"[11] (@VogelPaula February 22, 2016). Miranda replied the same day that he was "honored to be in YOURS, maestro, thank you," adding that he was "about to see our mutual homey Quiara [Alegría Hudes]" (@Lin_Manuel). Manuel's use of the masculine "maestro" rather than the feminine "maestra" and his reference to Hudes suggest he was thinking of Vogel both as professor and playwright. He used a term normally reserved for conductors of great orchestras, who are themselves considered both teachers and, especially, artists.[12]

On Saturday, June 18, 2016, I attended the penultimate performance of *Indecent* at New York's Vineyard Theatre.[13] The walls just outside the house were covered with references to Sholem Asch's *God of Vengeance*, for which Vogel has said that *Indecent* is "product placement" (Pollack-Pelzner), as well as articles and quotations from articles detailing the controversy, convictions, and successful appeals resulting from the Apollo production. A reprint of Miami University, Ohio, Professor of English Katie N. Johnson's 2007 *Gay and Lesbian Review* article, "When Lesbian Love Came to Broadway," was available near the box office. Johnson quoted 1922 newspaper pieces describing *God of Vengeance* as an "ugly story, hopelessly foreign to our Anglo-Saxon taste and understanding" and "one of the most terrible plays ever presented in New York." Johnson also proposed a "stunning fact: the lesbian love scene was never performed." Johnson's research strongly suggested that the same-sex kiss for which *God of Vengeance* is perhaps best remembered today did not actually take place on Broadway, although it had regularly been performed abroad and in New York's Bowery.

Inside the theatre were projected the words "the true story of a little Jewish play." All the way upstage sat ten people clad in old-fashioned attire who waited, looking impassively downstage, as the audience took our seats. Male and female, these ten people represented a feminist *minyan* of ghosts performing what Vogel, in a tweet, called "theatrical Kaddish"; what is more, this combination of characters and words imaginatively transported the audience to Asch's time and text. Although the program conspicuously lacked playwright's or director's notes, it did divide the performers into seven members of "The Troupe" and three of "The Musicians." Only Richard Topol garnered a specific association with a role, that of "Lemml, The Stage Manager." Given the first dialogue, a brief conversation about the play that Lemml says "changed my life" before concluding cryptically that "I can never remember the end," (10), Lemml, as Soloski notes, and his "air of rueful compassion conjure Thornton Wilder" (*Indecent*), whom Vogel has cited as an influence.[14]

Before Lemml could speak, however, the full cast rose from their chairs and began dancing to the klezmer music performed by Lisa Gutkin, Aaron Halva, and Mike Cohen. Sand "[fell] in thin streams," notes Isherwood ("Review: *Indecent*"), symbolizing the dust to which all humans return, the millennia of wandering by the Jewish people, and—for students of Vogel—perhaps the dusty copy of *God of Vengeance* in its 1918 Isaac Rosenberg translation that she read in the Cornell University Library stacks. Pollack-Pelzner describes the "ashes calling from the sleeves of the troupe ... as they rise from the dead to tell Asch's story" (@pollackpelzner) as a moment of stagecraft that has lingered beyond the performance.

The play presents an early image of Sholem Asch, in his apartment in 1906 Warsaw, reading his new play to his wife, Madje. She remarks upon the "purest, most chaste" (10) desire between Rifkele, the brothel owner's

Vogel in the Twenty-First Century

daughter who is improbably being groomed to be a rabbi's wife, and Manke, a prostitute. Identifying herself as a twentieth-century woman aware of Freud, Madje Asch adds, "We're all attracted to both sexes" (11), and jokes with her husband about what her affair with a woman or his with a man might (or might not) mean. Further suggesting the fluidity of gender and attraction, Madje ironically points out that the women's passionate declarations of their love for each other have come from Sholem Asch's seduction of his own wife. Thus, Vogel dramatically offers an explanation of how Asch, a young, heterosexual, newlywed male, may have produced the Sapphic language that so captivated her more than forty years earlier.

The play next shifts to the prestigious Warsaw salon of I. L. Peretz, where Nakhmen, one of the regulars, has brought his cousin from the country, Lemml, a tailor who has never seen a play. Lemml immediately becomes enraptured by the play world and cannot understand the argument that ensues about this play that depicts a Jewish pimp and Jewish prostitutes. Peretz, in particular, insists that producing this scandalous play would pour "fuel on the fires of anti-Semitism" (19). Asch's retort that his definition of a *minyan* has come to be "ten Jews in a circle accusing each other of anti-Semitism" (20) only angers Peretz further. His instructions to Asch come down to two dyspeptic words: "BURN IT" (20).

Disappointed by the reception from Peretz but with the support of Madje and, now, Lemml, Asch presses on to Berlin. Here, two women, violinist Lisa Gutkin and one of the actresses, provide the Vineyard production of *Indecent*'s first same-sex kiss. Later, when a gentile actress is slated to play Manke and mentions to her Rifkele cohort the need to learn some Yiddish before performing the part, the younger actress tells her, "I am Jewish" (23). "That is very brave of you," "Manke" replies in a laugh line that will later turn tragic.

This Vineyard Vogel reproduction of Asch performed the very end of *God of Vengeance* four times, facing stage left, stage right, upstage, and finally downstage toward us. In Asch's powerful ending, the father demands to know whether his daughter has remained a chaste Jewish maiden. Uncertain how to interpret her experiences with Manke, she replies, "I . . . don't know" (17). Enraged, Yekel declares that he knows how to make money and that the Torah in his hand has been earned by women performing on their backs and on their knees. Yekel then condemns Rifkele and her mother, a former prostitute, to repay the cost in a similar fashion.[15] He hoists the scroll as if to hurl it, as in Asch's play, but in Vogel's rendering Yekel never actually throws the stage property passing as a Torah. Indeed, the printed version of *Indecent* contains the stage direction, "*Yekel raises the Scroll but does not throw the Torah*" (27). The first three times the Vineyard's company performed this truncated version of the scene, it was met with rapturous applause from an imaginary audience. The fourth and final time, Yekel and company faced Vogel's live audience, which even after having witnessed the scene three times, audibly gasped at the scene's raw emotion.

Indecent occasionally flashes forward, and one of those times comes as the play moves forward to Ellis Island and "AN IMPOSSIBLY LONG LINE" (28), which here represents freedom and opportunity but will take on a more sinister meaning later. Lemml, in broken English, proclaims, "America! I here am!"(28). The carefully teased curls of young American women remind the immigrants of the *peyes* worn by Orthodox Jews back home. As the actors have done earlier, they continue performing *God of Vengeance*, in Yiddish, at The Bowery Theatre. Vogel then defamiliarizes metadrama, having the actresses who depict Rifkele and Manke falling in love "really" being in love but able to show this love only when enacting the love scene onstage. As do most immigrants, the actors, Lemml, and— foreshadowing his actions during the upcoming trial—Asch struggle with different languages. The play even offers a delightful pun over one actor's pronunciation so that "whore" and "hair" (32) sound virtually identical. Almost without the audience noticing, Vogel defamiliarizes "real" and "foreign" language themselves. To wit, when the actors would address each other in "Yiddish," they would speak what we heard as clear American English. Their "English" was heavily inflected by Yiddish. In fairly typical Vogel style, then, we were defamiliarized away from our own native language when we saw it experienced as a second or third or even fourth tongue by the characters before us.

By 1922, Lemml has been anglicized to "Lou," and the Provincetown Players[16] are ready to perform *God of Vengeance* in English, but with certain unwelcome changes expected. The "very brave" Jewish actress portraying Rifkele has been replaced by an American-born alumna of Smith College.[17] Although Adina Verson, who earlier played Madje Asch, portrayed both the "Jewish" Rifkele and the "American" Rifkele, a quick change of accents and physical demeanor alone sufficed to show the anguish felt by two women in love but now separated from their only means of displaying that love. Strikingly, however, Vogel has Verson's American Rifkele enthusiastically practice kissing Manke, with an "onstage" Provincetown Players kiss extending beyond the curtain.

Flush from the 1922 success of O'Neill's *The Hairy Ape* and their production of *God of Vengeance*,[18] The Provincetown Players take the Asch play uptown for its 1923 premier at the Apollo Theater. More changes are required. This time, the rain scene (which we have heard mentioned but have never actually seen) must go. The actress playing Manke protests to no avail, complaining that the production retains the sex while eviscerating the romance between Manke and Rifkele. Manke now seems not to love Rifkele but rather to sentence her to "a life of white slavery" (43).[19] The performers discuss the perennial Broadway dilemma between what the actress playing the mother calls the need to sell tickets versus artistic integrity. Lemml is dismayed to hear that Asch, whom we have seen being treated for "nervous exhaustion" (45) and prescribed the bedrest often useful to "women and writers" (46), has approved the changes. Then, a weird interlude of the song "Ain't We Got Fun" interrupted the Vineyard performance, conveying a sense of 1920s commercialism and a decade that famously roared. The play within the play next resumed, and the Broadway production brings both a tender same-sex caress and a policeman bearing orders to arrest the cast but to "wait until the end of the play" (49), presumably after a same-sex kiss has occurred. A kiss, or at least an expectation of it, that the rest of the cast have watched, touched deeply, from the wings many times now results in arrest and criminal charges. The rules differ uptown from those in the Bowery—and in Europe.

Ensuing events pass quickly and bring numerous surprises. We learn that the primary objection against the play has come not from an anti-Semite but from Rabbi Silverman of Temple Emanu-El, who boasts, "I registered the complaint" (52). Silverman denounces the play, sneering that it is possible two Jewish women will one day exchange wedding vows under the *chuppah*, but only in the sense that it is possible one day pigs will fly. Eugene O'Neill, from his perch at Hell Hole, a West Village bar, calls *God of Vengeance* "a corker of a play" (55)[20] and indicates a willingness to testify on behalf of the play. The prosecutors have cleverly blocked O'Neill and all the other witnesses to the play's literary worth by putting not the text on trial but rather the actual performance at the Apollo Theater. Since O'Neill saw the Provincetown Players version rather than the Apollo performance, he and many others are ineligible to testify. As O'Neill notes, "They say the script may have been tampered with on its way uptown" (55).

A significant surprise comes in Sholem Asch's unwillingness to testify on behalf of his own work. Lemml confronts the author, demanding, "Why did you agree to those cuts?" (60). In his defense, Asch claims barely to have understood the English revisions and to have accepted them while less than fully informed. Asch acknowledges to Lemml that he has not tried to testify for *God of Vengeance* because of the fear that his own broken and accented English would make him appear ignorant before the court. Ego seems to have prevailed over artistic vision. A broken-hearted Lemml takes his leave of Asch, saying again that the play "changed my life" (61) and returns to Europe. Lemml cannot know (but the audience knows only too well) the gravity and consequences of this decision. Meanwhile, after another unexpected interlude, this one by the Catskill performers billed as "The Bagelman Sisters," the play moves forward into the 1930s.

By now, *God of Vengeance* exists only in the Lodz ghetto and only because of the tremendous exertions by Lemml. Forced to wear the hated yellow star, constrained from staging a full performance by a curfew, and having to make do with a suggestion of a stage and threadbare costumes, Lemml still maintains, "On the seventh night . . . God created Yiddish theatre" (69). One act per week, Lemml manages to stage the first two acts, including our first view of a truncated rain scene and Manke's loving "you let me wash your breasts in the rain" (71). We even witness an ersatz wedding and *chuppah*.

Lemml's "God willing, next week we will still be here to perform Act Three" (70) is not to be, however. The Lodz actors join "*a single-file line*" as the production comes to its "*Kaddish*" (72). Now Lemml, eyes closed, pleads, "Please don't let this be the ending" (73). In a moment of theatrical magical realism, Rifkele and Manke escape, just before "LEMML OPENS HIS EYES" (74). The words "ASHES TO ASHES—THE TROUPE RETURNS TO DUST" (74) remind the audience starkly of the ovens of Auschwitz and call to mind the sand from the beginning in heartrending fashion. Yet the play does not end here.

Just as the intrusion of "Ain't We Got Fun" in the 1920s and Borscht Belt Catskills entertainment in the 1930s have struck a discordant note, so now do a few bars from *Oklahoma*. Vogel reminds her audience of the purely escapist fare that sold well throughout the entertainment industry while the ashes of *God of Vengeance*'s final European performers were irretrievably lost and the English translation of Asch's play gathered dust in American libraries. In such a library at Cornell, Vogel, at age twenty-two (Warner), would eventually discover it and begin the process that led to *Indecent*. Lemml's wish echoes in Act Two when we see Asch one last time. So, too, does a reminder that while his death in the Holocaust prevents a performance "next week" of Act Three, we may yet observe the still mostly withheld rain scene. Now an old man played by Tom Nelis, who has earlier portrayed Peretz and Yekel, Asch encounters a young scholar from Yale named Rosen,[21] played by Max Gordon Moore, who has earlier portrayed the young Asch. Asch quips that it is easier for a camel to pass through the eye of a needle than for a Jew to gain admission to Yale, laments that *God of Vengeance* has caused him decades of grief, and finally brings the story of the play full circle. Revealing that he is under investigation by the House Un-American Activities Committee (HUAC), an arm of the McCarthy era "red scare," because of favorable comments he made regarding socialism years earlier and that he is leaving the United States, Asch tells Rosen that he will repeat the words of a far wiser man: "burn it" (76).

Then, Vogel ends *Indecent* not with the chronological end of Asch's life but with an unexpected and transcendent moment from the scene of the true protagonist of *Indecent*, *God of Vengeance* itself. On that evening in 2016, I sat enraptured as water began gushing down a large area downstage, and Rifkele and Manke reappeared, dressed in white. With the cast and musicians watching from upstage and Lemml smiling, they performed the rain scene. After an hour and forty minutes of waiting without intermission, the audience could witness the "purest, most chaste" love Magde Asch, in 1906, read on the page. Manke and Rifkele frolicked. They embraced. They were a couple in love. When this scene ended, the water stopped pouring, and the play was over. The audience stood as one for an enthusiastic standing ovation and then slipped quietly into the June night.[22] This reaction resonated with theatre as sacrament. The play, as scheduled, then closed the following day.

Vogel achieved her goal of restoring interest in Asch's play, including New Yiddish Rep performing *God of Vengeance* in Yiddish, with English subtitles, in June 2016 (Chow). Just over two months after *Indecent* was closed at the Vineyard, Vogel told Talya Zax, "Would I like to see this show be on Broadway? You bet," adding, "I would put on a sandwich board and walk the street in front of the theater every night to see that happen" (Zax). Preliminary speculation about a Broadway future for *Indecent* transformed into concrete planning on October 26 when David Gordon reported, "Paula Vogel's acclaimed drama *Indecent* will move to Broadway this spring, producers Daryl Roth, Elizabeth Ireland McCann, and Cody Lassen have announced." By March 2017, *Indecent* was set for the Cort Theatre, with the entire cast from the Vineyard production returning. Michael Paulson noted that *Indecent* would be one of only two plays by women that Broadway season, the other being Lynn Nottage's *Sweat*, and wrote,

"The fact that these two writers are just now making their Broadway debuts raises uncomfortable questions for the theater industry, which season after season sees plays by men vastly outnumber plays by women in the all-important commercial spaces where money can be made, reputations burnished and Tony Awards won"[23] (Paulson). Reflecting the moment in both her biography and theatre history, Vogel stated, "You feel the ghosts in a really great way, . . . and they're the kind of ghosts that are saying, 'Welcome home'" (Paulson).

In bringing *Indecent* to Broadway, Vogel commented upon the anti-Semitism faced ninety years earlier by Asch's play as well as upon America's political climate of 2017. Vogel told a BroadwayCon audience that *God of Vengeance* "was a play in 1906 that said we are all lesbians and we are all Jews" (Fierberg). She continued that "theatre tells the truth, and we need the truth right now. Not alt-facts, but the truth" (Fierberg). Then, in "A Note from the Playwright" published in the *Playbill* for *Indecent,* Vogel wrote of not anticipating that *Indecent* "would be as relevant today as it is; we again are witnessing an upheaval of fear, xenophobia, homophobia, and yes, anti-Semitism." "In this moment of time," she went on, "we must say that we are all Muslim. . . . We must remember where the closing of borders in the 20th century led nations around the globe."

The Broadway reviews were less favorable than the ones of the Vineyard Theatre production. Sometimes, the reviewer seemed predisposed against the play, as did Jesse Green, who compared *Indecent* with *Sweat* and J. T. Rogers's *Oslo*, 2017 Broadway plays "taking a huge slice of cultural and social history as [their] subject," and called Vogel's play "in some ways the most ambitious of the three, and in all ways the least convincing." Later, Green disclosed "a problem with plays, however well-intentioned, that hitch their wagon of importance to the Holocaust" and even went so far as to add, "I would submit that the Holocaust in particular cannot yet be treated abstractly or aesthetically."[24] Green did attribute "one thing perfectly right" to the Cort production, namely the rain scene, which Green found "something shocking and sacred—and character-driven," as "[m]ost history is."

Although in 2016 *The New York Times* reviewer Charles Isherwood had made *Indecent* a Critics Pick, the 2017 reviewer from the same newspaper, Ben Brantley,[25] leavened his praise with less positive observations. Brantley recorded *Indecent* as a "long-awaited Broadway debut" that showed "four decades in the theater have not jaded Ms. Vogel" ("Review: *Indecent*"), and he termed the play a "heartfelt ode and elegy to a landmark of modern drama." Brantley termed *Indecent* "decent, in the most complete sense of the world," as well as "virtuous, sturdily assembled, informative and brimming with good faith." All the same, however, Brantley argued that "the ardor that must have informed the writing and early performances of *Vengeance* only occasionally blazes forth" in Vogel's recounting, and he thought the rain scene was "perhaps repeated once too often." In sum, Brantley concluded that *Indecent* "may not inhabit the lightning-struck stratosphere of the play it portrays," all but stating that he would have preferred reviewing a Broadway return of *God of Vengeance*.

Indecent earned three Tony Award nominations: Best Play, Best Director (for Taichman), and Best Lighting Design (for Christopher Akerlind). Despite these nominations, the play struggled for commercial success. In fact, "In the week ending June 11, the final week leading to the Tonys, the play brought in $277,395 in ticket sales—up from $227,045 the week before but still only 30 percent of its potential gross" in the "relatively large" Cort Theatre (Barone). June 11, the night of the Tonys, brought both success and disappointment to Vogel. Akerlind and Taichman won in their categories. The opportunity extended to Vogel, as a nominee, to speak offered her almost certainly the single largest audience she had ever addressed. Then, three days later the June 25th closings of both *Indecent* and—despite its Pulitzer Prize victory—*Sweat*, the two new 2017 Broadway plays by women, were announced. Joshua Barone noted that *Indecent*, after fifteen previews and seventy-nine regular performances, would be the first Tony Award-winning play of 2017 to close.

Vogel and Nottage took to social and other media to denounce what they perceived as Brantley's role in closing the two plays. Vogel tweeted, "Brantley&Green 2-0. Nottage&Vogel 0-2. Lynn, they help close us down,&gifted str8 white guys run: ourplayswill last.B&G#footnotesinhistory"[26] (@VogelPaula June 14, 2017), to which Nottage replied, "The patriarchy flexing their muscles to prove their power" (@LynnBrooklyn June 14, 2017). Then, unexpectedly came "an upsurge in ticket sales" for *Indecent* that led producer Daryl Roth to "keep the show open through August 6 (for a total of just sixteen weeks)" ("A Collective Call"). This increase of "more than a $100,000 difference from the previous week," followed by "[t]his number then doubl[ing] the following week," led Roth to what Olivia Clement called the "gutsy" decision to extend the play's run ("Daryl Roth").

Describing herself as "very instinctive about everything I do in the theatre" and a veteran of more than sixty Broadway productions, Roth "suddenly regretted the decision to close." She explained, "I had been so unhappy since posting the notice and I just couldn't really live with myself because I just wanted this play to be seen by more people, . . . I felt it hadn't lived its life." A combination of the rise in ticket sales and the availability of both the Cort Theatre and the performers helped Roth persuade the other producers to give *Indecent* six more weeks to reach a live audience. This potential audience then grew exponentially when, after this "outpouring of support from the theatre community and pushing back [of] its closing date" (McPhee), *Indecent* was filmed by BroadwayHD on August 3, just three days before the production's eventual closing. BroadwayHD announced plans to make the film "available on the theatre streaming service in January 2018 in honor of International Holocaust Remembrance Day" (McPhee). The likely audience then grew yet again when PBS announced that this film of *Indecent* would "air on PBS *Great Performances* November 17" (Hetrick "Broadway's"). The PBS broadcast likely has attracted more viewers than all live performances of Vogel's plays combined to date.

Jennifer-Scott Mobley's 2018 *Theatre Journal* review of *Indecent* on Broadway delved into both Vogel and Taichman's play and its Asch inspiration. Perhaps echoing Katie N. Johnson, Mobley noted that the same-sex kiss in *God of Vengeance* "was excised . . . before the play moved to Broadway, which effectively changed the relationship between the women from one of love to that of prurient manipulation." *Indecent*, however, noted Mobley, "recovered the lesbian love scene in all of its purest beauty and finally brought it to Broadway." Not only that, but the scene was "conjured" and "elicited a palpable catharsis for the audience" (251). Hence, Mobley implied, Vogel and Taichman resurrected Asch's lovers in a magical way and to an effect that was both visceral and fantastical.

Despite the 1923 obscenity convictions for the major players in *God of Vengeance*, the record appears to indicate that the kiss from Asch's (and Goldberg's) original script was literally "obscene" in the sense Vogel dramatizes in *Hot 'N' Throbbing*, which is to say off the stage. Asch's Broadway audience never saw it. By not only including but even highlighting the kiss in *Indecent*, Vogel rights a historical wrong, and she also pays dramatic tribute to the young lovers as envisioned by Asch and staged across Europe and even the Lower East Side. *Indecent* also manifests the "piety" observed by reviewer Ben Brantley.

God as referenced in Sholem Asch's title is a god of "vengeance," but it is not God who takes vengeance upon Rifkele; rather, it is Yekel. Yekel concludes the play by shouting to Rifkele, "down into the brothel! Down below!" and adding, "Take the Holy Scroll along with you! I don't need it anymore!" (60). His attempt to buy his daughter's way into society by purchasing a Torah having failed, Yekel rejects not only Rifkele but even God Himself. Yekel's view does not prevail, however, for Vogel and Taichman or for their audience. The fact that Vogel's Yekel does not throw the Torah serves as a symbol that Vogel and Taichman do not throw away the idea of God.

Bert States did not send young Paula Vogel to the Cornell University library so that she could read about a father disowning his daughter for her Sapphic longings and behaviors. What Vogel's Madje calls a "chaste" and even "spiritual" love (10) triumphs instead. By having Lemml, in his imagination, pull Manke and Rivkele from what may well be the very line to a gas chamber and watch them frolic in a purifying rain, Vogel foregrounds romantic love and provides her characters and her audience what is in every way a mercy. Yekel has probably never read the Torah he has paid to have inscribed, and he is almost certainly unaware of the ongoing Jewish discussion involving justice, which is traditionally masculine, and mercy, which has generally been understood as a feminine principle. *Indecent* is, as Fornés said of *Fefu and Her Friends*, a feminine play, and so even if it can only hold the Holocaust at bay for a moment, it fills that moment with grace. From dust we—and *Indecent*—may come, but to it we need not return during however brief a period we or Lemml's grace note endures.

Having turned seventy in November 2021, Vogel enjoys relevancy and continues to reach new audiences through her relationships with younger people. Vogel has told Olivia Clement, "One of the gifts that these younger writers have given me is a total acceptance of who I am. I may feel uneasy in my own peer group, but I don't feel uneasy with younger people. It's almost nostalgic to think of me as a lesbian in a way. They don't even blink" ("The Myth"). Although Vogel granted, "All playwrights should be angry in their twenties," she indicated that in *Indecent*, she identified most closely with the young, polemical, idealistic, and love struck Asch, not his struggling middle aged or frustrated older incarnations (or with any of the women). "I still continue to be angry," she continued, "but I don't see myself as an angry person. I think that we've created a myth of feminism that involves anger versus involving love—a love to make things different for the next generation." Expressing her joy over the Pulitzer winners she has taught, Vogel stated that she has "now been able to scream and jump up and down thanks to" their success. Rather than seeing playwriting as competitive, per the business model, Vogel concluded, "I want [other playwrights] to be brilliant so that I can try and catch up with them" (Clement "The Myth").

125

The Theatre of Paula Vogel

While theatres closed during the 2020 Covid-19 pandemic, Vogel found a new way to promote what she considered brilliant plays virtually. She identified "works that have been overlooked and never produced, along with plays that deserve a larger audience." Deeming these plays "too ambitious, too quirky, and too smart to be contained," Vogel created a series, "Bard at the Gate," and curated a series of plays "by BIPOC [Black, Indigenous, and people of color], women, LGBTQ, and disabled artists" ("Paula Vogel's Bard") for readings streamed over the internet. *The New York Times* described the series as "brilliantly cast" (Paulson) as it brought Vogel favorites such as Eisa Davis's *Bulrusher*, Kermit Frazier's *Kernel of Sanity* (directed by Gregg Daniel), and Meg Miroshnik's *The Droll* (directed by Devin Brain) to worldwide audiences during the 2020–1 season and continued into new seasons. In March 2022, Vogel won an American Connected Theater Award for Pandemic Year 2 for her work with Bard, earning praise for what began as a "simple idea" (Mandel) and grew into yet another tour de force of mentoring and promoting emerging playwrights.

Vogel has dropped at least one hint regarding what she has written since *Indecent*. In February 2022, I tweeted my praise of her treatment of both Jewish (*Indecent*) and Southern (*How I Learned to Drive*) subject matter, asking if Vogel might have plans to address Southern Jewish characters. She replied that her New Orleans Spanish, French, and German Catholic side continues to battle with her Russian and German Jewish side from New York, adding, "I am currently writing about Maryland" (@VogelPaula). Since Vogel's comment coincided closely with the start of rehearsals for *How I Learned to Drive*'s Broadway debut, I began contemplating characters such as L'il Bit and Uncle Peck with a touch of Yiddish, but then I almost immediately realized the futility of trying to limit her ever-expanding vision.

On July 6, 2021, Lynn Nottage tweeted that Twitter had "decided that I'm not verifiable." The only woman ever to win two Pulitzer Prizes for Drama added, "Guess I have not quite yet accomplished enough to be of public interest" (@LynnBrooklyn). Vogel replied, "Same" (@VogelPaula). Within a few days, Twitter acquiesced to requests that Nottage be verified, prompting her to begin a campaign to verify Vogel. On July 16, Vogel tweeted, "Well, my friends, I appreciate your support. The request for me to be verified by twitter has been denied. As long as my friends and family Continue to love me, I will survive!" (@VogelPaula).

As she indicated in her tweet, Vogel has, indeed, survived. Her Twitter biography proclaims her "Proudly unverified by gatekeepers." Then, a link for Bard at the Gate strongly suggests that Vogel understands well the audience she seeks to reach and how to appeal to it. Nearly five decades after she arrived as a new graduate student at Cornell, Vogel has developed a reputation as a clear, independent voice from Broadway to the furthest reaches "off." Not only that, but she has also built a sturdy "House of Paula Vogel" that has not relied upon building permits or the permission of gatekeepers to grow and expand. Where the path has not been clear, she has nevertheless forged ahead and created a path not only for herself but for the countless playwrights she has taught and promoted. Now in her eighth decade, Vogel shows no signs of putting down her tools or quieting her urgent, sometimes "indecent" voice.

CHAPTER 6
CRITICAL PERSPECTIVES

THE ALCHEMY OF INFLUENCE: PAULA VOGEL AND SARAH RUHL

Amy Muse

Sarah Ruhl is refreshingly free of the so-called anxiety of influence. She has no fear of diminishing her own artistry by praising another's accomplishments and their inspiration to her. In interviews and essays she warmly acknowledges what she has learned from Anton Chekhov, Virginia Woolf, Maurice Maeterlinck, María Irene Fornés, and, most of all, her living teacher, Paula Vogel. Vogel, in turn has humbly claimed, Wren notes, that her "most significant contribution to the American theatre" will be having convinced Sarah Ruhl to become a playwright. (In a 2007 conversation between them for *BOMB* magazine Ruhl observes, "There are so many incredible writers out there right now, and much of it, Paula, is due to your teaching. There's a renaissance going on.") The effect of Vogel's teaching and mentorship of Ruhl is apparent in matters of craft that originated in classroom exercises: experimentation with non-linear storytelling and bunraku puppets, for instance, or stage directions as whispered love notes, which Ruhl made her own signature. More subtle are the deep aesthetic and ethical affinities between their plays, what we might call sensibilities or dispositions toward playwriting—and toward life. They share boldly theatrical imaginations, both preferring fabulation to kitchen-sink realism as a means of getting to the truth of our experience of life. Bigsby, in *Contemporary American Playwrights*, quotes Vogel saying that "fantasy and imagination are realer" than realism (284). Ruhl adds in her *Bomb* interview that "If you excavate people's subjectivity and how they view the world emotionally, you don't get realism." "I like plays that have revelations in the moment, where emotions transform almost inexplicably," Ruhl has told John Lahr in the aptly titled "Surreal Life"; in writing characters, too, she learned to resist a mapped-out psychological journey, arguing in *100 Essays*

The Theatre of Paula Vogel

I Don't Have Time to Write that "clear steps seem more appropriate for a manual on how to put together furniture from another country" than for playwriting. Boundaries and borders, between life and death, comedy and drama, are permeable in their work, which has led Vogel's to be described as camp, Ruhl's as whimsy—that is, camp with the rough edges smoothed out.

Neither of those labels adequately captures the poignancy of their work nor appreciates the aesthetic of these playwrights, which is also an ethical statement about being in the world. As Ruhl puts it in *100 Essays*, building upon Italo Calvino's concept of lightness, "A suspicion that lightness is not deeply serious (but instead whimsical) pervades aesthetic discourse. But what if lightness is a philosophical choice to temper reality with strangeness, to temper emotion with humor. Lightness is then a philosophical victory over heaviness." Ruhl and Vogel have written some of our most profound plays about grief (*The Baltimore Waltz, The Long Christmas Ride Home, Eurydice*) that are also disarmingly funny. Ruhl's "habitual tightrope act," Celia Wren has written, is her "flair for joining humor to sadness." Sarah Rasmussen, artistic director of the McCarter Theatre Center, recalls Vogel saying "laughter allows us to open our hearts a little bit more so that we can go deeper."[1] Both playwrights delve into the complications of our longings: Vogel's *How I Learned to Drive* is about desire rather than pedophilia; Ruhl's *How to Transcend a Happy Marriage* is about intimacy rather than orgies. What Vogel and Ruhl are really aiming for, I think, is moving us into a state of *wonder*. Ruhl, writing for the Ben Hodges volume *The Play That Changed My Life*, calls this Vogel's "alchemical" power. When Vogel comes into your orbit, transformations ensue.

As first meetings go, theirs was an auspicious one. In 1993, Ruhl, then an undergraduate at Brown, saw a campus production of *The Baltimore Waltz*. Ruhl's father had very recently died of cancer, and Vogel's devastating, funny, imaginative tribute to her brother Carl, who had died just a few years before of AIDS, transported Ruhl emotionally and, later, vocationally from poet to playwright. She enrolled in Vogel's playwriting course, and listening to Vogel lecture, thought, "This is the first genius I have ever met"; later she reflected for Hodges, "I think there was something about meeting Paula, and having been so affected by her work, that made it possible for me to write."

In *The Play That Changed My Life*, Ruhl beautifully encapsulates Vogel's and her own playwriting. Here, she writes, is what she may have "unconsciously absorbed" from *The Baltimore Waltz*:

> How Paula created a modern architecture for grief. How she transmuted personal loss into something formal, and how she both stepped back

from the grief formally, but laid the grief bare in an extraordinary, transparent way at the end. How Paula laughs at terrible, terrible things. How she uses gesture and language in that play, and how there was no fourth wall. How she used fragment. How she changed modes and styles quickly, seamlessly. How language itself can be a source of solace but also a mode of alienation. How the personal can coexist up against the iconic and become even more personal for the contrast. [...] [H]ow arbitrary are our distinctions between the real and the unreal. How she sees theatre as a place for memory, and for ghosts. (121)

Nearly all of these qualities and theatrical choices are features of Ruhl's own playwriting. Charles Isherwood's rave *New York Times* review of *Eurydice*, Ruhl's first major play, describes Ruhl's work in a way that sounds like *her* description of Vogel's; Isherwood "warns" audiences that Ruhl's "offbeat style, which mixes colors and tones in ways that can be delightful but occasionally jarring, requires some re-education for audiences used to the contemporary theatre's steady diet of naturalism and relatively straightforward demarcations between comedy and drama."

We can watch Ruhl trying out this style as early as *Dog Play*, the one-act she wrote for her first playwriting course with Vogel. Ruhl, grieving the death of her father, wanted to write about it but felt blocked. Vogel suggested she write about it *indirectly*. Echoing Ruhl's reflection on *The Baltimore Waltz*, Vogel instructed her to transmute her personal loss into something formal, and by stepping back from that grief formally, she would—and did—lay that grief bare in an extraordinary, transparent way. *Dog Play* presents us with a dog as protagonist. The dog (a human actor in a dog mask) talks directly to the audience about missing the father of the family, who has died. The daughter of the family is grieving deeply and cannot be consoled. When Dog and Daughter sit outside and look at the moon, they are joined by Father, who leans against the moon ("You're smart enough to know there's no heaven or hell," he tells the Dog; "I live on the moon mostly"), but only Dog can see him. Dog tells the audience, "I dreamed last night that I could speak and everyone could understand. I was telling them that he is not dead, that I can see him. No one believed me."[2] Recalling *Dog Play*, Vogel told Ruhl for *Bomb* about how Ruhl approached her father's death from a:

> unique angle: a dog is waiting by the door, waiting for the family to come home, unaware that the family is at his master's funeral, unaware

of the concept of death. And, oh yes, the play was written with Kabuki stage techniques, in gorgeous, emotionally vivid language. I sat with this short play in my lap in my study, and sobbed.

As Vogel did in *How I Learned to Drive*, *The Baltimore Waltz*, and *The Long Christmas Ride Home*, Ruhl "creates sites for the audience for mourning," which is what she explains to Hodges as "at the root of why we make theatre, in an ancient, ancient way" (123). Both playwrights create ritual spaces of remembrance where the living and the dead can reunite, replay moments of their lives, and enjoy each other's company again. Like Vogel, whose plays pay tribute to and continue conversations with her brother, Carl ("Even if he can no longer write letters to me, I can write letters to him, and so I do in every play [. . .] 'Carl' is inscribed in every manuscript," Vogel writes in *The Long Christmas Ride Home* [80]). Ruhl has woven portraits and remembrances of her father into many of her plays. In *Eurydice* (2001), a "transparently personal" work written to have "a few more conversations" with her father, she uses the story of Orpheus and Eurydice as a formal distancing device; as Weckirth writes, the "myth exploring the underworld and the connection between the dead and the living was a way to negotiate that terrain" (30). Similar to Vogel's use of a letter from Carl as a "document" for productions of *The Baltimore Waltz* to put in their playbills, Ruhl gives the Father in *Eurydice* dialogue spoken by her father in real life, most memorably in the letter that Father writes to Eurydice on her wedding day, offering advice, including "continue to give yourself to others because that's the ultimate satisfaction in life—to love, accept, honor and help others" (344). *The Oldest Boy*, a play about attachment and letting go, allowing both the living and the dead to be released from worry and grief, ends with a magical moment in which the protagonist's son reveals that he is a reincarnation of her father from an earlier lifetime, and that he remembers holding her just as the son is now holding his baby sister: "I've done this before. I used to be your father, remember? [. . .] Many lifetimes ago I held you in my arms, like this" (131). *For Peter Pan on Her 70th Birthday* features the ghost of a father walking casually around the family home, reading the newspaper, patting the ghost of the family dog, while his children sit around the kitchen table holding a wake for him, reminiscing about his life.

Both *The Oldest Boy* and *For Peter Pan on Her 70th Birthday* are stylistically affiliated with Vogel's *The Long Christmas Ride Home*, a play that Ruhl has said she would like to direct; she has been deeply inspired by how it shows us theatre as "a place where you can actually look at the invisible," a space of what Weckwirth calls "invisible terrains" (31). *The Oldest Boy* borrows *The Long Christmas Ride Home*'s use of puppetry; the character of the Oldest Boy is played by a puppet, allowing us to see the duality in him, both the current three-year-old child and his adult self from his previous life, at the same time. *For Peter Pan* borrows *The Long Christmas Ride Home*'s Japanese Noh form; Ruhl calls it a "contemporary Midwestern Noh drama," "the protagonist meets the ghost, then recognizes the ghost, then dances with or embraces the ghost" (xvii). Like *The Long Christmas Ride Home*, *For Peter Pan* lingers on the relationships among adult children, the changing relationships they had with their parents as they grew, and the struggle to enter adulthood. A central moment in the play is the characters' comparative stories of when they knew they were grown up: from the trivial (getting to move from the kids' card table to the big dining room table for holiday dinners) to the profound (running toward rather than away from an emergency situation). Its third movement transforms from naturalistic (an unusual style for Ruhl) into the fantastical: a highly theatrical, children's-theatre style re-enactment of *Peter Pan*, with the adults comically straining to fly with their aging bodies, devolving into the adult children crying, "I don't want to grow up!"

Ruhl resolves these plays in ways that are quite different from her mentor, however. *The Long Christmas Ride Home* swerves sharply from what could have been a sentimental ending in which the Man and Woman reconcile, and the Man's love and care for his wife inspire him to steer the car away from the edge of the cliff. They do pause, and in this extended moment onstage (split-second moment in real time), the Man prays, "God. Let me start over. Let me take back this day." He looks at his children ("My children are good children") and his wife ("My wife is . . . my wife"), while the Woman thinks of how she could change ("If I try harder—if I have another child—[. . . .] If I dress a bit younger—if I say softer things—"). The stage directions tell us "*The Man and Woman almost turn to each other*" (my emphasis). But they don't. Instead, the Man thinks of his mistress, Sheila; his desire for her—his desire to live *for her*—causes him to get control of the car and ease it away from the ledge. It is a happy ending in the sense that the family members come out of that scrape alive. And Vogel gives the audience a final image of a certain amount of peace, the Ghosts of Stephen, Claire, and Rebecca "cran[ing] their necks up into a beautiful shaft of light. Upon their upturned faces, it begins to snow" (73–6). Yet she leaves us with mixed, sad feelings of foreboding for this family and for the painful outcomes of the three adult children, which we witness earlier in the play.

The ending of Ruhl's *For Peter Pan on Her 70th Birthday*, in contrast (and *The Oldest Boy*—and, for that matter, nearly all of her plays, from *Eurydice* to *The Clean House* to *Dead Man's Cell Phone* to *In the Next Room or the vibrator play* to *Stage Kiss* to *How to Transcend a Happy Marriage*), shows us unalloyed love. *For Peter Pan* ends with a layered moment of time "in the theater's disconcerting liminal space between ordinary and extraordinary worlds" (x) in which protagonist Ann is simultaneously the seventy-year-old Ann mourning the death of her father, and seventeen-year-old Annie, whose father has come to her premiere of *Peter Pan* at the Davenport Children's Theatre. Her father comes onstage as his younger self, carrying a bouquet of flowers for Annie. Ann talks to him in the present, asking:

> Did you die?
> What was it like?
> Your breathing was terrible.
> It seemed like you didn't want to go.
> Was it awful? (99)

At the end of the scene "*They embrace. He exits*" and "*She watches him go*" (100). Ann turns to the audience and tells us she stayed in the theatre just a little while longer because in the theatre "you don't have to grow up" (101).

Ruhl resists sentimentality by tempering the sweetness with the awareness and weight of loss, but her plays ultimately soothe; they seek to bring the characters and the audience into the deep, if complicated and always in flux, enchantment of being in the world and with each other. Vogel's plays keep us in a place of greater tension. As David Savran puts it, Vogel's plays "do not make easy reading—or playing. They demand that readers, actors and director approach them with a genuine commitment to exploring their desires and fears as well as the laws, both spoken and unspoken, of the society in which they live (in the understanding that it is the law that produces desire and fear in the first place)" (xiv). What we might call Ruhl's history plays—*Passion Play* and *Scenes from Court Life or the Whipping Boy and His Prince*, have more of a Vogelian grain in their sharper endings because of the very real fears of real life, such as leaders who will lie and send us into wars over and over again, as expressed in *Scenes from Court Life*'s final song, which concludes, "Let the wars come to an end. / Let the whipping and the torture end. / Oh let us all pretend—/ Please oh Lord / If there be a Lord / Let the killing end."[3]

Critical Perspectives

At Brown, Pollack-Pelzner wrote for *The New Yorker*, "rather than cultivate a house style," Vogel "sought out voices that would challenge her aesthetic." And so it should be, for "one repays a teacher badly if one remains always a pupil," as Nietzsche's famous observation has it. Sarah Ruhl absorbed many qualities of Paula Vogel's playwriting but transformed them into her own signature style, which may be nowhere more apparent than in the most immediately visible and remarked-upon feature of a Sarah Ruhl play: her use of stage directions. On the page they appear like lines of verse calling us to attend to them, rather than being "hidden away in parentheses" where they might get treated as mere "filigree."[4] Ruhl traces the origin of this aesthetic choice to a class at Brown; as Ruhl tells interviewer Bess Rowen, Vogel "sat us down and she read the first stage directions from a Tennessee Williams play," and told the students, "these aren't stage directions, these are a love letter from Tennessee Williams to his reader, over time" ("Ruhl's"). Vogel gave her permission to think of stage directions as an opportunity to create "intimacy of contact with a reader." Bess Rowen has labeled these "affective stage directions," which don't tell an actor which way to move on stage but are instead "more concerned with internal mechanisms than their external expressions," designed to "put the actor in the same physical and emotional mood as the character is in the play" ("Undigested" 310, 311). For instance, in *The Clean House*, sisters Lane and Virginia are often in opposition; Lane is a doctor whose marriage is breaking up and whose cleaning lady is too depressed to clean her house, while Virginia, who is lonely and enjoys cleaning, would love to clean her sister's house. At a moment of intense feuding, Virginia accuses Lane of driving her husband away, snapping, "No wonder Charles left. You have no compassion." Lane retorts, "I traded my whole life to help people who are sick! What do you do?" Ruhl follows these lines with this stage direction for the actors:

> *Virginia and Lane breathe.*
> *Virginia and Lane are in the state of silent animal warfare,*
> *a brand of warfare particular to sisters.* (83)

Later, Lane gives medical attention to Ana, the woman that Charles fell in love with. Ruhl's stage directions to the actor playing Lane capture the essence of Lane's wary care; as Lane watches Ana sleep, "*She guards her the way a dog would guard a rival dog, / if her rival were sick*" (103). The stage directions evoke precisely how these characters feel; they spark actors to contribute their art in finding a way to show this through their bodies onstage.

Ruhl's love letters extend to designers and directors as well, collaborating with them to use the mechanics of the stage to help the audience experience what the characters experience. In *Dead Man's Cell Phone*, to convey the wonder of falling in love felt by Jean and Dwight, who share an affection for fine paper, Ruhl's stage directions instruct:

> *Embossed stationery moves through the air slowly,*
> *like a snow parade.*
> *Lanterns made of embossed paper,*
> *houses made of embossed paper,*
> *light falling on paper,*
> *falling on Jean and Dwight,*
> *who are also falling.* (56)

To transmit the experience of sudden lightness when obstacles between spouses seem to fly away and they can take joy and see beauty in one another again, Ruhl's stage direction for the end of *In the Next Room or the Vibrator Play* envisions, "*Although the domestic space seemed terribly permanent—a settee, a statuette—suddenly it disappears and we are in a sweet small winter garden. Snow covers trees that in the spring flower with pink flowers*" (142). And, to conclude *How to Transcend a Happy Marriage* with a sweeping feeling of transcendence rooted in the details of our everyday family lives, "*the sound of Bach's minuet being played on a small violin*" builds throughout the theatre as "*more violins are added*" and Ruhl whispers to the sound designer (and casting director!), "*If possible, one hundred children onstage are revealed playing the violin together in the forest*" (123).

Most innovative of all, Ruhl employs stage directions in *Dear Elizabeth* to provide the emotional force of the play. Constructed from the letters of poets Elizabeth Bishop and Robert Lowell, *Dear Elizabeth* uses only their language for its dialogue. The stage directions are the only place in the play that Ruhl uses her own language, to imagine scenes that Bishop and Lowell refer to obliquely, yet with enormous longing or tinged with regret, in their letters. Ruhl calls these "Interludes" because they are interludes in the letter-writing, when Bishop and Lowell actually see one another in person and therefore aren't writing (and also therefore are not recording their lives for the curiosity of future readers). The Interludes physicalize in the present moment what is merely alluded to in the letters, the most significant of which was when Lowell visited Bishop at her house in Maine (it was early in their friendship; he was just divorced from his first wife); the letters tell us they spent the weekend together, at once point "swimming, or rather standing, numb to the waist in the freezing cold water, but continuing to talk," and Lowell thought about but did not propose marriage to Bishop. It is a moment that returns elliptically in the letters. Ruhl imagines it through stage directions:

They see each other in Maine.
Suddenly the stage is full of water and a rock.
They stand waist high in cold water, holding hands, looking out.
A silence.
She turns to him.

BISHOP
When you write my epitaph, you must say I was the loneliest person who ever lived.

She starts laughing at herself.
Suddenly it's not funny.
He stops laughing and touches her face.
A moment.

A SUBTITLE FLASHES:
He thinks the question: Will you marry me?
She thinks: What did you say?
The gulls, the sea, and a wave almost engulf them.
They come up for air.
The water dries rapidly. (18)

Bishop's line is from the letters. We don't know the full context, though. Ruhl's stage directions evoke the sorrow and rueful humor, and how they were almost engulfed emotionally during this weekend, pulled into a romance that would have been disastrous for both, but metaphorically "came up for air" and developed a long and deep friendship instead. These Interludes are what catapult *Dear Elizabeth* beyond mere adaptation; like Vogel's many plays responding to other writers, Ruhl's is an imaginative conversation, filling in the gaps of her curiosity and expressing her appreciation for what these writers have brought to her life. Ruhl turns these unspoken moments into "moments of being" (inspired by Woolf): moments where characters, and audiences, step outside of regular time to experience connectedness and wonder.

Perhaps we can say that Ruhl's "moments of being" aesthetic has influenced Vogel as well. The famous "rain scene" in Vogel's *Indecent* is so magical and radiant that it feels Ruhlian: "*Manke softly taps for Rifkele,*" calling her out into the night and washing her hair in the rain; the stage directions tell us "*Manke leads Rifkele into a flood of light. They turn their faces up to the light. They feel the rain*" (70–1). Vogel's earthy eroticism and Ruhl's airy transcendence, the intimacy and hope against the dark backdrop of anti-Semitic violence, is powerfully felt. That the particular magic of that scene onstage is also a result of Vogel's collaboration on the play with Rebecca Taichman, a frequent director of Ruhl's work, feels apt, because the playwriting of Paula Vogel and Sarah Ruhl is clearly conceived *in relationship with* its readers: actors, directors, designers, and everyone else who likes to read as well as see plays. Vogel, discussing working with actor Cherry Jones on *The Baltimore Waltz*, remarked that Jones taught her to "under-write" her plays "so that the actors can make more choices" (In Herren 13), a decision we can see in Ruhl's plays as well. The artists of Profile Theatre in Portland, Oregon, who created a "Sarah Ruhl Season" in 2015, relished that Ruhl "does not tell artists how to realize her vision. According to Lauren Bloom Hanover, she furnishes the idea, the image, the moment, and then trusts those handling her plays to find their own unique way to share the soul of her stories." Ruhl's ideal for the stage and life is an "I/Thou" mutuality, inspired by Martin Buber, in which individuals acknowledge their bondedness to one another—acknowledge that we exist because of and in connection to one another. She and Vogel are playwrights building webs of mutuality with their theatre collaborators, audiences, students, and one another.

In Ruhl's *100 Essays I Don't Have Time to Write* meditation "Is playwriting teachable?: the example of Paula Vogel," she writes, "What strikes me most when I remember Paula's teaching is her *presence* as much as the content of her teachings. [. . ..] Paula has a tremendous gaze, a tremendous listening power, and the most intelligent curiosity of anyone I have ever met. She took me seriously" (167). Ruhl, who now teaches at Yale School of Drama, has become a mentor as well, and we will likely see her influence on a next generation of playwrights. Where it has surfaced most visibly so far is in her friendship with the late poet Max Ritvo; very reminiscent of Ruhl's mutually nourishing relationship with Paula Vogel, her relationship with Ritvo moved from teacher-student friendship to writing collaborator in

Letters from Max, a collection of their emails to one another during the years leading up to Ritvo's death in 2016. In an interview with Nick Tabio for the *Yale Daily News* on her influences, Ruhl said,

> I think my top five influences would be Paula Vogel, who was an incredibly important teacher for me, Virginia Woolf, Elizabeth Bishop, Katherine Mansfield and Shakespeare. And because we're talking about teachers and students, I would add Max to that list. I think that our students impact us as teachers, and we impact our students. And that is an incredibly generative cycle that goes on infinitely.

Vogel's model of mentoring playwrights, encouraging their experimentation and the development of their own dramatic voices and not stamping them with her own, generously offering them financial as well as moral support for production, should be the standard for playwriting education. But how do we teach love? "When I reflect on all the things Paula taught me," Ruhl writes, "among them, Aristotelian form, non-Aristotelian form, bravery, stick-to-itiveness, how to write a play in forty-eight hours, how to write stage directions that are both impossible to stage and possible to stage—the greatest of these is love. Love for the art form, love for fellow writers, and love for the world" (169).

The Theatre of Paula Vogel

DRAWING NEW CIRCLES: ON PAULA VOGEL'S MAIEUTICS, QUIARA ALEGRÍA HUDES'S BROKEN LANGUAGE AND THE SEEDS OF BORICUAN INSPIRATION

Ana Fernández-Caparrós

Drawing Circles: Success in Circuit Lies

At seventy, the always vivacious and indefatigable Paula Vogel is now recognized as one of the greatest living American playwrights. Christopher Bigsby wrote of her plays, over twenty years ago, that in them audiences are taken on a journey they would not ordinarily take and what "is unusual about that journey is not only that it frequently takes them into the world of the fantastic and the bizarre but that it liberates them from a Manichean frame of mind, from a binary mode of thought" (*Contemporary* 289). If her writing politics were always, as Bigsby says, "more inclusive than exclusive" (289), a firm belief in and defense of inclusiveness has also shaped and defined Paula Vogel's dedicated role as a mentor in the past four decades. So much so that, in welcoming so many fellow writers to her "house" in Providence, she might be the playwright to have more strongly influenced and nurtured a whole new generation of twenty-first-century American playwrights who have revitalized and redefined the American theatre produced in this millennium. As important as the singularity of Vogel's dramatic oeuvre is, then—as Lee Brewer Jones insightfully illustrates in Chapter 4 of this book—the impressive richness of her legacy as a "brilliant mentor" (Savran, "Loose Screws," xii), as a friend, and as a glittery beacon for those who took part in her intensive advanced playwriting seminars of the MFA Playwriting Program at Brown University, which she founded in 1985.

Vogel's reputation as a mentor is firmly established. Several scholars and former students have given glimpses of her techniques and have openly expressed their gratitude to their *maestra*. Both Lynn Nottage and Sarah Ruhl, for instance, have extensively acknowledged how much their playwriting was shaped and indebted to their encounter with Paula Vogel, how it literally changed their lives. In this chapter I want to examine Vogel's influence on yet another outstanding, successful, and Pulitzer Prize-winner playwright who is, for David Román, "at the forefront of a new dramaturgy that suggests that the first few decades of the twenty-first century might just be remembered as among the most significant in the history of American theatre": Quiara Alegría Hudes (149). Hudes was likewise trained by Vogel, "that monster of mischievous theatrical form who taught her playwriting"[5] at Brown, where she earned her MFA in playwriting in 2004. Like her fellow playwrights, she has often expressed gratitude to her mentor in interviews and in the Acknowledgments sections of her plays.[6] It is, however, in her recently published memoir, *My Broken Language* (2021), where Hudes provides a profuse and intimate account of her relationship with Vogel. Hudes's personal chronicle of her training as a playwright in the fourth section of her memoir, entitled "Break Break Break My Mother Tongue," gives a most valuable record not only of Vogel's unique personality and style as a teacher but also of the challenges and difficulties Hudes met in the path toward finding her creative voice. This section is particularly interesting for drama lovers and scholars, but the book as a whole creates a new context for reading Hudes's oeuvre and for understanding that perhaps Vogel's greatest gift to her student was to help her find the confidence and space to confront her fears and find the vocabulary to articulate in the theatre an already powerful, latent legacy. As Hudes later explained in the online launch of her memoir at the Free Library of Philadelphia in conversation with her teacher and friend, Paula gave her the blessing of "having permission to make something creative and artistic out of something broken" ("Quiara"): her imperfect Spanish. No less importantly, Vogel also dispelled her of the notion that she must be loyal to English or even her second language Spanglish.[7]

Through the exploration of the open and ongoing dialogue between Vogel and Hudes in the past two decades—which can be traced in Hudes's plays, in her memoir, in published interviews or in the public conversations they have had, such as the live-streamed launching of *My Broken Language* in April 2021—a sharper image emerges of Vogel's pedagogical philosophy and its effects on her mentees. Ann Pellegrini argues that Paula Vogel "believes in ghosts" (473). In this chapter I want to argue that she also believes in circles, and that an intuitive, complex reliance on what Emerson might call "the copious sense of this first of forms" (403) likewise permeates Quiara Alegría Hudes's dramaturgy. Allusion to circles permeates the discourse of both these playwrights and can also be traced in their formal experimentations, in the way that they represent communal relationships on the stage and in how they relate as members of a community of theatre makers.

Circles are inclusive, reciprocal, and spiritual.[8] As the transgender character of Kes claims in Stacey Gregg's 2015 dramatic monologue *Scorch*, "a circle is about trust" and "*for* trust" (16). Or, as Emerson claimed in the "First Series" of his *Essays* (1841), believing in circles means believing "in the circular and compensatory character of every human action" (403). And not to a lesser extent, in the truth that "around every circle another can be drawn; that there is no end in nature, but every end is a beginning" (Emerson 403). Vogel is a playwright who has consistently refused throughout her playwriting "the niceties of linear narration in favor of circular structures that up-end, or at least muddle, neat distinctions among past, present and future" (Pellegrini 474). Her first major success, *The Baltimore Waltz* (1993), her Pulitzer Prize-winning play *How I Learned to Drive* (1998), and the more conceptual and poetic *The Long Christmas Ride Home* (2003), all use circular dramatic structures with different purposes. Be they the conflation of the real and the imagined, or of remembered and real events, in all of them the fluid shaping of time that the circular form grants reveals a resistance to tell things "straight" (Pellegrini 474). In fact, as Joanna Mansbridge notices, Vogel's use of the circular form

> poses a new way of seeing and, by extension, a new way of thinking about the historical constitution of cultural issues and social identities. She takes audiences on round-trip journeys that bring them back to the place from which they began, although with perspectives that have been inevitably changed by what they have seen along the way. ("Memory's" 212)

The richness and complexities of circularity that Vogel advocates for on the stage might have been molded by having slowly but solidly forged a career as a playwright in the 1980s and 1990s at the margins of a male-dominated mainstream theatre and American dramatic tradition. Being a self-declared lesbian, moreover, increased her sense of exclusion but gave her also, crucially, as Bigsby observes, "a place to stand, a perspective on mainstream values." It might have been this standing at the limits of a circumference that shaped Vogel's belief that "drama works by indirection" (*Contemporary* 291). And thus her determination to find ways to create a vocabulary for the stage to embody in it the Dickinsonian credo that, if one is to tell the truth, they have to tell it slant: "Success in Circuit lies."[9] This contention seems to be literally true for Vogel in many senses: her circumvention of mainstream theatrical conventions was eventually recognized with perhaps the highest distinction for dramaturgy in the United States, a Pulitzer Prize; this and other recognitions granted her sufficient pecuniary rewards to buy herself a house and other goods. The measure of Vogel's success, however, relies also, crucially, on her having established and sustained a powerful circuit of fellow playwrights around her—in other words, in having shared her own success by drawing new circles, which in turn extended success to a whole community of dramatists.

Vogel's generous ways of mentorship, I want to further claim, can also be seen as being circular in nature because they are based on a firm belief in reciprocity. Indeed, Quiara Alegría Hudes refers to an "Oft-repeated Paula scripture" which states, "*When a door opens for you, bring another person through*" (280).

Circular Teachings: A Pedagogical Philosophy of Reciprocity

The existing sources describing Vogel's pedagogical methods for playwriting reveal that she is no conventional teacher. She trusts the necessity of training and, as Joanna Mansbridge explains in her volume on Vogel, her pedagogy "emerges from her belief that we are not, as Lady Gaga would have it, 'born this way,' but rather, to borrow the words of Rodgers and Hammerstein, 'we have to be carefully taught'" (8). However, rather than imposing a rigid, established method, or fixed ideas about what makes a good play, Vogel has her trainees engage in challenging creative tasks that will force them to exercise their "writing muscle," such as drafting a full play in forty-eight hours;[10] writing a play that is impossible to stage; or drawing "from a real-life profile on the FBI's 'Most Wanted' list and then writing a scene that defies the profile" (Mansbridge 8). The end of these formalist lessons aimed at structuring "negative empathy" (Mansbridge 8) is, as David Savran beautifully puts it,

> getting her students to write not about what they are sure of, but what they don't know, what terrifies them, what they desire madly, what they have to fight to comprehend. As she explains it, she longs, both in her own writing and that of her students, to unleash the confusion in the hope that this will lead both writer and reader to understand the confusion, to make sense out of a world—and a society—gone terribly awry. (xiii)

I want to reflect here not so much on the specific features of Vogel's writing techniques and exercises, but rather on the humble nature of her open, cooperative "philosophy" of teaching that, in unleashing confusion as the path to self-discovery, could be seen as an intuitive, contemporary, and personal reinterpretation of the art of maieutics proper of the Socratic Method. The latter was described by Plato in his *Theatetus* (c. 369 BCE). There are, naturally, patent dissimilarities: the context is radically different and Vogel is certainly no philosopher. Interestingly, however, she sees her role as that of "a facilitator" (Mansbridge 8), a description of her purposes that is not essentially different to that of the Greek philosopher who, being in fact the "son of a strapping midwife called Phaenarete," saw himself as applying the art of midwifery with his disciples (Plato 11). In Plato's dialogue Socrates tells the young Theatetus that no midwife "attends other women while she's still conceiving and bearing children herself"; that it is only "those past being able to give birth who do it"; and that they are "the cleverest of match-makers" (11–12). A well-known and delightful anecdotal happenstance is that, as a matter of fact, the childless Paula Vogel and her wife Ann Fausto-Sterling introduced their then students at Brown, Sarah Ruhl, and now psychiatrist Tony Charuvastra, and later served as officiants at their wedding.[11] One can imagine both these intelligent women provided with a sharp sense of humor laughing at this ironic coincidence. Regardless of our understanding of it as hazardous or as proof of ancient popular wisdom, it is rather the art of intellectual midwifery that Vogel seems to have developed and mastered over the years: an art in which, as she might likely agree with her Greek forebearers, the role of a mentor who essentially lacks wisdom is instead to have their mentees make progress by prolonged "association" with them: not, hence, because they have learnt anything from their teacher, "but because they have themselves discovered many admirable things in themselves, and given birth to them" (Plato 11).

Vogel's stamina and generosity of spirit are quite uncommon. She is obviously not the only American playwright to have trained aspiring playwrights: the Playwrights Unit program founded by Edward Albee, Richard Barr, and Clinton Wilder supported writing and production of new plays by John Guare, Adrienne Kennedy, Lanford Wilson, Leonard Melfi, and many others between 1963 and 1971; Sam Shepard and María Irene Fornés were regular teachers at the summer Padua Hills Playwrights Workshop and Festival founded by Murray Mednick outside of Los Angeles in 1978; Fornés then founded and ran the seminal INTAR Hispanic Playwrights-in-Residence Laboratory in New York City from 1981 to 1992. Vogel's career as a mentor might be very close in spirit to that of her "hero" Fornés—whose profound legacy for several generations of contemporary Latina playwrights, including Quiara Alegría Hudes, has been critically assessed by playwright and scholar Anne García-Romero in her 2016 book

The Fornés Frame. What might be quite unique about Vogel's pedagogical approach to teaching playwriting, though, is not only her extended dedication to it for over three decades but also her uncompromising trust in equality and reciprocity. This confidence in circular and reciprocal teaching is one that dismantles inherited dichotomies and fixed categories, as it essentially blurs the distinction between teacher and learner, or rather, turns teaching into a rewarding act of learning. In a blatant reversal of the expectations about teaching, still often perceived as a vertical relationship of power in which an elder imparts knowledge to a younger pupil, Vogel has always been grateful for the wisdom that her students grant her. Significantly, she does not refer to them as mentees or students, but as her fellows. Already in the Acknowledgments section of *The Baltimore Waltz and Other Plays,* published by Theatre Communications Group in 1996, she confessed how much her own writing was indebted to a decade of Brown University playwrights. There, she listed alphabetically forty-three names, including those of Adam Bock, Nilo Cruz, Edwidge Danticat, Lynn Nottage, and Sarah Ruhl. She also recognized how many other writers and colleagues had "instructed this instructor to dance on the page by their example."[12]

In the online conversation she had with Hudes as part of the launching of *My Broken Language,* Vogel naturally confesses to having invited Quiara to Brown because she wanted to learn from her: she wanted Quiara to be her teacher. Hudes's memoir confirms this and provides a delightful account of their first encounter: how Paula, after reading the musical she had submitted, had run straight to the phone because she wanted to know everything about the language, the process, and how Ogun had become part of her life. And how Paula then invited her to "crash on [her] sofa for a night" to convince her to make Providence her two-year home. Hudes's remembrance of that first weekend at Paula's house is extremely valuable for the vivid and intimate portrait it paints of her future mentor as an exceptionally charming and close person, described as she drove her prospective student to Horseneck Beach in her new Honda del Sol as "a lithe conversationalist, lacking pretension, all curiosity and exclamation points" (*My Broken Language* 264–6).

In hindsight Vogel has admitted that she thinks of the time she and Quiara spent together in Providence as a "chapter in [her] learning: that [she] never saw theater or plays the same [and she] didn't see language in the same way."[13] As Vogel told Sarah Ruhl for *BOMB,* "Most of us do not know what place we possess as students in our teachers' thoughts. Unless we ourselves teach, how could we know? That we teachers share our students, bring the work home, mention their names over the dinner table until they become household words." Interestingly, as a response, Hudes *literally* endorsed the "inclusive" notion of "teaching being circular and being intergenerational" as being "wonderfully freeing" and not necessarily contradicting the notion of "respecting one's elders" (Vogel "Sarah Ruhl").

Perhaps no one has better transformed the Vogel-inspired notion that teaching is always circular to the language of the stage than her distinguished disciple Sarah Ruhl in *The Oldest Boy* (2014), a delicate and very spiritual play, formally indebted to Vogel's *The Long Christmas Ride Home*, about an American mother and her Tibetan husband having to come to terms with the news that their son is a reincarnated lama teacher. Hudes no doubt also learned the benefits of circular teaching through the "warm ebullient enthusiasm"[14] of her mentor but she admits that she was in turn only fully aware of being part of a chain of reciprocal learners when she became a thirteen-year-older sister to Gabi, who taught her about life. As important, however, for her intuitive apprehension of the rewards of circularity was her upbringing among the matrilineal descendants of her Puertorican grandmother, Obdulia Pérez.

AZADA, AZADA, AZADA! On (Circular) Gardens, Cropping, and Healing

For all the relevance of her encounter with Paula Vogel, which was decisive to forge the conviction that she could become a professional playwright, Quiara Alegría Hudes's path toward finding her creative voice had started much earlier and it was not without its obstacles. In 2018—after having produced three musicals and four plays she confesses to being proud of; two early plays she is fond of; and a handful of work she would rather forget about—in the keynote address that Hudes delivered together with her sister Gabriela Sánchez at the ATHE conference, she claimed that it hurt to get to theatre, and that only then she saw "the nature of the wound," that only recently she had "acquired the vocabulary to describe the affliction, the clarity to admit the hurt."[15] In this section I want to briefly look into the circuitous paths that Hudes took in the past fifteen years to rebel against an institutional theatrical landscape dominated by what she and Sánchez called "stubbornly entrenched, atheist white male aesthetics." As relevant as exploring in which ways she was influenced by her mentor is how much she was likewise influenced by her extended family circle and particularly by her mother Virginia Sánchez (née Pérez). When Hudes and Vogel crossed paths, she was "digesting a cosmos and building [her] own":[16] that she did it transgressing, like her teacher, mainstream portrayals of the American family and linear narratives reveals elective affinities but Hudes's oeuvre also reveals very personal ways of representing and seeing cyclical transformations.

Should we single out two features that distinguish the style of Quiara Alegría Hudes's drama, they would be bringing center stage the stories of characters of Puerto Rican descent inspired by her own family in North Philadelphia, and the significant presence of music. With a close reading of the trilogy including *Elliot, A Soldier's Fugue* (2006), *Water by the Spoonful* (2012) and *The Happiest Song Plays Last* (2013) in light of its critical reception, and enriched with the intimate and vivid portrait that Hudes makes of herself and her family in *My Broken Language*, we can better understand how she crafted her unique vision. Could it be said that Hudes, like Vogel, believes in circles? It might be argued that she does, but that she draws them differently. One way of relying on circles in complex and unexpected ways is by creating dramatic structures inspired by musical forms. The other is by bringing to the stage what might be regarded as an "earthly wisdom" inherited from Hudes's matrilineal descendance, whose clearest symbol to be found in the plays mentioned above is Ginny's garden in *Elliot, A Soldier's Fugue*, later on tended by the character of Yaz in *The Happiest Song Plays Last*.

That Hudes became a playwright is somehow an unexpected turn of events, as she was trained in music from an early age and in fact earned a BA in musical composition from Yale University. A detailed account of her experience at college is given in Chapters 24 and 25 of *My Broken Language*. It was only while at university that she realized that her most important musical influences, such as Celina and Reutilio, which she named and recognized for the first time, were excluded models in a curriculum centered on canonical Western classical, where Music "was synonym for 'white'" (213). A slow yet sharp process of self-awareness started from the first lessons:

> I had already begun craving an uglier language, one that expressed the Perez resilience and maelstrom. North Philly's too young death and mucky girlhood and gorgeous dance were eager to key their way out of my cage. There was a poetics I longed to share with my mom at home and the world at large, one messier than dainty Mozart, more

syncopated than Chopin, more guttural than elegant Bach. But I hadn't yet found it. Schoenberg and Ruggles were too bleak. I needed dissonance that spoke of love, too. A turbulent woman's tongue. (206–7)

In the barrio in *My Broken Language*, music meant "Nigeria and Senegal, Cuba and Brazil, PR and DR, and Harlem, U.S.A." and thus she craved for a richer conversation with her peers, one that did not blindfold itself to her culture, one that "didn't other entire hemispheres of art" (212, 215–16). It was only when Hudes heard of a scholarship for students of color across disciplines that she saw an escape from Yale's insularity and composed a salsa musical called *Sweat of the River, Sweat of the Ocean*. She wrote a story about the agnostic daughter of a Santera that has nine days to dismantle her mom's altars, with music inspired by Celia's montunos and Bongo Santamaria's jam. She had to make do with the help of amateur Latinx actors, actresses, and musicians recruited across the campus and with the help of her aunt and uncle. But the musical was finally performed in a 45-seat-black box theatre, and happily, it got the blessing of her mother and her family.

Hudes's formative years at Yale did not lead her to forge a life out of music: or perhaps they did, only not just in the most conventional ways, as a soloist or as an arranger. She crossed paths with legendary Philadelphia producer Larry Gold, and even opened for Gil Scott-Heron, but she did not set off the ground. As hard as it was to admit that she was not good enough, her musical higher education was a most enriching detour, one that would give her the key to understand, as her mother Virginia told her, that she had stories to tell. That she was a writer. That *their* stories had not been told and could be meaningful. The salsa musical written at Yale was eventually read by Vogel in the process of candidates' selection for her playwriting seminar, and Vogel, like Virginia, saw an enormous potential in the cultural and musical baggage that Quiara could bring to the stage.

Hudes has written the books and lyrics for very successful musicals: *In the Heights* (2005) with music by Lin-Manuel Miranda and recently adapted to the cinema, and *Miss You Like Hell*, with music by Erin McKweon (2016). It might be, however, in her dramatic plays where Hudes most originally "recycled" her impressive knowledge of music in a sophisticated creative process that shall be understood not just as using something for a different purpose but also as a means to giving it a new life. As Hudes told Harvey Young, music is a basic relationship that she has with the world, one of the lenses through which she experiences things: as a theatre practitioner, thus, in "thinking about that primal circle that we enter to tell a story for theatre, to separate music out seems potentially artificial" (187). *Elliot, A Soldier's Fugue* is the first play in which the playwright "consciously incorporated music" first as an organic discovery and then also "as an intellectual decision-making process": her main endeavor was "exploring music in drama" and using Bach's fugues as a compositional model to tell the stories of Latinx characters, thus conflating seemingly clashing worlds, Hudes has told Kathleen Potts, felt very different to conventional writing models but also "like home" for her.[17] The play premiered at Page 73 Productions in New York City in 2006 and is, essentially, a war play that centers on eighteen-year-old Lance Corporal Elliot Ortiz's return to his hometown, Philadelphia, after a first tour of duty in Iraq in 2003. Elliot, a war veteran, has to make the decision of whether to return or not for a second tour of duty, after having been severely wounded in the leg. Hudes uses the polyphonic structure of the fugue to stage different episodes of Elliot's experience as a combatant by counterpointing Elliot's voice with that of his grandpop, who served in Korea; his father, who served in Vietnam; and his mother, who also served in Vietnam as a nurse. The play has fourteen scenes, titled either a fugue or a prelude. In the "Fugue" scenes, where the playwright orchestrates major events in Elliot's life as a marine (i.e., preparing to ship off for Iraq; the first time he kills a person there; his leg injury and his next departure), different temporal and spatial frames are conflated—a dramatic technique that Hudes surely learnt from Vogel. When Elliot steps in them, he is in 2003 in Iraq, Pop in the late 1960s, and Grandpop in 1950 in Korea. In these scenes, "people narrate each other's actions and sometimes narrate their own" (Potts). The character of Grandpop explains in Scene Eight, a prelude in the garden area of the stage, how he played the flute "light as feather, free as a bird" to his platoon in Korea because it was "very soothing after the bombs settle down," and how he only played Bach, because its cold music could be approached like a "calculation. An exercise. A routine" (35–6). He provides a definition of the fugue, and with it, Hudes deftly describes its dynamics while asserting its metaphorical possibilities:[18]

> The fugue is like an argument. It starts in one voice. The voice is the melody, the single solitary melodic line. The statement. Another voice creeps up on the first one. Voice two responds to voice one. They tangle together. They argue, they become messy. They create dissonance. Two, three, four lines clashing. You think, Good god,

they'll never untie themselves. How did this mess get started in the first place? Major keys, minor keys, all at once on top of each other. It's about untying the knot. (35)

The different voices in the fugues open up a possibility for all characters to utter each other's truths starkly and slantly, thus enabling each of them to circumvent their unutterable stories. This choral technique for confronting *together* analogous experiences becomes a ritual aimed more at strengthening the bonds of a community than at disclosing the horrors and betrayals of combat, although the dissonance created might certainly allude to the complexities of war. The knots, as García-Romero claims, may possibly refer instead to their personal entanglements resulting from military service and, on the other hand, to how characters throughout the play also try to untie themselves from each other to clarify their past and move on (168). This is enacted in the preludes interspersed among the fugues, which all take place in Philadelphia and are often more lyrical monologues or short dialogues in which each character is given their own space.

As important as Hudes's innovative musical composition in *Elliot* is her conception of two different playing areas that do not exclude one another. One is a minimal, stark "empty space" that transforms into many locations, including war scenarios. This is a "sad space": "when light enters, it is like light through a jailhouse window or through the dusty stained glass of a decrepit chapel." Then there is Ginny's garden, the dumping lot Elliot's mother bought for one dollar upon her return from serving in the Army Nurse corps and turned into a lush image of Arecibo in Puerto Rico. The "garden space" teems with life: "a verdant sanctuary, green speckled with magenta and gold." However different, they are both regarded as "holy" in their own way.

The significance of the garden here and in the following plays cannot be underestimated, as it is one of the clearest symbols of the cultural values of Hudes's Boricuan ancestry, one that symbolizes natural life cycles that grant germination, growth, blooming, and, after decay, as a new circle begins, transformation, survival, endurance, and resilience. Quiara's memory opening this section, Quiara's remembrance of her and her mother Virginia's cropping soil to design a circular garden in the horse farm in Malvern, where they moved in during a short period of Quiara's childhood, is one of the opening scenes of *My Broken Language*. Their garden as a living medicine wheel was planted with "Angelica. Rosemary. Eucalyptus. Rue. Lemon balm. Yerba bruja. Basil (albahaca). Verdolaga (purslane). Peony. Artemisa (wormwood). Varios types of mint. Parsley. Marjoran (mejorana). Hot peppers. Pazote. And many, many sages. Because of its strong personality and curative properties, sage was to be planted at center" (8–9). It was there that their rituals began. Later on, Hudes would learn from the formative theatrical readings that Paula Vogel assigned her how the empty space of the theatre allows her to summon and transform this and other rituals.

In *Elliot, A Soldier's Fugue* Ginny's urban garden is not explicitly described in stage directions as being circular in shape, but is nonetheless a sacred space—at once real and symbolic—for hope and healing, one whose very necessity and relevance are even greater within a war context. This is made clear in Scene Thirteen of the play, a prelude given the shape of a monologue in which Elliot opens up about his wounds, his guilt, his nightmares, and his father's reluctance to discuss their war experiences. In the last part of the scene Ginny enters the garden area and "*begins to braid vines around Elliot's body, from the garden*" and "*wraps his body in intricate, meticulous ways*," slowly adding leaves and other flora until the scene ends (57). This healing ritual mirrors symbolically and poetically counterpoints the previous covering of Elliot's legs in barbed wire in Scene Ten, a Fugue performed by all the characters in the empty space to represent Elliot's excruciating pain after getting seventy-four thorns dug deep into his skin.

In an earlier prelude scene Hudes has the character of Ginny expand on the powerful meanings and rewards of a garden:

> When Elliot left for Iraq, I went crazy with planting. Begonias, ferns, trees. A seed is a contract with the future. It's saying, I know something better will happen tomorrow. I planted bearded irises next to palms. I planted tulips with a border of cacti. All the things the book tells you: "Don't ever plant these together," "Guide to Proper Gardening." Well, I got on my knees and planted them side by side. I'm like, you have to throw all the preconceived notions out the window. You have to plant wild. When your son goes to war, you plant every goddamn seed you can find. It doesn't matter what seed is. So long as it grows. I plant like I want and the hell with the consequences. (22)

As a powerful locale and trope symbolizing hope, healing and renewal, Ginny's garden in *Elliot, A Soldier's Fugue* represents Hudes's dialogue with and recognition of traditional Latinx writing and its values, what Jorge Huerta calls "a search for a better life" (466) and an artistic vision "inextricably linked to matters of community building."[19] More specifically, as García-Romero contends, Hudes echoes the dynamic in a number of Latinx plays with roots in the Caribbean "in which the American characters' utopian yearnings for island life often drive the action of the play" (167–8). Ginny's personal guide to gardening, however, shall also be read metatheatrically, thus reflecting Hudes's originality as a dramatist, for she also challenges and reimagines the tradition of both Latinx and American plays alike, and audiences have, as with Vogel plays, to throw all the preconceived notions out the window when entering these stage worlds.

Hudes has explained how, having found an idiom she felt comfortable with, that is, bringing musical composition to playwriting, she felt compelled to keep exploring it through Elliot's fictional story. In subsequent plays following Elliot Ortiz's life from 2003 to 2011, she would explore other musical forms: John Coltrane's free jazz in *Water by the Spoonful* and traditional Puerto Rican music played with cuatro in *The Happiest Song Plays Last*. The exploration of these other musical forms would further enable Hudes to draw new circles for the creation of novel aesthetic paradigms attuned to the exploration of wider, non-conventional familial and affective bonds. In *Water by the Spoonful* we find again the character of Elliot in 2009, working at a Subway sandwich shop in Philadelphia and confronting the death of Ginny, whom we learn to be his aunt, and getting in touch again with his birth mother, Odessa, who runs a chat for recovering crack addicts like herself. The stories of Elliot and his cousin Yaz, a music professor, interlock with those of characters relating on the "online world." As Alvarez and Ortuzar have shown, the free jazz dramaturgy allows Hudes to open up "new spaces of representation for the irreducible particularities of Latinx experience" (148) and for the spatial articulation of expanded families that reject a patriarchal model which values biological motherhood the most to explore instead matriarchal models based on the "reproduction of kindness,"[20] regardless of bloodline. Alvarez and Ortuzar rely on the "Coltrane circle," a diagram that the musician created in 1960 combining musical scales from all over the world as a conceptual image of music that can shed light on the structure of Hudes's play and indeed invites to overlay worlds that appear separate in the play. This circle, they explain, "outlines a variation of movements in a geometric pattern that looks like a clock, each hour represented by a cluster of three notes. Within these three-note clusters we find notes that outline the cycle of fifths, which in music theory represents the relationship among twelve tones of the chromatic scale and their corresponding key signatures" (150). Alvarez and Ortuzar very successfully use this complex circular diagram for a close reading of a play whose episodic scenes featuring clusters of predominantly three to five characters in split scenes juxtapose disparate, simultaneous worlds (the real and the virtual) that are eventually brought together. As they claim, Hudes's reliance on Coltrane's expansive polyphony and aesthetic opposition challenges expectations about order and beauty and thus she demands from audiences to put expectations aside: "this is not a play where everything goes together, much less a play that can be easily compartmentalized and reduced to the label 'Latinx.' Hudes's free jazz dramaturgy . . . shatters and transforms, asking us to pay attention to forms of social life made possible by radical and often unpredictable relationalities" (152).

The tough stories of these memorable characters, Elliot and Yaz, only come full circle at the end of *The Happiest Song Plays Last*, when Elliot, now an actor, soon to be a father, digs a grave for the passport of Taarek Taleb, the civilian he killed in Iraq, in Ginny's garden, now Yaz's. Elliot, memorably performed throughout a decade by Armando Riesco, was first seen taking Taleb's wallet, following military code, in a key scene in *Elliot, A Soldier's Fugue*. In *Water by the Spoonful* he was haunted by the ghost of Taarek demanding: "Momken men-fadluck ted-dini gawaz saffari," whose rough translation, he learns, is "Can I please have my passport back?" (11). His failed attempt to have it returned to the man's family while in Jordan in *The Happiest Song Plays Last* eventually leads him to finally put an end to his guilt, pain, and bereavement by giving this object symbolizing an irreparable loss a proper burial, so that healing will bring renewal and peace: "Taarek Taleb. It's been a long journey we've taken together, hasn't it. You and me, man . . . Taarek, may your little boy speak. Your son, my son," Elliot wishes (11).

At the end of her trilogy Hudes has likewise taken audiences and readers alike on a long journey whose circuitous paths demand thoughtful interpretation. Like the journeys in Vogel's plays, this one also liberates audiences from a binary mode of thought and grants eventual transformation and emotional healing. As a conclusion to this brief critical assessment of Hudes's innovative dramaturgical techniques, deftly used to draw new circles for the creation of a more expansive and open American theatrical tradition, it might be said that she uses her writing in the same fashion that her mother and her ancestors used their hoes. As told in a key scene of *My Broken Language*, her mother Virginia had the transformational vision to reverse an insult—having been called a whore—into its near homophone, a hoe—AZADA! AZADA! AZADA—and this gardening tool shall be seen as the perfect metaphor to understand how Hudes broke her imperfect language to dig into the soil of her wounds and those of her surrounding relatives. She wonders, at the end of her memoir, what use a utensil like that could have at all, when the Pérez women divorced mother nature long ago, her abuela's gandules harvest being over; her mom's sage, dead; her horse woods, gone; and those who had been one "earth women . . . now North Philly—treeless rubble, tire-strewn and derelict" (311). Hudes now understands that one plot of land persists in their bodies and how, by having named their pain and their imperfections in her writings, she declares their resilience and, in the theatre, brings it center stage. As simple as telling these stories seems, much courage and determination was needed to transform them into challenging and inspiring theatrical events, so much that they might be seen, echoing the playwright's name, as an unexpected "revolution masked as happiness" (24).[21] And perhaps both Virginia Pérez and Paula Vogel's greatest gift to Hudes was providing either confidence or models, a safe space and supporting circuit to write them down: Sí se puede! Sí se puede! Sí se puede!

Critical Perspectives

"THE FEMININE SPIRIT THAT REALLY I NEEDED": INTERVIEW BETWEEN LEE BREWER JONES AND LYNN NOTTAGE

Lee Brewer Jones
January 2021

Lee Jones: When I met Paula Vogel at that workshop at the Vineyard in 2017, I walked in with a cup of coffee, and the greeter said, "You are going to need that caffeine." That person was absolutely right! My first question, then, is whether you remember the first time you saw Paula Vogel, and do you retain any sense of that initial energy?
Lynn Nottage: You know, it is so interesting. I first met Paula Vogel when I was a senior at Brown University, and I had requested to be in her graduate playwriting class. She said no, but then generously permitted me to be in her senior playwriting seminar. I remember thinking at the time that she was spunky, passionate, and exuded warmth. However, I think the biggest impression that she left was the fact that she was a woman. Up until then, I had only studied with men, and I'd come to believe that playwriting was the realm of men, and I was merely an interloper. So when I walked into the classroom and saw Paula, I was surprised and immediately excited. I was so elated to finally have a woman help guide me through a discipline that I was passionate about, but never felt quite welcoming.
LJ: That was in the 80s, right?
LN: That would have been like 1986; I was a senior.
LJ: I hate to segue to the second question because it is about a man, but when she was speaking at the Vineyard, she talked a lot that day about Bert States and the influence he has had on her career. I wanted to ask you if she introduced you to States's work and if there were any other important scholars she introduced you to who have been an influence.
LN: No, I don't really recall her introducing me to Bert States, but the playwright whose work she was really high on when I was studying with her was Peter Barnes. I remember reading and responding to his historical plays, which I found to be irreverent and whimsical. Paula's sensibilities were quite different from my previous professors. She was very much part of a young movement of writers who were looking to each other for inspiration, and I think the ingredient that she introduced was the notion of breaking with the traditional canon and inviting us as students to read the works of

more contemporary writers like Eric Overmeyer, Mac Wellman, Connie Congdon, and Philip Kan Gotanda. They were outside of the mainstream, in that they used language and structure in really innovative and adventurous ways. What she gave me as a student was a more expansive way of looking at how plays could be written and who could write those plays.

LJ: Did she talk a lot with you about defamiliarization and negative empathy?

LN: She didn't. When I was at Brown University, I think that Paula was very much in the process of evolving as a playwriting teacher, so some of the vocabulary and the exercises that she continues to use while teaching students had not yet been codified. I have been teaching for twenty-one years, and it really takes time to fully come into your own as a professor, and when I met Paula she was in a nascent moment before her evolution into a master teacher.

LJ: I like that word nascent. She has tweeted that when she won a certain capital P prize, it of course being the Pulitzer, that she received a really nice note from August Wilson saying, "Welcome to the Club." Wilson had died by the time you won your first Pulitzer, but I wondered if she sent you a similar note about the club. If so, do you remember what it said?

LN: I recall that after I won the first Pulitzer, she did send a very nice warm email. I can't remember the specifics of what she wrote, but I remember her reaching out to say how proud she was of my accomplishment, which she has continued to do throughout the years. I always embrace those correspondences, and appreciate having her as a colleague and creative ally.

LJ: I can understand that. Also on Twitter, in her bio, she identifies herself as—and she uses these words—"playwright, mentor, teacher, New Englander." I wanted to ask you if she has remained a mentor for you after she was no longer officially your teacher, and if so, with what effect?

LN: After I studied with Paula, I went on to the Yale School of Drama where I was thrust, without emotional preparation, into an environment where I was being taught entirely by white male professors. So while I wasn't in touch with Paula at that time, she remained a distant guiding light that I clung to, because she was the first person who allowed me to envision playwriting as a possible profession for somebody who looked like me. We lost touch for a number of years, but the mere fact of her being was something that I clung to as a form of creative nourishment.

LJ: That's powerful. I noted that your Twitter handle is "Lynn Brooklyn," with a geographic identity, and her Twitter handle says, "New Englander." So I wonder if she has had any influence on the way a sense of geography has informed the way you identify yourself.

LN: I would say that Brooklyn has really shaped the way I think of my emotional and physical geography. When I was young, Brooklynites were treated like the provincial cousins of Manhattanites. We were the bridge and tunnel folk, marginalized working-class people who lived on the other side of the bridge from the real "New Yorkers." I think my sense of place really came from this desire to assert identity and to celebrate community, and as a result we wore our outsider status like a badge of honor. Like Paula, my writing is an extension, reflection, and interrogation of the community that I grew up within.

LJ: I think I know how you feel. I have often, when I have spoken to people outside of the South, had to apologize for being a Georgian, and these past few weeks have made me very proud to be a Georgian . . ..

LN: That's wonderful.

LJ: . . . because of the things we have been able to do.

LN: Yeah.

LJ: Was Paula able to address your concerns as a playwright of color, as a woman, and if not, was she able to point you to resources?

LN: Even at Brown as a Black writer, I felt a great deal of isolation. I was fortunate that while I was studying, I had a Black playwriting mentor, George Bass, who I believe was an important colleague, friend, and mentor to Paula Vogel as well. He was fiercely protective of her at a time when the academy was not welcoming to a young free-spirited woman hellbent on shifting the culture within the theatre department. George taught me a great deal about theatrical traditions that were outside of the Western canon. He very much embraced the notion of theatre as a sacred ritual that connected and uplifted the Black community. So it wasn't necessary for me to look to Paula for cultural guidance, because I had a nurturing relationship with George. For me it was the feminine spirit that really I needed, and Paula was instrumental in helping me locate the work of female playwrights whose work was absent in my classes. Paula's guidance opened up space for me to write from an authentic place, and invite characters on to the stage who were organic representations of my imagination.

LJ: Yes, absolutely. I was wondering if, whether as a student or any time later, you ever participated in one of her bakeoffs or boot camps.

LN: I haven't. She hadn't developed her bakeoffs or boot camps when I was studying with her. I certainly have had students who have done bakeoffs, and I've done exercises that are inspired by her bakeoffs. We overlapped at Yale School of Drama; we were both teaching at the same time, and she offered boot camps to help students entering graduate school expand their arsenal of tools. I did have discussions with her about her bakeoffs, but I feel badly that due to timing I never had the opportunity to participate in one of her workshops at the drama school.

LJ: Right, right. I certainly understand. Can you tell me about at least one significant assignment she gave you when you were a student and tell me what made it especially memorable or instructional?

LN: I was trying to think, but remember when I studied with Paula it was 1986, over thirty years ago. I can say in all honesty I can't remember specific exercises, but I remember how the class offered me a new way to think about the craft of playwriting. The fact is I can't even remember what classes I took in college, but I remember Paula's.

LJ: Yeah, I know the feeling, but I had to ask because . . .

LN: I know. I wish I could remember, I've searched my memory, but "Wow, it was a really long time ago."

LJ: I understand. Would you mind sharing whether she has read any early drafts of any of your published plays and any comments about what she was like as a reader.

LN: Yeah, I don't believe she's read any of the early drafts of my published plays.

LJ: Even after the fact, has she gotten in touch with you with commentary about a play where you felt she was offering something astute as a reader?

LN: Paula has consistently come to see my plays and at times given me helpful feedback and necessary encouragement, and her support has been a true gift. Over the years, she's made a point of seeing my work, and what I recall—and this is something that is the hallmark of Paula Vogel as a teacher and a person—is her abundance of generosity. She is able to provide words that are incredibly nurturing, soothing, and that are also about expanding the possibilities of your voice, rather than trying to get into your process and be prescriptive. I think she understands how to say just the right combination of words that can inspire you to dig deeper into your own voice and fully embrace your objectives as a writer.

LJ: Thank you. That's a powerful answer and I love the way you use the word "nurturing." Several people have described her in very similar terms. I was wondering if she has helped you to get in touch with any of her other former students whom she has nurtured and if so how that experience has shaped you as a playwright and as a mentor yourself.

LN: You know. I think one of the most significant contributions that Paula has made in my life is that of my husband, Tony Gerber, who was also her student at Brown University. While we were not in the same writing class, we definitely bonded over our interest in playwriting and our love for Paula. I think in terms of the indelible impact she has had on my life, it is the indirect role she played in bringing my husband and me together.

LN: Did she introduce you to your husband?

LJ: Well, she didn't introduce me to my husband; we actually met in acting class. But we bonded over playwriting and both being in Paula Vogel's class. And I know my husband considered Paula to be a very important teacher and mentor in his life, and in some ways I think that very early on he was part of that glue that connected me to Paula.

LJ: Thank you for clarifying that.

LN: But in terms of playwrights who Paula has touched, as we overlapped at Brown University, there are a number of playwrights who came through the program who I remain very close to. I respect and feel connected to their writing which is an extension of their work with Paula, and now I've become attached to them as human beings. Over the years, we have formed a community of playwrights, and there is an unspoken bond forged by our relationship to Paula Vogel. I am thinking about playwrights like Quiara Alegriá Hudes, Christina Anderson, Nilo Cruz, and Sarah Ruhl.

LJ: And that's a wonderful and very accomplished community. When you and she were scheduled for residencies during the Portland season a couple of years ago, were you able to participate, before the pandemic?

LN: No, I didn't get to attend. I think my play was scheduled after it started.

LJ: Moving on, then, you told the *New York Times* that both you and Paula Vogel write plays that, and these are your words, "tend to be unafraid of the darkness." I wanted to ask: How are your plays that explore the darkness similar to Paula's, and how are they different?

LN: I think as writers we are both very interested in tackling the unspoken dangers that women face in our culture, whether it be rape, child abuse, or sexual exploitation. I think that is the thematic glue that binds our work, though stylistically our approaches are quite different. I think that often Paula's work has great lyricism and poetry. Her work tackles difficult themes with a gentle, compassionate, and assured hand. I do think that both of us use humor to help ease the audience into subjects that are difficult or somewhat controversial. In that way our work is in dialogue. But, I would say that where our work tends to diverge is that I am really interested in the intersectionality between gender, race, and class, and I'm very interested in the complications of multiculturalism in America, and the way it impacts the lives of women from the African diaspora.

LJ: Right, right. Are there any moments in Vogel that you think are particularly lyrical or humorous that you would like to say a word about?

LN: Sure. One of your questions is, "What is your favorite Paula Vogel play and how has it affected you?" I think the play I really responded to and surprised me was *Indecent*, which I found to be beautiful, visceral, and political. It gave a voice and shape to characters we rarely see on the stage, and Paula has the incredible ability to invite the audience into an intimate space, challenge us in an unexpected way, and ultimately shift our perspective. This is one of the things I really love about theatre. In *Indecent* she tackled a very difficult subject matter, a forbidden love during a moment when it was quite dangerous for those two people to publicly express their desire. She did it in a way that was lyrical, humorous, emotional, and painfully true. I admired Paula's ability to balance humor and pathos in equal measures, while crafting a work that was unapologetically entertaining.

LJ: Okay, thank you. So speaking of *Indecent*, when you and Vogel arrived on Broadway at the same time in 2017, how did you celebrate your shared accomplishment, and was she still "mentoring" you then, or was the relationship different by then?

Critical Perspectives

LN: I feel like it was such a blessing on so many levels for me to share that moment with Paula because she is so wise, and she is such a generous and compassionate spirit. So I felt that in moments that I felt frightened or unsure, I could just lean on her, and it really felt that we had to approach it with a kind of intrepidness. I can't think of any better warrior to be in battle with than Paula Vogel, you know, and we spent a lot of time talking about what it meant for us to be on Broadway together and how difficult it was for us to finally get there after years of being in the trenches. And so just on a very personal level, I felt very thankful and blessed to have a shoulder to lean on, to have someone I could commiserate with, and to have a fellow traveler with whom I could celebrate.

LJ: Is there anything you'd like to add to the question about your favorite Paula Vogel play?

LN: What would I add about *Indecent*? I mean, one of the things that I also really admired about that particular play and its arrival on Broadway is that it was so unabashedly romantic and emotional, sort of the antithesis of many plays that you see on Broadway that are written by men. I felt like it was a feminist play and a feminine play in all of the best ways, and I really admired those aspects.

LJ: Right. Thank you, I appreciate that. And of course the question I have stems from seeing the Thanksgiving parade: Would Paula Vogel make a good mermaid, and why or why not?

LN: I think Paula would make a wonderful mermaid. The mermaid parade is really about folks who dwell outside the mainstream, who embrace their idiosyncrasies and freely fly their freak flag, and I think that Paula would be a glorious mermaid.

LJ: Okay. Well, thank you. You've answered all of my questions. Is there anything else you would like to add to this interview?

LN: I think I have put it there, and thank you for doing this book. It is sort of long overdue, and I am glad there is an opportunity to really collate all the voices.

LJ: I know you are very busy, and I take it as a real tribute to her that you were willing to give time to me. Thank you.

NOTES

Chapter 1

1. In his "Production Notes" for *Six Degrees of Separation*, Guare tells the story of how Stockard Channing came to be cast at Ouisa. He writes of a "casting error" that left the production with "sixteen actors and no lead." "One morning," however, Guare writes, "we read in the papers that a play starring Stockard Channing expected to open on Broadway would instead terminate its run in San Diego." Offered the role of Ouisa, Channing accepted, "closed in San Diego on a Sunday and came to us on Tuesday and we didn't miss a beat." "Has any other actress," Guare asks, "been scheduled to open in New York at a certain time and, indeed, did however in another play?" (9).
2. Will Smith was in the middle of a six-season run as television's *Fresh Prince of Bel-Air*. Playing Paul afforded him a chance to show his skills as a serious actor.
3. Fornés died on October 30, 2018.

Chapter 2

1. Bigsby reports that *Desdemona* "had been successfully staged" in 1979 "at the New Plays Festival in Louisville and before that, in 1973, in a staged reading at Cornell University" (*Modern* 390). The 1973 date is problematic, given that Vogel did not enroll at Cornell until 1974, and Vogel, when she published the play in *The Baltimore Waltz and Other Plays*, in 1996, did not list a Louisville production (see Chapter 1).
2. Vogel's 1998 *Bomb* magazine interview given to Mary-Louise Parker suggests Vogel did have a playwright in mind. Asked for her five ideal dinner guests, Vogel included Aphra Behn, whom she described as "the first professional playwright in England during the Restoration. She wrote plays, but they were all condemned by the critics." This comment also gives a sense of what Vogel would have written in her 1970s Cornell doctoral dissertation.
3. This situation makes Vogel's 2017 debut on Broadway all the more astonishing.

Notes

4. Perhaps Vogel had these reviews in mind when she lamented to David Savran, "Tom Stoppard can do Rosencrantz and Guildenstern, but Paula Vogel can't do Desdemona" (Savran, "Driving" 16).
5. In *Modern American Drama, 1945–2000*, Bigsby cites Louisville as the city where *Desdemona* was staged at the New Plays Festival. Although Bigsby does not mention Jon Jory or Actors Theatre of Louisville, this city and Vogel's subsequent rupture with Jory may hint at why Vogel does not mention a Louisville production in *The Baltimore Waltz and other Plays*, where, in 1993, *Desdemona* was finally published.
6. Storyville, on which Storeyville seems based, was the name for the New Orleans section where prostitution thrived at the time of Mae's childhood.
7. Prostitution, although not exactly legal, was tolerated in the Storyville section of New Orleans until the district was officially closed in 1917.
8. According to Mansbridge, Mae's line was a Signature Theatre addition not in the published version (202).
9. One of America's foremost Shakespeare scholars, Kahn, taught at Brown and served in 2009 as president of the Shakespeare Association of America.
10. Katherine Helmond played 83-year-old Mae when she was 75, Joyce Van Patton 79-year-old Ursula at 70, Carlin Glynn 75-year-old Lillian at 64, Marylouise Burke 74-year-old Edna at 63, and Priscilla Lopez 72-year-old Vera at 56. While Rooney described Lopez as "perhaps too young to be a contemporary of the other gals," the ages of the actors compared with their characters appear to have gone unnoted.
11. Although George Washington has long been called the "Father of His Country," his and Martha's marriage, like that of the George and Martha in Albee's play, was childless. Washington did help bring up Martha's children by her deceased husband, Daniel Parke Custis.
12. A clear sign that Peter, at this point, feels "in the way" (73) or excluded from the "Woman Creating" activity comes in his response to this phrase: he tells both women, "Shut the fuck up!!" (71).
13. Whether in an intentional or unintentional homage to this word choice, Vogel will later write a play called *Hot 'N' Throbbing*, which I will discuss in Chapter 3.
14. Providing further support to Pellgrini's assertion that Vogel eschews the "add same-sex couple and stir" possibilities in *Baby*, Peter manifests a sexuality more complicated than that of the gay friend sperm donor. As already noted, he engages in heterosexual coitus with Anna, and he tells her that "the fantasies weren't . . . necessary" (73) for him to achieve orgasm, adding, "I really miss breasts." Scene Two ends with a tableau of Peter and Ruth at Anna's breasts.
15. Gussow, who Mansbridge says also reviewed the 1984 production, cryptically refers to "an earlier version, which was presented by the playwright under a pseudonym."

Notes

Chapter 3

1. Bigsby notes that the name is German for "death rattle" (*Contemporary* 310).
2. Mansbridge notes that the letter from Carl included in the *Playbill* might have told Rich Carl's identity (161).
3. If a Vogel equivalent to David Mamet's famous "Mamet Mafia," numbering such stage and screen luminaries as William H. Macy, Felicity Huffman, and Joe Mantegna, existed, Cherry Jones would undoubtedly be a charter member.
4. By the time Vogel and Jones spoke with *The Advocate*, both were history-making figures. Jones, in 1995, "became the first lesbian actor to thank her partner from the stage as she accepted a Tony Award for Best Actress for her role in the play *The Heiress*. And in 1998, in recognition of her smash hit *How I Learned to Drive*, Vogel became the first out lesbian to win the Pulitzer Prize for drama" ("Role"). Both in their collaborations and in the professional results of their deciding to work apart, Vogel and Jones each enjoyed success, albeit success tempered by momentary failure.
5. Covid-19 comes to mind.
6. Bigsby says Vogel considered the obscenity pledge "a deliberate affront" (*Contemporary* 312). Given the tone both of Vogel's introduction and of the play itself, plus Bigsby's report that Vogel sent "a copy to Jesse Helms with a note thanking him for his work in destroying civil rights," Vogel seems to have regarded the pledge more as an assault than an affront.
7. Charlene's work is a forerunner of what Jill Soloway, inspired by feminist theorist Laura Mulvey, describes as the "female gaze" (Nussbaum) and tries to film in her Emmy Award-winning television series *Transparent*.
8. When Charlene asks, "What are P.L.s?", the only answer she receives is Leslie Ann's "Nothin'" (238). Perhaps the most P.G. interpretation of what the abbreviation means is "panty lines."
9. *The Baltimore Waltz* and *How I Learned to Drive* contain direct references to teenage male sexuality. Neither, however, describes a boy quite as young as Calvin or clearly calls the teenager "Boy."
10. Teenaged Harrison in the 2021 Showtime series *Dexter: New Blood* endures a similar trauma when even younger, with violent consequences and an almost verbatim plea.
11. Mansbridge writes that Vogel so disapproved of Smith's staging that this "conflict of opinion" ended playwright and director's professional relationship (87).
12. Rousuck's generally favorable review suggests that a reassessment of the 1999 Arena Stage production, directed by Molly Smith may be appropriate.
13. For purposes of this discussion, I will include only elements where the film is true to the original source.
14. The 2008 film *The Reader* drew some critical remarks because of its portraying a graphic sexual relationship between thirty-something Hanna

165

Notes

Schmitz and fifteen-year-old Michael Berg, but most of the criticism focused on Kate Winslet's Oscar-winning performance as Hanna.

15. *Drive* contains a very brief scene, *Implied Consent* (76), that nominally refers to an agreement to take a sobriety test but that, in the context of the play, clearly suggests sexual conduct.
16. Anna's follow up, "Because if you feel it, you'll remember it. And then maybe you'll remember me" (41), may be influenced by the final line of *Tea and Sympathy*, "Years from now, when you speak of this, and you will, be kind."
17. Vogel also told Clay that "she wrote [*Drive*] picturing longtime American Repertory Theatre actor and current queen of the New York stage Cherry Jones," the Obie-winning actress whose performance of Vogel's characters I have already discussed. *Drive* would have been Jones's fourth Vogel play, but she was unavailable, and so the part went to Mary-Louise Parker.
18. The possibility of memory residing in the glands calls to mind William Faulkner's Nobel Acceptance Speech criticism of the author who "writes not with the heart but with the glands." Significantly, the hypothetical author addressed is a "he." If Vogel is moving the location of a woman's memories to her mammaries, she is making a strong feminist statement consistent with the "biological rupture" she described to Clay.
19. Heilpern, it must also be noted, has written of *Lolita* that the brilliance of Nabokov's novel "surely resides in its metaphor of old crumbling Europe (Humbert Humbert) being seduced by the lollipop charms of young, irresistible, uncultured America" (Lolita) (135), an interpretation I have already explored as problematical.
20. Margaret Edson's Pulitzer for *Wit* in 1999 marked the first time ever that women had won the Drama Pulitzer in consecutive years. In comparison, three women—Willa Cather, Margaret Wilson, and Edna Ferber—won the Pulitzer Prize for Fiction consecutively in 1923–25. Women have been more successful in winning Pulitzers for Fiction and Poetry than for Drama.
21. Johanna Day, as Female Greek Chorus, also returned from the 1997 Vineyard production.
22. Phillips's choice of "awed" calls to mind the way the audience responded when I saw *Indecent* at the Vineyard. Such a silence at this Broadway performance of a Vogel play suggested that her skill for intimacy translates to larger theatres.
23. Mary-Louise Parker, after playing L'il Bit while in her thirties, returned to the part at fifty-seven when *Drive* premiered on Broadway in 2022. David Morse played Peck at approximately forty-five and again at sixty-eight.

Chapter 4

1. Both *How to Transcend a Happy Marriage*, by Ruhl, and *Indecent*, by Vogel, were directed by Rebecca Taichman.

Notes

2. Much *Mud* criticism discusses the play in socioeconomic and feminist terms, at times portraying it as of a piece with such other English-language plays as Churchill's *Top Girls* and Vogel's *The Oldest Profession*.
3. Although the anecdote about *Dancing on My Knees* appears in several sources, I could find no record of the play ever having been produced.
4. Another way Cruz resists pigeonholing has to do with sexuality. Although identified as "openly gay" at least as early as 2003, Cruz reportedly was "not focused on gay issues as an author" (Abarbanel). This characterization has held true over the following decades.
5. Rose uses the term "marriage" loosely or even ironically because one of the relationships she discusses is the unconsummated union of John Ruskin and Effie Gray, which was annulled after Ruskin could not overcome his revulsion to his wife's pubic hair.
6. Zeus and Hera argued over which sex took more pleasure from coitus, with Zeus attributing more pleasure to the woman and Hera to the man. Tieresias, who had lived and had sex as both a man and a woman, was uniquely qualified to answer the question. After Tieresias sided with Zeus, Hera struck him blind; however, Zeus gave some recompense by awarding Tieresias second sight, or prophecy.
7. Vibrators became victims of their own success when they began appearing in pornography. They were banished from mainstream sales papers around 1930 and avidly outlawed by many state legislatures.
8. Later in this volume, Amy Muse, author of the Methuen Drama volume *The Drama and Theatre of Sarah Ruhl*, offers extended thoughts on Vogel and Ruhl.
9. Presciently anticipating Lucas Hnath's straight-to-Broadway 2017 drama, the critically acclaimed *A Doll's House, Part 2*, Zoglin singled out "experimental reworkings of Ibsen" as the fare likely to run onstage in New York.
10. *In the Heights* numbered among its supporting actors Jimmy Smits and Daphne Rubin-Vega, who had featured in the 2003 Broadway production of Nilo Cruz's *Anna in the Tropics*, creating another "House of Paula Vogel" moment.
11. For more on Hudes and Vogel as well as Hudes and music, see the Ana Fernández-Caparrós essay later in this volume.
12. The fact of Nilo Cruz interviewing Nottage for *The Dramatist*, like that of Vogel interviewing Sarah Ruhl for *BOMB*, is a moment of "House of Paula Vogel" congruence.
13. Believing that lukewarm reviews by male reviewers helped close *Sweat* and doom *Indecent* to an announcement it would close on the same day, June 25, 2017, Paula Vogel used Twitter to denounce the critics and declare her solidarity with Nottage. Chapter 5 will discuss this story in more detail.
14. For Nottage's impressions of Vogel as playwright, professor, and friend, see the 2021 interview later in this volume.

Notes

15. Nottage shared the experience of writing for musicals with fellow "House of Paula Vogel" members Cruz and Hudes.
16. All quotations in this section of this chapter, unless noted otherwise, are transcribed from the notes I made during the May 22, 2017, workshop. Any errors are inaccuracies result from writing and listening simultaneously.
17. Vogel noted that audience is not among Aristotle's essentials of drama and added, perhaps half ironically (given the chuckles from the workshop participants), that she has written many plays without an audience.
18. This suggestion calls to mind critics' comments about none of Vogel's "gods"—Guare, Fornés, and Churchill—writing the same play twice.
19. Vogel also enumerated, under "Circle" plays, "every faculty meeting I've ever attended."
20. Vogel's comments about some well-made plays may have suggested that Ibsen, Chekhov, and others have cloyed for her, a possibility she undermined by saying that "good directors have to defamiliarize" the scripts of classics.
21. Going back at least as far as Freud colleague and biographer Ernest Jones's *Hamlet and Oedipus*, the highly individuated psychology of Hamlet has been the topic of so much criticism as to become a cliché.
22. Apropos of the Greeks' use of wounded speech, Vogel commented that the eye hears and the ear sees in theatre. Our ears "see" what is told of Medea's treacherous gifts and their effects. Likewise, Sam Shepard's *The Killer's Head*, Vogel commented, is a play that has the audience "see" through their ears. Vogel also mentioned but did not elaborate upon a story of crossed perspectives when attending a performance of *Who's Afraid of Virginia Woolf?*
23. It is largely a reflection of her desire not to direct her own plays from the page, Vogel said, that prevents her from using the words "stage directions."
24. Carol Reed's 1949 film noir *The Third Man* plays an important role in Vogel's *The Baltimore Waltz*, discussed in Chapter 3.
25. Kellyanne Fitzpatrick Conway, born 1967, is the first woman to run a winning US presidential campaign.
26. In an interview on August 22, 2017, Silverstein told me he believed he may have been the first graduate student to have had Vogel on his dissertation committee. Vogel, in a August 23, 2017, tweet, affirmed, "I think so too" (@vogelpaula).
27. All quotations and paraphrases about Silverstein's experience with Vogel derive from a personal interview on August 22, 2017.
28. Among the Vogel anecdotes Silverstein shared, one involved her recommending Bert States's *Great Reckonings in Little Rooms*. This story documents Vogel's admiration for States enduring for several decades.

Notes

Chapter 5

1. The audience at the performance I attended in November 2014 in Dallas did not sing along.
2. On March 2, 2022, the Cort was renamed the James Earl Jones Theatre, prompting Vogel to tweet, "So proud to have had Indecent produced in the James Earl Jones theatre (also place where The Diary of Anne Frank premiered) 'Yes!'" (@VogelPaula).
3. Margulies won the 2000 Pulitzer Prize for Drama for *Dinner with Friends*.
4. Although the convictions were eventually overturned, the damage to the play was done.
5. Klein also noted that Taichman's work was facilitated greatly by the fact that Yale University's Beinecke Rare Book and Manuscript Library is "the repository for Asch manuscripts, memorabilia and books," including "the trial transcripts, too."
6. Vogel told the *HowlRound* livestreaming that this conversation took place five years earlier, or around 2011.
7. Observing Lemml's devotion, I tweeted to Vogel that it "suggests theatre as a sacrament that counters darkness," including censorship and anti-Semitism, to which Vogel replied, "Thank you!" Vogel then retweeted my remarks, tagging the production and *Playbill* as she did so (@VogelPaula, @IndecentBway, @playbill April 25, 2017).
8. The asterisk is Vogel's.
9. As of March 2022, this list remained available at Vogel's website.
10. *Shuffle Along, or, the Making of the Musical Sensation of 1921 and All That Followed* was a 2016 Broadway production that retold the story of *Shuffle Along*, the 1921 Black-written and Black-directed unexpected Broadway hit that helped promote several careers, including those of Josephine Baker and Paul Robeson.
11. The missing spaces between words are Vogel's, a necessity of completing her message in the 140 keystrokes then allowed per tweet.
12. Miranda indirectly supports the thesis that Vogel is the foundation of a literary "house," all but acknowledging her as the patriarch (in her case, of course, matriarch) of a theatrical "family."
13. Both *How I Learned to Drive* and another 1990s Pulitzer Prize-winning play, Edward Albee's *Three Tall Women*, premiered Off-Broadway at the Vineyard.
14. Wilder remains the only writer to win the Pulitzer for both fiction (*The Bridge of San Luis Rey* in 1927) and drama (*Our Town* in 1938 and *The Skin of Our Teeth* 1942). Lemml seems directly inspired by the narrator in *Our Town*.
15. This scene contains a departure from Asch's text, which sentences the daughter but not her mother to the brothel.

Notes

16. Beginning with the memorable 1915 season, the Provincetown Players produced some of the most important early works by Susan Glaspell, George Cram Cook, Paul Green, and a young Eugene O'Neill. Many scholars, including C. W. E. Bigsby, consider the Provincetown Players seminal in the development of modern American theatre.
17. Dramaturgically, Smith College has the most Anglo-sounding name Vogel could have chosen.
18. Many volumes have been written on the importance of 1922 as the year Sylvia Beach published James Joyce's *Ulysses* and T. S. Eliot's *The Waste Land* came out first in magazine and later in book form. The Provincetown Players' English-language performance of *God of Vengeance* belongs alongside such major literary events as these and O'Neill's *The Hairy Ape*.
19. Perhaps this line contains a reference to the infamous Zwi Migdal, an actual white slavery racket based in Buenos Aires that preyed on young Jewish women in Eastern European shtetls, promising them lives of New World wedded bliss but actually sending them to servitude and sex trafficking in a foreign country.
20. My notes indicate that O'Neill used "cracking good" at the Vineyard performance.
21. I have been unable to verify the existence of Rosen. Perhaps he is a purely imaginary character or a composite of eager fans who may have contacted Asch during his later years. The tone of Asch's response to Rosen, however, is a documented historical fact. In May 1946, Asch "announced that he ha[d] prohibited the production of his play . . . in any language in the United States and in other countries." Asch stated that "the situation described in the play is dated and exists no longer" ("Sholem Asch Bans").
22. I estimate conservatively that I have witnessed or acted in more than 200 performances of plays, and I have never seen a response like the one this evening to *Indecent*. The audience's near silence while exiting was like that of a group leaving a particularly moving temple Sabbath service.
23. "It's about damn time," Pulitzer-winner Marsha Norman (*'night, Mother* 1983) told Paulson, adding, "Thank you, universe."
24. Why, one might reasonably wonder, was this review assigned to Green by the editor at nymag.com offsoot *Vulture*?
25. *The New York Times* dismissed Charles Isherwood in February 2017.
26. Vogel was referencing Jesse Green, also of *The New York Times*.

Chapter 6

1. Rasmussen is quoted in Amy Muse, *The Drama and Theatre of Sarah Ruhl* (London: Bloomsbury Methuen Drama, 2018), 131.

Notes

2. *Dog Play* is cited, courtesy of the author, from the unpublished manuscript, 2 and 4.
3. The unpublished manuscript is quoted (20) by permission of the author.
4. This sentiment, from *100 Essays* (199), echoes Vogel's frequently declining to offer separate stage directions.
5. "Bio." *Quiara Alegría Hudes, Quiara.com.* http://www.quiara.com/bio> Accessed January 12, 2022.
6. In the published edition of Hudes's first major play, *Elliot, A Soldier's Fugue*, the writer expresses her gratitude to her mentor, specifically, for "reading Scene 1 and saying, 'Write Scene 2,' and then championing this play." Quiara Alegría Hudes, *Elliot, A Soldier's Fugue* (New York: Theatre Communications Group, 2012), viii.
7. Hudes discusses Spanglish in *My Broken Language*, 273.
8. Medieval theologians defined God as a circle of which the center is everywhere and the circumference. Emerson, for instance, attributes this statement to St. Augustine at the beginning of his essay "Circles." For an exploration of how the Elizabethan theatre constructed a secular circularity, see Charlotte Spivak, "The Elizabethan Theatre: Circle and Center" (*The Centennial Review*, 13.4: 1969), 424–43).
9. Helen Vendler, *Dickinson: Selected Poems and Commentaries* (Cambridge, MA: The Belknap Press of Harvard University Press, 2010), 431. Quotations of Emily Dickinson's poems are cued to the poem numbers of Franklin's *Reading Edition* (1999). Vendler here refers to poem 1263.
10. Quiara Alegría Hudes, *My Broken Language*, 267.
11. See Amy Muse, *The Drama and Theatre of Sarah Ruhl* (London: Methuen Drama, 2018), 70.
12. Paula Vogel, *The Baltimore Waltz and Other Plays* (New York: Theatre Communications Group, 1996), n.p.
13. "Quiara Alegría Hudes / My Broken Language." *Free Library of Philadelphia Author's Events*, 12:40.
14. Gabriela Serena Sánchez and Quiara Alegría Hudes, "Two Sisters Deliver the ATHE 2018 Conference Keynote Address" (*Theatre Topics* 29.1), March 2019, n.p. https://www.proquest.com/scholarly-journals/pausing-breathing-two-sisters-deliver- athe-2018/docview/2295413167/se-2?accountid=14777.
15. Gabriela Serena Sánchez and Quiara Alegría Hudes, "Two Sisters Deliver the ATHE 2018 Conference Keynote Address," n.p.
16. Quiara Alegría Hudes, *My Broken Language*, 278.
17. Kathleen Potts. "Water by the Spoonful: An Interview with Quiara Alegría Hudes," *Guernica: A Magazine of Art and Politics*, July 2, 2012. https://www.guernicamag.com/interviews/water-by-the-spoonful/
18. Anne García-Romero, *The Fornés Frame*, 168.

Notes

19. Tiffany Ana Lopez, "Writing Beyond Borders: A Survey of US Latino/a Drama," *A Companion to Twentieth-Century American Drama*, edited by David Krasner (Malden, MA: Blackwell Publishing, 2005), 371.
20. Patricia Ybarra, "How to Read a Latinx Play in the Twenty-first Century: Learning from Quiara Hudes" (*Theatre Topics* 27.1, 2017), 52. Alvarez and Ortuzar build on Ybarra's critical reading of lateral relationality of Hudes trilogy in her representation of extended families.
21. The name Quiara Alegría was not chosen for its meaning of joy and happiness, but to honor Puerto Rican anthropologist Ricardo Alegría, who uncovered and documented Taíno ceremonial grounds that had been silenced.

REFERENCES

Abarbanel, Jonathan. 2003. "A Conversation with Playwright Nilo Cruz." *Windy City Times*, July 9, 2003, http://www.windycitytimes.com/lgbt/A-Conversation-with-Playwright-Nilo-Cruz/3243.html.
Adams, James Trulow. 1931. *The Epic of America*. New York: Triangle Books, 1931.
Alleva, Richard. 2001. "How Sick Can We Get?" *Commonweal*, vol. 128, no. 13, July 13, pp. 17–18.
Als, Hilton. 2004. "Unnatural History." *The New Yorker*, Apr 19, 2004, https://www.newyorker.com/magazine/2004/04/19/unnatural-history-2.
Als, Hilton. 2009. "Life during Wartime." *The New Yorker*, Feb 23, 2009, www.newyorker.com/magazine/2009/03/02/life-during-wartime. Accessed Sept. 16, 2022.
Als, Hilton. 2010. "Feminist Fatale." *The New Yorker*, Mar 15, 2010, https://www.newyorker.com/magazine/2010/03/22/feminist-fatale.
Alvarez, Natalie, and Jimena Ortuzar. 2021. "Quiara Hudes's Water by the Spoonful and the Dramaturgy of Free Jazz." *Critical Perspectives on Contemporary Plays by Women: The Early Twenty-First Century*, edited by Penny Farfan and Leslie Ferris. Ann Arbor: University of Michigan Press, p. 148.
Asch, Sholem. 2021. *The God of Vengeance*. Translated by Isaac Goldberg. 1918. Rpt. Adansonia Publishing.
Aston, Elaine, and Elin Diamond, editors. 2009. *The Cambridge Companion to Caryl Churchill*. Cambridge: Cambridge University Press, 2009.
Bacalzo, Dan. 2005. "*Hot 'N' Throbbing*." *TheaterMania*, Mar 29, 2005, http://www.theatermania.com/new-york-city-theater/reviews/03-2005/hot-n-throbbing_5830.html.
Barone, Tony. 2017. "Despite Tony Wins, *Indecent* Announces Its Broadway Closing." *New York Times*, June 14, 2017, https://www.nytimes.com/2017/06/14/theater/despite-tony-wins-indecent-announces-its-broadway-closing.html.
Bigsby, C. W. E. 1982–1985. *A Critical Introduction to Twentieth-Century American Drama*, 3 vols. Cambridge: Cambridge University Press.
Bigsby, C. W. E. 1999. *Contemporary American Playwrights*. Cambridge: Cambridge University Press.
Bigsby, C. W. E. 2000. *Modern American Drama, 1945–2000*. Cambridge: Cambridge University Press.
Brantley, Ben. 1993. "Iago's Subterfuge Is Made the Truth." *New York Times*, Nov. 12, 1993, http://www.nytimes.com/1993/11/12/theater/review-theater-iago-s-subterfuge-is-made-the-truth.html.

References

Brantley, Ben. 1997. "A Pedophile Even Mother Could Love." Rev. of *How I Learned to Drive*. New York Times, Mar. 17, 1997, http://www.nytimes.com/1997/03/17/theater/a-pedophile-even-mother-could-love.html.

Brantley, Ben. 2003. "The Poetry of Yearning, The Artistry of Seduction." *New York Times*, Nov. 17, 2003, http://www.nytimes.com/2003/11/17/theater/theater-review-the-poetry-of-yearning-the-artistry-of-seduction.html.

Brantley, Ben. 2004. "Portrait of Working Girls Who Work No More." *New York Times*, Sept. 27, 2004, http://www.nytimes.com/2004/09/27/theater/reviews/portrait-of-working-girls-who-are-girls-no-more.html?r=0.

Brantley, Ben. 2008. "Ladies Who Lunch? No, Here's to the Power Players." *New York Times*, May 8, 2008, http://www.nytimes.com/2008/05/08/theater/reviews/08girl.html.

Brantley, Ben. 2009. "War Terrors, Through a Brothel Window." Review of *Ruined*, by Lynn Nottage. *The New York Times*, Feb. 10, 2009, http://www.nytimes.com/2009/02/11/theater/reviews/11bran.html.

Brantley, Ben. 2015. "Review: Cloud Nine, a Comedy of Fluid and Complicated Couplings." *New York Times*, Nov 1, 2015, https://www.nytimes.com/2015/10/06/theater/review-cloud-nine-a-comedy-of-fluid-and-complicated-couplings.html?rref=collection%2Ftimestopic%2FChurchill%2C%20Caryl&action=click&contentCollection=timestopics&region=stream&module=stream_unit&version=latest&contentPlacement=3&pgtype=collection.

Brantley, Ben. 2017. "Review: *Indecent* Pays Heartfelt Tribute to a Stage Scandal." *New York Times*, Apr. 18, 2017, https://www.nytimes.com/2017/04/18/theater/indecent-review-paula-vogel-broadway.html.

Brunner, Jeryl. 2017. "Broadway's Greatest Stars and Their Creatives Reveal Their Inspirations." *Parade*, July 3. 2017, https://parade.com/582638/jerylbrunner/broadways-greatest-stars-and-creatives-reveal-their-inspirations/.

Bryer, Jackson R. 1995. *The Playwright's Art: Conversations with Contemporary American Dramatists*. New Brunswick: Rutgers University Press, 1995.

Bryer, Jackson R., and Mary C. Hartig. 2010. *The Facts on File Companion to American Drama*, 2nd ed. New York: Facts on File, Inc., 2010.

Casey, Carolyn Craig. 2004. *Women Pulitzer Playwrights*. Jefferson: McFarland, 2004.

Chow, Andrew R. 2017. "Paula Vogel to Host Free Playwriting Workshop." May 14, 2017, https://www.nytimes.com/2017/05/14/theater/paula-vogel-to-host-free-playwriting-workshop.html?smid=tw-nytimesarts&smtyp=cur&_r=0.

Churchill, Caryl. 1982. *Top Girls*. London: Methuen, 1982.

Churchill, Caryl. 1994. *Cloud 9*. New York: Theatre Communications Group, 1994.

Churchill, Caryl. 1999. "Poem for María Irene Fornés." *Conducting a Life: Reflections on the Theatre of María Irene Fornés*. New York: Smith and Kraus, p. xiv.

Clay, Carolyn. 1998. "*Drive*, She Said." *The Boston Phoenix*, May 14–21, 1998, http://www.bostonphoenix.com/archive/theater/98/05/14/PAULA_VOGEL.html.

Clement, Olivia. 2017. "Daryl Roth on the 'Gutsy' Move to Extend *Indecent* after Announcing Its Closing." *Playbill*, July 13, 2017, http://www.playbill.com/

References

article/daryl-roth-on-the-gutsy-move-to-extend-indecent-after-announcing-its-closing.

Clement, Olivia. 2017. "How One Hopeful Cold Call Became Broadway's *Indecent*." *Playbill*, Apr. 10, 2017, http://www.playbill.com/article/how-one-hopeful-cold-call-became-broadways-indecent.

Clement, Olivia. 2017. "The Myth of Angry Feminism." *Lenny Letter*, Aug. 11, 2017, http://www.lennyletter.com/culture/interviews/a948/paula-vogel-playwright-interview/.

"A Collective Call against Critical Bias." *HowlRound*, June 26, 2017, http://howlround.com/a-collective-call-against-critical-bias.

Cruz, Nilo. 2003. "The Alphabet of Smoke." *Anna in the Tropics*. New York: Dramatists Play Service, 2003, pp. 5–12.

Cruz, Nilo. 2003. *Anna in the Tropics*. New York: Dramatists Play Service, 2003.

Cruz, Nilo. 2016. "Art Talk with Playwright Nilo Cruz." Rebecca Sutton. *Art Works Blog*, Oct. 20, 2016, https://www.arts.gov/art-works/2016/art-talk-playwright-nilo-cruz.

Cruz, Nilo. 2004. "Nilo Cruz by Emily Mann." *Bomb*, Winter 2004, http://bombmagazine.org/article/2626/nilo-cruz.

Cruz, Nilo, and Erika Munk. 2003. "The Children are the Angels Here." *Theater*, vol. 33, no. 2, pp. 62–3. Project MUSE, muse.jhu.edu/article/44363.

Cummings, Scott T. 2013. *María Irene Fornés*. London: Routledge.

Cummings, Scott T. 2013. "María Irene Fornés." *The Methuen Drama Guide to Contemporary American Playwrights*, edited by Martin Middeke, Peter Paul Schnierer, Christopher Innes, and Matthew C. Roudané. New York: Bloomsbury.

Daniels, Robert L. 1997. "Review: *How I Learned to Drive*." *Variety*, Mar. 29, 1997, http://variety.com/1997/legit/reviews/how-i-learned-to-drive-2-1200449074/.

Decaul, Maurice. 2017. "David Rabe and Quiara Alegría Hudes Enter the Breach." *American Theatre*, Mar. 2017, http://www.americantheatre.org/2017/02/22/david-rabe-and-quiara-alegria-hudes-enter-the-breach/.

Dickinson, Peter. 2010. *World Stages, Local Audiences: Essays on Performance, Place, and Politics*. Manchester: University of Manchester Press, 2010.

Dolan, Jill. 1998. "*How I Learned to Drive* – Performance Review." Rev. of *How I Learned to Drive*, by Paula Vogel. *Theatre Journal*, vol. 50, no. 1, pp. 127–8.

Egan, Caroline. 1998. "The Playwright's Playwright: Who's Best at Making a Drama Out of a Crisis?" *The Guardian*, Sept. 21, 1998. ProQuest, http://ezproxy.gsu.edu/login?url=http://search.proquest.com/docview/244533528?accountid=11226. Accessed Jan. 26, 2017.

Emerson, Ralph Waldo. 1983. *Essays & Lectures*. New York: The Library of America, 1983.

Emmrich, Stuart (@StuartEmmrichNY). 2016. "Celeb spotting at #Indecent, picking up tix at Vineyard box office. 'John Guare. That's G-U-A-R-E.' The Woman at Window didn't Blink an Eye." *Twitter*, May 21, 2016, 11:55 a.m., https://twitter.com/StuartEmmrichNY/status/734095312042790912.

"Esteemed Playwright Named 2007 'Genius.'" *NPR*, Sept. 25, 2007, http:www.npr.org/templates/story/story.php?storyId=14683563.

References

Falconer, Morgan. 2010. "Sidney Poitier Was My Father, Believe It or Not." *Times, the (United Kingdom)*, Jan 9, 2010, p. 4. EBSCOhost, ezproxy.gsu.edu/login?url-http://search.ebscohost.com/login.aspx?direct=true&db=nfh&AN=7EH31320077&site=eds-live.

Fierberg, Ruthie. 2017. "Playwright Paula Vogel Examines Her Jewish Identity Through *Indecent*." *Playbill*, Apr. 24, 2017, http://www.playbill.com/article/playwright-paula-vogel-examines-her-jewish-identity-through-indecent.

Fornés, María Irene. 1984. "María Irene Fornés by Allen Frame." *Bomb*, Oct. 1, 1984, https://bombmagazine.org/articles/maria-irene-Fornés/. Accessed Feb. 19, 2022.

Fornés, María Irene. 1986. "*Mud*." *Maria Irene Fornés Plays*. New York: PAJ Publications, pp. 3–40.

Fornés, María Irene. 1990. *Fefu and Her Friends*. New York: PAJ Publications.

García-Romero, Anne. 2016. *The Fornés Frame: Contemporary Latina Playwrights and the legacy of Maria Irene Fornés*. Tucson: The University of Arizona Press.

Gener, Randy. 2005. "Paula Vogel Faces Her Critics." *American Theatre*, Apr., p. 15.

Gener, Randy. 2010. "In Defense of *Ruined*: 5 Elements That Shaped Lynn Nottage's Masterwork." *American Theatre*, Oct., pp. 118–22.

Gerard, Jermy. 1993. "Review: *And Baby Makes Seven*." *Variety*, May 11, 1993, http://variety.com/1993/legit/reviews/and-baby-makes-seven-1200432275/.

Gerard, Jermy. 1993. "Review: *Desdemona: A Play about a Handkerchief*." *Variety*, Nov. 21, 1993, http://variety.com/1993/film/reviews/desdemona-a-play-about-a-handkerchief-1200434290/.

Glab, Keith. 2013. "Review of *Desdemona: A Play about a Handkerchief*." *Chicago Theatre Beat*, Mar. 16, 2013, http://chicagotheaterbeat.com/2013/03/16/review-desdemona-a-play-about-a-handkerchief-sea-change-theatre/#review.

Goldenberg, Suzanne. 2006. "Too Pretty for Prison." *The Guardian*, Mar. 23, 2006, https://www.theguardian.com/world/2006/mar/24/usa.gender.

Gordon, David. 2016. "Paula Vogel's Acclaimed Drama *Indecent* Will Move to Broadway." *TheaterMania*, Oct. 26, 2016, http://www.theatermania.com/broadway/news/indecent-paula-vogel-broadway_78936.html?utm_source=twitter&utm_medium=social&utm_campaign=26oct2016.

Green, Jesse. 2017. "Theatre Review: A Holocaust Meta-History, in Paula Vogel's *Indecent*." *Vulture*, Apr. 18, 2017, http://www.vulture.com/2017/04/theater-a-holocaust-meta-history-in-paula-vogels-indecent.html.

Gregg, Stacey. 2016. *Scorch*. London: Nick Hern Books.

Grode, Eric. 2013. "Vogel's *And Baby Makes Seven* Is Revived." *New York Times*, Apr. 12, 2013, https://www.nytimes.com/2014/03/26/theater/paula-vogels-and-baby-makes-seven-is-revived.html.

Guare, John. 1971. *The House of Blue Leaves*. New York: S. French.

Guare, John. 1994. *Six Degrees of Separation*. New York: Vintage.

Gussow, Mel. 1993. "Parents-to-Be Regress to Childhood." *New York Times*, May 7, 1993, http://www.nytimes.com/1993/05/07/theater/review-theater-parents-to-be-regress-to-childhood.html.

References

Gussow, Mel. 2003. "Nilo Cruz's 'Anna Karenina' Lights the Cubans' Cigars." *New York Times*, Sept. 14, 2003, http://www.nytimes.com/2003/09/14/theater/theater-nilo-cruz-s-anna-karenina-lights-the-cubans-cigars.html.

Hanover, Lauren Bloom. 2016. "Leaving Us in the Light: The Power of Sarah Ruhl." *Breaking Character: A Concord Theatricals Publication*, Oct. 18, 2016, https://www.breakingcharacter.com/home/2019/4/8/leaving-us-in-the-light-the-power-of-sarah-ruhl.

"Hans Hofmann Biography, Art, and Analysis of Works." 2017. *The Art Story*, The Art Story Foundation, www.theartstory.org/artist-hofmann-hans.htm.

Hardy, Thomas. 2015. "The Ruined Maid." Edited by Edgar V. Roberts and Robert Zweig. *Literature: An Introduction to Reading and Writing*. Compact 6th ed. London: Pearson, pp. 907–8.

Heilpern, John. 2000. *How Good Is David Mamet, Anyway? Writings on Theatre and Why It Matters*. London: Routledge.

Hemingway, Ernest. 2021. "Soldier's Home." *In Our Time*. Independently Published, pp. 41–47.

Herren, Graley. 2010. "Narrating, Witnessing, and Healing Trauma in Paula Vogel's *How I Learned to Drive*." *Modern Drama*, vol. 53, no. 1, pp. 103–14.

Herren, Graley. 2013. "A Conversation with Paula Vogel." *Text and Presentation 2012*. McFarland & Company. Comparative Drama Conference Series. EBSCOhost, ezproxy.gsu.edu/login?url=http://search.ebscohost.com/login.aspx?direct=true&db=nlebk&AN=509391&site=eds-live.

Hetrick, Adam. 2017. "Broadway's *Indecent* Sets November Air Date on PBS *Great Performances*." *Playbill*, Aug. 16, 2017, http://www.playbill.com/article/broadways-indecent-sets-november-air-date-on-pbs-great-performances.

Hodges, Ben. 2009. "Nilo Cruz: Distilled to Its Essence." *American Theatre Wing Presents "The Play That Changed My Life,"* edited by Ben A. Hodges, 13–19. Milwaukee: Hal Leonard Corporation.

Holmberg, Arthur. 1998. "Through the Eyes of Lolita." *American Repertory Theater*. Mag., Sept. 18, 1998, http://americanrepertorytheater.org/inside/articles/through-eyes-lolita.

Horwitz, Simi. 2001. "Paula Vogel, Not Pulitzer Winner, But Playwright Getting Out of the Way." *Backstage*, 21, 2001, https://www.backstage.com/news/paula-vogel-not-pulitzer-winner-but-playwright-getting-out-of-the-way-this-is-the-second-part-of-a-two-part-interview-which-began-in-last-weeks-issue/.

Hudes, Quiara Alegría. 2012. *Elliot, A Soldier's Fugue*. New York: Theatre Communications Group.

Hudes, Quiara Alegría. 2012. *Water by the Spoonful*. New York: Theatre Communications Group, 2012.

Hudes, Quiara Alegría. 2014. *The Happiest Song Plays Last*. New York: Theatre Communications Group.

Hudes, Quiara Alegría. 2016. "An Interview with Quiara Alegría Hudes." *Victoria Myers*, May 16, 2016, http://theintervalny.com/interviews/2016/05/an-interview-with-quiara-alegria-hudes/.

Hudes, Quiara Alegría (@quiarahudes). 2017. "This Week in Broadway Feminist Joy: 1. @Lynnbrooklyn Receives Second Pulitzer 2. @VogelPaula Opens

References

Indecent Pens Out, Historians!" *Twitter*, Apr. 18, 2017, 5:56 p.m., https://twitter.com/quiarahudes/status/854499024568815616.

Hudes, Quiara Alegría. 2017. http://www.quiara.com/bio. Accessed Sept. 14, 2017.

Hudes, Quiara Alegría. 2021. *My Broken Language*. London: William Collins.

Huerta, Jorge. 2008. "From the Margins to the Mainstream: Latino/a Theater in the U.S." *Studies in Twentieth and Twenty-First Century Literature*, vol. 32, no. 2, p. 463.

Hull, Deborah. 2016. Love on the Stage, War on the Page: Evaluating the Role of War Trauma in "How I Learned to Drive." Thesis, Georgia State University, http://scholarworks.gsu.edu/english_theses/200.

Iqbal, Nosheen. 2010. "Lynn Nottage: A Bar, a Brothel and Brecht." *The Guardian*, Apr. 20, 2010, https://www.theguardian.com/stage/2010/apr/20/lynn-nottage-ruined.

Isherwood, Charles. 2006. "A Comic Impudence Softens a Tale of Loss." *New York Times*, Oct. 3, 2006, https://www.nytimes.com/2006/10/03/theater/reviews/03eury.html.

Isherwood, Charles. 2009. "Beyond Electricity, Toward Female Emancipation." Rev. of *In the Next Room*, by Sarah Ruhl. *The New York Times*, Nov. 20, 2009, http://www.nytimes.com/2009/11/20/theater/reviews/20innextroom.html.

Isherwood, Charles. 2013. "An Extended Family, Sharing Extended Pain." Rev. of *Water by the Spoonful*, by Quiara Alegría Hudes. *New York Times*, Jan. 8, 2013, http://www.nytimes.com/2013/01/09/theater/reviews/water-by-the-spoonful-at-the-second-stage-theater.html.

Isherwood, Charles. 2016. "Review: *Indecent* Revisits a Play Colliding with Broadway Mores and More." *New York Times*, May 17, 2016, https://www.nytimes.com/2016/05/18/theater/review-indecent-revisits-a-play-colliding-with-broadway-mores-and-more.html.

Janardanan, Dipa. 2007. *Images of Loss in Tennessee Williams's "The Glass Menagerie," Arthur Miller's "Death of a Salesman," Marsha Norman's "'night, Mother," and Paula Vogel's "How I Learned to Drive."* Diss. Georgia State University, English Dissertations.

Johnson, Katie N. "When Lesbian Love Came to Broadway." *The Gay & Lesbian Review*, glreview.org/article/article-54/.

Johnson, Malcolm L. 1993. "Yale Rep's *Baltimore Waltz* Fluid But Drawn Out." May 8, 1993, http://articles.courant.com/1993-05-08/features/0000102321_1_baltimore-waltz-vogel-wojewodski.

Johnson, Reed. 2003. "'Anna in the Tropics' a Combustible Drama." *Los Angeles Times*, Oct. 6, 2003, http://articles.latimes.com/2003/oct/06/entertainment/et-johnson6.

Jones, Chris. 2011. "At Victory Gardens, the Pleasures and Perils of Electrified Desire." Rev. of *In the Next Room*, by Sarah Ruhl. *Chicago Tribune*, Sept. 21, 2011, http://www.chicagotribune.com/ct-ent-0921-vibrator-review-20110921-column.html.

Jones, Chris. 2022. "Broadway Review: Sex Abuse Drama "How I Learned to Drive" is as Unsettling Now as It was When It Broke Ground 25 years Ago." *New York Daily News*, Apr. 19, 2022, https://www.nydailynews.com

References

/entertainment/broadway/ny-broadway-review-how-i-learned-to-drive-20220420-sxxk7oietbem5i2tglbag3bowm-story.html.

Karinthy, Frigyes. 2014. "Chain-Links." Translated by Adam Makkai, Nov. 17, 2014, http://djjr-courses.wdfiles.com/local--files/soc180%3Akarinthy-chain-links/Karinthy-Chain-Links_1929.pdf.

Kennedy, Mark. 2017. "Don't Ask Where Paula Vogel Is, Ask Where Isn't She." *AP News*, Apr. 19, 2017, https://apnews.com/3d5086dc60624332b8889833994cd963/dont-ask-where-paula-vogel-ask-where-isnt-she.

Kent, Assunta Bartolomucci. 1996. *Maria Irene Fornés and Her Critics*. Westport: Greenwood Press.

Kimbrough, Andrew. 2002. "The Pedophile in Me: The Ethics of *How I Learned to Drive*." *Journal of Dramatic Theory and Criticism*, vol. 16, no. 2, Spring, pp. 47–67.

Klein, Alvin. 2000. "Theater; Another Take on a Yiddish Play." *New York Times*, Apr. 30, 2000, http://www.nytimes.com/2000/04/30/nyregion/theater-another-take-on-a-yiddish-play.html.

Krasner, David. 2006. *American Drama 1945–2000: An Introduction*. Hoboken: Blackwell Publishing.

Kritzer, Amelia. 1991. *The Plays of Caryl Churchill: Theatre of Empowerment*. London: Palgrave Macmillan, 1991.

Lahr, John. 2008. "Surreal Life: The Plays of Sarah Ruhl." *New Yorker*, Mar. 17, 2008, https://www.newyorker.com/magazine/2008/03/17/surreal-life.

Lahr, John. 2009. "Good Vibrations." Rev. of *In the Next Room*, by Sarah Ruhl. *The New Yorker*, Nov. 30, 2009, https://www.newyorker.com/magazine/2009/11/30/good-vibrations-2.

Lahr, John. 2016. "Act of Grace." *The New Yorker*, Dec. 19 and 26, 2016, pp. 52–64.

Levitt, Hayley. 2018. "Paula Vogel's National Ubu Roi Bake-Off Blends Playwriting With Activism." *TheaterMania*, Jan. 26, 2018, www.theatermania.com/new-york-city-theater/news/paula-vogel-national-ubu-roi-bake-off_83853.html.

Lewis, Christian. 2022. "'How I Learned To Drive' is a Nuanced Exploration of Memory." *Did They Like It?* Apr. 19, 2022, https://didtheylikeit.com/shows/how-i-learned-to-drive-2/how-i-learned-to-drive-is-a-nuanced-exploration-of-memory/.

"Livestreaming a Reading of Paula Vogel's *Indecent*." Martin E. Segal Theatre Center, Apr. 18, 2016, http://howlround.com/livestreaming-paula-vogels-indecent-martin-e-segal-theatre-center-mon-april-18.

Lopez, Tiffany Ana. 2005. "Writing Beyond Borders: A Survey of US Latino/a Drama." *A Companion to Twentieth-Century American Drama*, edited by David Krasner. Malden: Blackwell Publishing.

Low, David. 2015. "Writing the Untold Stories." *Wesleyan*, May 5, 2015, http://magazine.wesleyan.edu/2015/05/05/writing-the-untold-stories/.

Lunden, Jeff. 2017. "Yale Repertory Marks 50 Years as a Theater Incubator." *NPR*, Jan. 18, 2017, http://www.npr.org/2017/01/18/509734619/yale-repertory-marks-50-years-as-a-theater-incubator.

Maines, Rachel. 1999. *The Technology of Orgasm*. Baltimore: The Johns Hopkins University Press.

References

Mandell, Jonathan. 2022. "American Connected Theater Awards for Pandemic Year 2." *New York Theater*, Mar. 11, 2022, newyorktheater.me/2022/03/11/american-connected-theater-awards-for-pandemic-year-2/.

Mansbridge, Joanna. 2012. "Memory's Dramas, Modernity's Ghosts: Thornton Wilder, Japanese Theater, and Paula Vogel's The Long Christmas Ride Home." *Comparative Drama*, vol. 46, no. 2, Summer, pp. 209–35. doi:10.1353/cdr.2012.0022.

Mansbridge, Joanna. 2013. "Paula Vogel." *The Methuen Drama Guide to Contemporary American Playwrights*, edited by Martin Middeke, Peter Paul Schnierer, Christopher Innes, and Matthew C. Roudané. London: Bloomsbury, pp. 372–90.

Mansbridge, Joanna. 2014. *Paula Vogel*. Ann Arbor: University of Michigan Press.

"Mary-Louise Parker and David Morse Revisit Roles in 'How I Learned To Drive.'" 2022. *Spectrum News NY1*, Apr. 30, 2022, https://www.ny1.com/nyc/all-boroughs/on-stage-episodes/2022/04/30/mary-louise-parker-and-david-morse-revisit-roles-in--how-i-learned-to-drive-#.

McAuliffe, Jody. 2000. "Interview with Nilo Cruz." *South Atlantic Quarterly*, vol. 99, no. 2–3, pp. 461–70.

McCasland, Steven Carl, Drama Book Shop. 2016. "Live with Paula Vogel and Beck Taichman." *Facebook*, June 10, 2016, 5:00 p.m., https://www.facebook.com/dramabookshop/videos/1045287582225464. Accessed June 20, 2016.

McPhee, Ryan. 2017. "*Indecent* Will Be Film for Future Broadway HD Release." *Playbill*, Aug. 3, 2017, http://www.playbill.com/article/indecent-will-be-filmed-for-future-broadwayhd-release.

Miller, Stuart. 2014. "A Sort of Homecoming." *American Theatre*, Jan 2014: 86–90.

Miranda, Lin-Manuel (@Lin_Manuel). 2016. "@VogelPaula @Lynnbrooklyn @beyondabsurdity honored to be in YOURS, maestro, thank you. About to see our mutual homey Quiara!" *Twitter*, Feb. 22, 2016, 9:01 a.m., https://twitter.com/lin_manuel/status/701814134363570176.

Mobley, Jennifer-Scott. 2018. "Review of *Indecent*, by Paula Vogel." *Theatre Journal*, vol. 70 no. 2, pp. 249–51. Project MUSE, doi:10.1353/tj.2018.0037.

Moroff, Diane Lynn. 1996. *Fornés: Theater in the Present Tense*. Ann Arbor: University of Michigan Press.

Morse, David. 1997. "Charlie Rose June 19, 1997: A Conversation about the Play, How I Learned to Drive." Charlie Rose, 2007. DVD.

Muñoz, José Esteban. 2007. "'Chico, what does it feel like to be a problem?' The Transmission of Brownness." *A Companion to Latina/o Studies*, edited by Juan Flores and Renato Rosaldo. Hoboken: Blackwell, pp. 441–51.

Murphy, Brenda, ed. 1999. *The Cambridge Companion to American Women Playwrights*. Cambridge: Cambridge University Press.

Muse, Amy. 2018. *The Drama and Theatre of Sarah Ruhl*. London: Bloomsbury Methuen Drama.

Nabokov, Vladimir. 1973. *Strong Opinions*. New York: McGraw-Hill.

"National UBU ROI Bake-Off." *Paula Vogel*, paulavogelplaywright.com/ubu-bake-off.

"Nilo Cruz & Lynn Nottage." *Dramatist*, Mar 2010, pp. 20–8.

References

Noh, David. 2017. "Paula Vogel on Broadway with *Indecent*." *Gay City News*, Mar. 16, 2017, https://gaycitynews.nyc/paula-vogel-broadway-indecent/.

Nottage, Lynn. 2006. *Intimate Apparel*. New York: Theatre Communications Group.

Nottage, Lynn. 2010. *Ruined*. New York: Dramatists Play Service.

Nottage, Lynn (@Lynnbrooklyn). 2016. "Just Saw #Indecent @VogelPaula new play @vineyardtheatre Poetic & poignant. Gorgeously staged. Was totally taken." *Twitter*, June 9, 2016, 7:33 a.m., https://twitter.com/Lynnbrooklyn/status/740914600871395328.

Nottage, Lynn (@Lynnbrooklyn). 2017. "The Patriarchy Flexing their Muscles to Prove their Power." *Twitter*, June 14, 2017, 1:36 p.m., https://twitter.com/Lynnbrooklyn/status/875089690143203328.

Nottage, Lynn (@Lynnbrooklyn). 2021. ".@Twitter has Decided that I'm not Verifiable. 🙄 . Guess I have not Quite yet Accomplished Enough to be of Public Interest." *Twitter*, July 6, 2021, 1:17 p.m., https://twitter.com/lynnbrooklyn/status/1412460772131753988.

Nussbaum, Emily. 2016. "Inside Out." *New Yorker*, Jan. 4, 2016, https://www.newyorker.com/magazine/2016/01/04/inside-out-on-television-emily-nussbaum.

Paran, Janice, moderator. 2011. "An Evening with Nilo Cruz." *TCG Playwrights in Conversation: Discussions and Readings*, Dec. 5, 2011, http://www.thegreenespace.org/events/thegreenespace/2011/dec/05/evening-nilo-cruz/.

Parker, Mary-Louise. 1997. "Paula Vogel." *BOMB Magazine 61*, Fall 1997, http://bombmagazine.org/article/2108/paula-vogel.

"Paula Vogel on The Baltimore Waltz." *YouTube*, Mar. 27, 2017, https://www.youtube.com/watch?v=Mkj7NC9AU4w.

"Paula Vogel Explains the Magic of The Vineyard." *YouTube*, June 28, 2016, www.youtube.com/watch?v=T9lq0fWs33c.

"Paula Vogel to Receive Lifetime Achievement Award at the 62nd Annual Obie Awards." *Obie Awards*, Apr. 27, 2017, http://www.obieawards.com/2017/04/2017-lifetime-achievement-paula-vogel/.

"Paula Vogel's BARD AT THE GATE Is a Startup Play-Reading Series." *Bard at the Gate*, www.bardatthegate.org/about.

Paulson, Michael. 2017. "Two Female Playwrights Arrive on Broadway: What Took So Long?" *New York Times*, Mar. 22, 2017, https://www.nytimes.com/2017/03/22/theater/lynn-nottage-paula-vogel-broadway.html?smid=tw-share&_r=0.

Paulson, Michael. 2020. "Advocating, Agitating, Connecting, Inventing: [Arts and Leisure Desk]." *New York Times*, Dec. 27, 2020. ProQuest, https://www.proquest.com/newspapers/advocating-agitating-connecting-inventing/docview/2472756641/se-2?accountid=11226.

Pellegrini, Ann. 2005. "Repercussions and Remainders in the Plays of Paula Vogel: An Essay in Five Moments." *A Companion to Twentieth-Century American Drama*, edited by David Krasner. Hoboken: Blackwell, pp. 473–85.

Phillips, Maya. 2022. "'How I Learned to Drive' Review: Many Miles to Go Before a Reckoning." *New York Times*, Apr. 19, 2022, https://www.nytimes.com/2022/04/19/theater/how-i-learned-to-drive-review.html.

References

Plato. 1973. *Theatetus*, translated with notes by John McDowell. Oxford: Clarendon Press.

Plunka, Gene A. 2001. *The Black Comedy of John Guare*. Dover: University of Delaware Press.

Poandl, Michael. 2015. "*The Oldest Profession* at Rainbow Theatre Project." *DC Metro Theater Arts*, June 8, 2015, http://dcmetrotheaterarts.com/2015/06/08/the-oldest-profession-at-rainbow-theatre-project/.

Polin, Sophia. 2014. "Review *And Baby Makes Seven*." *StageBuddy*, Mar. 31, 2014, https://stagebuddy.com/theater/theater-review/review-baby-makes-seven.

Pollack-Pelzner, Daniel (@pollackpelzner). 2017. "With Her Eerily Timed *Indecent*, Paula Vogel Unsettles American Theatre Again." *New Yorker*, May 12, 2017, https://www.newyorker.com/books/page-turner/with-her-eerily-timely-indecent-paula-vogel-unsettles-american-theatre-again.

Pollack-Pelzner, Daniel (@pollackpelzner). 2021. "The Ashes Falling from the Sleeves of the Troupe at the Top of @VogelPaula's INDECENT as They Rise from the Dead to tell Asch's Story." *Twitter*, Mar. 19, 2021, 11:44 p.m., https://twitter.com/pollackpelzner/status/1373118267351441408.

Potts, Kathleen. 2012. "Water by the Spoonful: An Interview with Quiara Alegría Hudes." *Guernica: A Magazine of Art and Politics*, July 02, 2012, https://www.guernicamag.com/interviews/water-by-the-spoonful/

"A Prize-Winning Playwright: Interview with Paula Vogel." *PBS NewsHour*. Introduction by Elizabeth Farnsworth. MacNeil/Lehrer Productions, Apr. 16, 1998, http://www.pbs.org/newshour/bb/entertainment-jan-june98-play_4-16/.

"Pulitzer Prize Winning Playwright Lynn Nottage Celebrates Having 3 Shows Running In NYC At The Same Time." *CBS News*, Jan. 13, 2022, www.cbsnews.com/newyork/news/lynn-nottage-clydes-mj-the-musical-intimate-apparel/.

Purcell, Carey. 2014. "Paula Vogel's *And Baby Makes Seven* Opens March 23 at New Ohio Theatre." *Playbill*, Mar. 23, 2014, http://www.playbill.com/article/paula-vogels-and-baby-makes-seven-opens-march-23-at-new-ohio-theatre-com-216304.

"Quiara Alegría Hudes / My Broken Language." 2021. *Free Library of Philadelphia Author's Events, YouTube*, Apr. 8, 2021. https://www.youtube.com/watch?v=63Rl3Xe8BtQ, (46:53).

Rebellato, Dan. 2009. "On Churchill's Influences." *The Cambridge Companion to Caryl Churchill*, edited by Elaine Aston and Elin Diamond. Cambridge: Cambridge University Press, pp. 163–79.

Rich, Frank. 1992. "Play About AIDS Uses Fantasy World To Try To Remake The World." *New York Times*, Feb. 12, 1992, http://www.nytimes.com/1992/02/12/theater/review-theater-play-about-aids-uses-fantasy-world-to-try-to-remake-the-world.html.

"Role Models." *Advocate*, no. 778, Feb 2, 1999, p. 42. EBSCOhost, ezproxy.gsu.edu/login?url=http://search.ebscohost.com/login.aspx?direct=true&db=fth&AN=1484532&site=eds-live.

Román, David. 2014. "The Happiest Song Plays Last by Quiara Alegría Hudes, directed by Edward Torres, and Water by the Spoonful by Quiara Alegría

References

Hudes, directed by Davis McCallum" (performance reviews). *Theatre Journal*, vol. 66, no. 1, p. 149.

Rooney, David. 2004. "Review: *The Oldest Profession*." *Variety*, Sept. 26, 2004, http://variety.com/2004/legit/reviews/the-oldest-profession-1200530792/.

Rosenfeld, Megan. 1999. "One 'Hot' Property." *The Washington Post*, Sept. 12, 1999, https://www.washingtonpost.com/archive/lifestyle/style/1999/09/12/one-hot-property/cb2d4e37-5b22-4aae-badf-438b7ebe255d/?utm_term=.e26e5fa45a6f.

Roudané, Matthew. 1996. *American Drama Since 1960*. Woodbridge: Twayne.

Rousuck, J. Wynn. 1992. "*Baltimore Waltz* Is a Funny, Moving Drama about AIDS." *Baltimore Sun*, Apr. 9, 1992, http://articles.baltimoresun.com/1992-04-09/features/1992100211_1_baltimore-waltz-set-in-baltimore-dutch-boy.

Rousuck, J. Wynn. 1999. "Taking on Domestic Violence." Review *Hot 'N' Throbbing*. *The Baltimore Sun*, Sept. 13, 1999 http://articles.baltimoresun.com/1999-09-13/features/9909130082_1_rhea-seehorn-charlene-hot-n-throbbing.

Rousuck, J. Wynn. 2008. "A Critic Infiltrates Paula Vogel's Boot Camp." *American Theatre*, Dec. 2008: 48–52.

Rowen, Bess. 2014. "Ruhls of Play: An Interview with Sarah Ruhl." *Huffington Post*, Feb. 17, 2014, https://www.huffpost.com/entry/ruhls-of-play-an-intervie_b_4805944.

Rowen, Bess. 2018. "Undigested Reading: Rethinking Stage Directions Through Affect." *Theatre Journal*, vol. 70, no. 3, Sept., pp. 307–26.

Ruhl, Sarah. 2006. "Eurydice." *The Clean House and Other Plays*. New York: Theatre Communications Group, pp. 325–435.

Ruhl, Sarah. 2008. *Dead Man's Cell Phone*. New York: Theatre Communications Group.

Ruhl, Sarah. 2009. "*The Baltimore Waltz* and the Plays of My Childhood." *The Play That Changed My Life*, edited by Ben A. Hodges. New York: Applause Books. pp. 119–28.

Ruhl, Sarah. 2010. *In the Next Room or the Vibrator Play*. New York: Theatre Communications Group.

Ruhl, Sarah. 2014. *100 Essays I Don't Have Time to Write*. New York: Faber & Faber.

Ruhl, Sarah. 2014. *Dear Elizabeth*. New York: Faber and Faber.

Ruhl, Sarah. 2016. *The Oldest Boy*. New York: Farrar, Straus and Giroux.

Ruhl, Sarah. 2016. *Scenes from Court Life or the Whipping Boy and His Prince*. Unpublished play manuscript, courtesy of the author, 1.

Ruhl, Sarah. 2018. *For Peter Pan on Her 70th Birthday*. New York: Theatre Communications Group, p. xvii.

Ruhl, Sarah. 2019. *How to Transcend a Happy Marriage*. New York: Theatre Communications Group.

Saddik, Annette J. 2007. *Contemporary American Drama*. Edinburgh: Edinburgh University Press.

Sánchez, Gabriela Serena, and Quiara Alegría Hudes. 2019. "Two Sisters Deliver the ATHE 2018 Conference Keynote Address." *Theatre Topics*, vol. 29, no. 1, 2019, n.p., https://www.proquest.com/scholarly-journals/pausing-breathing-two-sisters-deliver-athe-2018/docview/2295413167/se-2?accountid=14777.

Savran, David. 1998. "Driving Ms. Vogel." *American Theatre*, vol. 15, no. 8, p. 16.

References

Savran, David. 1988. *In Their Own Words: Conversations with American Playwrights*. New York: Theatre Communications Group.

Savran, David. "Loose Screws, 1996." Paula Vogel. *The Baltimore Waltz and Other Plays*. New York: Theatre Communications Group, pp. ix–xv.

Schulman, Michael. 2017. "The Listener." *The New Yorker*, Mar. 27, 2017, pp. 30–3.

Shakespeare, William. 1974. *Othello. The Riverside Shakespeare*. Edited by G. Blakemore Evans, Harry Levin, Herschel Baker, Anne Barton, Frank Kermode, Hallett Smith, Marie Edel, and Charles H. Shattuck. Boston: Houghton Mifflin, pp. 1198–248.

Shepard, Alan, and Mary Lamb. 2002. "The Memory Palace in Paula Vogel's Plays." *Southern Women Playwrights: New Essays in Literary History and Criticism*, edited by Robert L. McDonald and Linda Rohrer Paige. Tuscaloosa: University of Alabama Press, pp. 198–217.

Shklovsky, Viktor. 2016. *Viktor Shklovsky: A Reader*. Edited by Alexandra Berlina. Bloomsbury Academic & Professional. ProQuest Ebook Central, https://ebookcentral-proquest-com.ezproxy.gsu.edu/lib/gsu/detail.action?docID=4707040. Accessed Oct. 10, 2016.

"Sholem Asch Bans His Own Play; Prohibits Staging *God of Vengeance* in Any Language." *Jewish Telegraphic Agency*, May 27, 1946, https://www.jta.org/1946/05/27/archive/sholem-asch-bans-his-own-play-prohibits-staging-god-of-vengeance-in-any-language.

Shuler, Catherine A. 1990. "Gender Perspectives and Violence in the Plays of Maria Irene Fornés and Sam Shepard." *Modern American Drama: The Female Canon*, edited by June Schlueter. Teaneck: Fairleigh Dickinson University Press.

Signature Voices. "VIDEO: IN THE HEIGHTS' Quiara Alegria Hudes Recalls First Meeting with Lin-Manuel Miranda and Thomas Kail," https://www.broadwayworld.com/videoplay/VIDEO-IN-THE-HEIGHTS-Quiara-Alegria-Hudes-Recalls-First-Meeting-with-Lin-Manuel-Miranda-and-Thomas-Kail-20160116. Accessed Sept. 14, 2017.

Silverstein, Marc. Personal Interview. Aug. 22, 2017.

Six Degrees of Separation. Directed by Fred Schepisi. 1993. DVD.

Soloski, Alexis. 2011. "Who Is the Greatest Living Playwright?" *The Village Voice*, Nov. 2, 2011, https://www.villagevoice.com/2011/11/02/who-is-the-greatest-living-playwright/.

Soloski, Alexis. 2016. "*Indecent* Review: Broadway's First Lesbian Kiss Locks Lips Once More." *The Guardian*, May 17, 2016, https://www.theguardian.com/stage/2016/may/17/indecent-broadway-review-lesbian-kiss.

Stasio, Marilyn. 2016. "Off-Broadway Review: *Indecent* by Paula Vogel." *Variety*, May 17, 2016, http://variety.com/2016/legit/reviews/indecent-review-play-1201777035/.

Stasio, Marilyn. 2022. "'How I Learned to Drive' Review: Mary-Louise Parker, David Morse Star in Sterling Revival of Paula Vogel's Shocker." *Variety*, Apr. 20, 2022, https://variety.com/2022/legit/reviews/how-i-learned-to-drive-review-broadway-mary-louise-parker-1235235443/.

References

Stewart, Zachary. 2014. "Review: *And Baby Makes Seven.*" *TheaterMania*, Mar. 23, 2014. http://www.theatermania.com/new-york-city-theater/reviews/03-2014/and-baby-makes-seven_67961.html.

Tabio, Nick. 2018. "A Friend Like a Comet: An Interview with Sarah Ruhl," *Yale Daily News*, Sept. 28, 2018. https://yaledailynews.com/blog/2018/09/28/a-friend-like-a-comet-an-interview-with-sarah-ruhl/

Taylor, Markland. 1994. "Review 'Resident; *Hot 'N' Throbbing.*'" *Variety*, May 2, 1994. http://variety.com/1994/film/reviews/resident-hot-n-throbbing-1200437376/.

"Theatre Uncorked Episode 2 – Paula Vogel and Rebecca Taichman," https://www.stitcher.com/podcast/eric-pargac/theatre-uncorked/e/44726361.

Tichler, Rosemarie, and Barry Jay Kaplan. 2012. "Paula Vogel." *The Playwright at Work: Conversations*. Chicago: Northwestern University Press, 2012, pp. 113–35.

Timpane, John. 2012. "An Upset Pulitzer Win for West Philly's Quiara Alegría Hudes." *The Inquirer*, Apr. 16, 2012, http://www.philly.com/philly/business/20120417_An_upset_Pulitzer_win_for_West_Phillys_Quiara_Alegr_iacute_a_Hudes.html.

"The Top 10 Most-Produced Plays: 1994–2014." *American Theatre*, Sept. 23, 2014, www.americantheatre.org/2014/09/23/top-10-most-plays-1994-2014/.

Turina, Ana Fernández-Caparrós. 2011. "The Geography of Imagination: Urban Mapping of Social Networks in John Guare's *Six Degrees of Separation*." *South Atlantic Review*, Fall, pp. 57–74.

Umansky, Ellen. 2007. "Asch's Passion." *Tablet*, Apr. 24, 2007, http://www.tabletmag.com/jewish-arts-and-culture/books/801/aschs-passion.

Urban, Ken. 2013. "John Guare." *The Methuen Drama Guide to Contemporary American Playwrights*, edited by Martin Middeke, Peter Paul Schnierer, Christopher Innes, and Matthew C. Roudané. London: Bloomsbury, pp. 58–75.

Vendler, Helen. 2010. *Dickinson: Selected Poems and Commentaries*. Cambridge, MA: The Belknap Press of Harvard University Press.

Viagas, Robert. 2016. "Paula Vogel's *Indecent* Books a Broadway Theatre." *Playbill*, Oct. 31, 2016, http://www.playbill.com/article/paula-vogels-indecent-books-a-broadway-theatre.

Vogel, Paula. 1996. *And Baby Makes Seven: The Baltimore Waltz and Other Plays*. New York: Theatre Communications Group, pp. 59–125.

Vogel, Paula. 1996. *The Baltimore Waltz*. The Baltimore Waltz and Other Plays. New York: Theatre Communications Group, pp. 1–57.

Vogel, Paula. 1996. *Desdemona: A Play about a Handkerchief*. The Baltimore Waltz and Other Plays. New York: Theatre Communications Group, pp. 173–224.

Vogel, Paula. 1996. *Hot 'N' Throbbing*. The Baltimore Waltz and Other Plays. New York: Theatre Communications Group, pp. 225–95.

Vogel, Paula. 1998. *How I Learned to Drive*. New York: Theatre Communications Group.

Vogel, Paula. 1996. *The Oldest Profession*. The Baltimore Waltz and Other Plays. New York: Theatre Communications Group, pp. 127–72.

References

Vogel, Paula. 1998. "A Prize-Winning Playwright." Interview with Elizabeth Farnsworth. *PBS Newshour*, Apr. 16, 1998, www.pbs.org/newshour/bb/entertainment/jan-june98/play_4-16.html. Accessed Mar. 2, 2014.

Vogel, Paula. 2004. *The Last Christmas Ride Home*. New York: Theatre Communications Group.

Vogel, Paula. 2007. "Sarah Ruhl." *Bomb*, 99, Apr. 1, 2007, https://bombmagazine.org/articles/sarah-ruhl/.

Vogel, Paula. 2012. *A Civil War Christmas: An American Musical Celebration*. New York: Theatre Communications Group.

Vogel, Paula. 2012. "Paula Vogel on Negative Empathy." *YouTube*, Aug. 26, 2012, www.youtube.com/watch?v=7iVrFCZ6bY0.

Vogel, Paula (@VogelPaula). 2016. "@Lynnbrooklyn @Lin_Manuel @beyondabsurdity Congrats LMfor Kennedy Prize: Hope to see all nominations in 2016. Honored to be in Your Midst!" *Twitter*, Feb. 22, 2016, 8:51 a.m., https://twitter.com/VogelPaula/status/701811557060186112.

Vogel, Paula (@VogelPaula). 2016. "thanks so very much Lynn! Looking forward to seeing SWEAT. Xxp." *Twitter*, June 9, 2016, 7:39 a.m., https://twitter.com/VogelPaula/status/740916291775660032.

Vogel, Paula 2017. *Boot Camp*. http://paulavogelplaywright.com/boot-camp/. Accessed Sept. 14, 2017.

Vogel, Paula (@VogelPaula). 2017. "Brantley&Green 2–0. Nottage&Vogel 0–2. Lynn, they help close us down,&gifted str8 white guys run: ourplayswill last.B&G#footnotesinhistory." *Twitter*, June 14, 2017, 9:24 a.m., https://twitter.com/VogelPaula/status/875026258710736897.

Vogel, Paula. 2017. "A Note from the Playwright." Program for *Paula Vogel's Indecent at the Cort Theatre, New York, Playbill*, Apr 2017, p. 33.

Vogel, Paula (@VogelPaula). 2017. "O &ps for folks who can't read tweets much less plays: Hnath deserves every rave ALL give him. Alas, have not yet seen OSLO! Congrats JT!" *Twitter*, June 14, 2017, 9:53 a.m., https://twitter.com/VogelPaula/status/875033522657951744.

Vogel, Paula. 2017. "Playwriting Workshop." May 22, 2017, Vineyard Theatre, New York.

Vogel, Paula (@VogelPaula). 2017. "Please buy a ticket soon to Indecent, asking your support. This show is the best i got in me. Want to share while we can." *Twitter*, May 25, 2017, 11:43 a.m., https://twitter.com/VogelPaula/status/867813466698121217.

Vogel, Paula (@VogelPaula). 2017. "Thank You!" *Twitter*, Apr. 25, 2017. https://twitter.com/elbyjay/status/856892156719620097.

Vogel, Paula. 2017. "The Urgency of Indecent Art." Interview with Helen Eisenbach. *The Huffington Post*, June 07, 2017, http://www.huffingtonpost.com/entry/the-urgency-of-indecent-art-paula-vogel-on-love-creation_us_59375a70e4b04ff0c46682bf.

Vogel, Paula (@VogelPaula). 2021. "My theatrical Kaddish, INDECENT, now gives me a bittersweet joy: This is the last week in London. We must say the Kaddish for Our Kaddish. Colds and bugs have stopped my return but grateful to have seen this magnificent company: dayenu! Sending all my love.

References

@MenChocFactory." *Twitter*, Nov. 23, 2021, 2:01 p.m., https://twitter.com/VogelPaula/status/1463221269420249088.

Vogel, Paula (@VogelPaula). 2021. "Same." *Twitter*, July 6, 2021, 3:53 p.m., https://twitter.com/VogelPaula/status/1412500025972867073.

Vogel, Paula (@VogelPaula). 2021. "Well, my friends, I appreciate your support. The request for me to be verified by twitter has been denied. As long as my friends and family. Continue to love me, I will survive!" *Twitter*, July 13, 2021, 4:07 p.m., https://twitter.com/VogelPaula/status/1415040116729552905.

Vogel, Paula (@VogelPaula). 2022. "So Proud to have had Indecent produced in the James Earl Jones Theatre (also place where The Diary of Anne Frank premiered) Yes!" *Twitter*, Mar. 2, 2022, 8:23 p.m., https://twitter.com/VogelPaula/status/1499193644657614853.

Vogel, Paula (@VogelPaula). 2022. "Thank you for your kind words. (My New Orleans Spanish, French &German Catholic side still battles with my Russian &German Jewish side from New York!) I am currently writing about Maryland. Best to you." *Twitter*, Feb. 9, 2022, 4:05 p.m., https://twitter.com/VogelPaula/status/1491518731473797131.

Vogel, Paula, and Rebecca Taichman. 2016. "Drama Book Shop Discussion." June 2016, https://www.facebook.com/dramabookshop/videos/1045287582225464/.

Walker, Jeffrey. 2015. "Paula Vogel's *The Oldest Profession* Review." *DC Theatre Scene*, June 11, 2015, https://dctheatrescene.com/2015/06/11/paula-vogels-the-oldest-profession-review/.

Warner, Sara. 2016. "Playwright Vogel Returns to Campus for Ph.D." *Cornell Chronicle*, Mar. 29, 2016, http://news.cornell.edu/stories/2016/03/playwright-vogel-returns-campus-phd.

Weckwirth, Wendy. 2004. "More Invisible Terrains." *Theater*, vol. 34, no. 2, p. 30.

Weinert-Kendt, Rob. 2009. "A War on Women: Lynn Nottage's Pulitzer Prize-winning *Ruined*." *America Magazine*, July 20, 2009, https://www.americamagazine.org/issue/703/theater-review/war-women.

Wren, Celia. 2005. "The Golden Ruhl." *American Theatre*, vol. 22, no. 8, Oct., p. 31.

Ybarra, Patricia. 2017. "How to Read a Latinx Play in the Twenty-First Century: Learning from Quiara Hudes." *Theatre Topics*, vol. 27, no. 1, p. 52.

Yeğenoğlu, Meyda. 2017. "Cosmopolitan Europe: Memory, Apology and Mourning." *European Cosmopolitanism: Colonial Histories and Postcolonial Societies*, edited by Gurminder K. Bhambra and John Narayan. London: Routledge, pp. 17–30.

Young, Harvey. 2015. "An Interview with Quiara Alegría Hudes." *Theatre Survey*, vol. 56, no. 2, May, p. 187.

Zax, Talya. 2016. "Sholem Asch's Scandalous *God of Vengeance* to Get Yiddish Rep Revival." *Forward*, May 24, 2016, http://forward.com/schmooze/341302/sholem-aschs-scandalous-god-of-vengeance-to-get-yiddish-rep-revival/.

Zinoman, Jason. 2004. "Lynn Nottage Enters Her Flippant Period." *New York Times*, June 13, 2004, http://www.nytimes.com/2004/06/13/theater/theater-lynn-nottage-enters-her-flippant-period.html.

References

Zinoman, Jason. 2005. "Pornography to Prop Up Family Values." Review of *Hot 'N' Throbbing*. *New York Times*, Mar. 29, 2005, http://www.nytimes.com/2005/03/29/theater/reviews/pornography-to-prop-up-family-values.html.

Zoglin, Richard. 2013. "*Water by the Spoonful*: The Acclaimed Play Too Good for Broadway." *Time*, Jan. 24, 2013, http://entertainment.time.com/2013/01/24/water-by-the-spoonful-the-acclaimed-play-too-good-for-broadway/.

Zunshine, Lisa. 2006. *Why We Read Fiction: Theory of Mind and the Novel*. Columbus: Ohio State University Press.

CONTRIBUTORS

Lee Brewer Jones is Professor of English at Georgia State University, USA. He is the co-author, with Alyse W. Jones, of the Longman textbooks *College Writing: Keeping It Real* (2001) and *A World of Writing* (2005).

Ana Fernández-Caparrós is Senior Lecturer of English and American literature at the University of Valencia, Spain. Her current research focuses on contemporary US drama and the representation of twenty-first-century crises, and it has been published in major journals such as *Studies in Theatre and Performance*, *Cultura Lenguaje y Representación*, *Studies in the Literary Imagination*, *Contemporary Theatre Review*, *Atlantis*, and others. She is the author of the monograph *El teatro de Sam Shepard en el Nueva York de los sesenta* (2015) and her latest publication is a chapter in the book *Staging 21st Century Tragedies: Theatre, Politics and Global Crisis*, edited by Avra Sidiroloupou (2022).

Amy Muse is Professor of English at the University of St. Thomas in Minnesota, USA. She is the author of *The Drama and Theatre of Sarah Ruhl* (2018) and essays on dramatic literature published in *The Journal of Dramatic Theory and Criticism* and *Text & Presentation*.

INDEX

Adams, James Truslow 27
   "American Dream" 27–9
   The Epic of America 27
Albee, Edward 2, 5, 10, 13, 16, 33–5, 38, 61, 84, 88, 144, 164 n.11, 169 n.13
   The American Dream 34
   Who's Afraid of Virginia Woolf? 2, 33–5, 61
   The Zoo Story 38
Als, Hilton 9–10
Alvarez, Natalie and Jimena Ortuzar 152, 172 n.20
American College Theater Festival's National Student Playwriting Award 3, 15
Apollo Theatre 108, 119
Asch, Sholem 5, 13, 108–9, 111–12, 114–22, 124–5, 169 n.15, 170 n.21
   God of Vengeance 108–12, 115–24, 170 n.18

bakeoff 80, 83, 95, 102–3, 112–13, 158
"Bard at the Gate" 126–7
Bass, George 90, 157
Beckett, Samuel 9, 24, 29, 98, 112
   Waiting for Godot 9
Behn, Aphra 18, 163 n.2
Bierce, Ambrose 5, 13, 42
   "An Occurrence at Owl Creek Bridge" 5, 42
Bigsby, C. W. E. 3, 15–19, 24, 28, 34–5, 39, 42–3, 46, 52, 55–9, 61, 64, 66–8, 74, 77, 79, 109, 129, 140, 142, 163 n.1, 164 n.5, 165 nn.1, 6, 170 n.16
Bolt, Robert 3, 5, 15
   A Man for All Seasons 3, 18
boot camps 80–1, 95–7, 105, 157
Brantley, Ben 12–13, 22, 30–1, 73, 111, 122–4
Brecht, Bertolt 16–17, 30, 91–2, 115

Broadway 1, 5–7, 10, 12, 18, 34, 50, 74–6, 79–80, 90, 93–4, 107–8, 110–11, 114, 116, 119, 121–4, 126–7, 160–1, 163 n.3, 166 n.22, 167 nn.9–10, 169 n.10
Brokaw, Mark 32, 72–5, 78
Brown University 2, 4, 15, 30, 47, 79, 83, 85, 87, 90, 95, 104, 130, 135, 140–1, 144–5, 155–7, 159

capitalism 24–5, 29
Channing, Stockard 7, 163 n.1
Churchill, Caryl 4–5, 8, 11–13, 76, 167 n.2, 168 n.18
   Cloud Nine 4–5, 12–13, 76
   "A Poem for Irene Fornés" 11
   Top Girls 5, 12, 167 n.2
Circle Repertory 21–2, 48–9
Clay, Carolyn 71–2, 166 n.18
Clement, Olivia 109–10
Congdon, Connie 80, 95, 155
Cornell University 3, 15, 97, 108, 114, 116, 120, 125, 127, 163 n.2
Cort Theatre 5, 79, 93, 107–8, 121–4, 169 n.2
Craig, Carolyn Casey 1–2, 95–6, 104
Cruz, Nilo 4, 10, 79–85, 90, 92–5, 104, 145, 159, 167 n.15
   Anna in the Tropics 80, 83–4, 90, 167 n.10
Cummings, Scott T. 9–11

Day, Johanna 73, 166 n.21
defamiliarization 13, 17–21, 23–4, 33–5, 42–3, 52, 97, 100, 111, 118, 156, 168 n.20
Derrida, Jacques 47
Dickinson, Emily 81, 142
Dolan, Jill 35, 73–4
Dr. Strangelove 36, 46

Index

Edelstein, Gordon   80, 95, 103
Emmrich, Stuart   8

Farnsworth, Elizabeth   1, 4, 11, 28, 62
Fausto-Sterling, Ann   2, 50, 144
feminism   3, 9–10, 15–16, 20, 23, 35, 94, 108, 116, 125, 161
Forbes Heermans and George McCalmon playwriting competition   3, 15
Fornés, María Irene   5, 8–11, 19, 76, 80, 82–3, 85, 125, 129, 144–5, 163 n.3, 168 n.18, 171 n.18
  Fefu and Her Friends   9–11, 19, 76, 125
  Mud   81, 83
  La Viuda   9
Freud, Sigmund   39, 45, 47, 117, 168 n.21

García-Romero, Anne   144, 150, 152, 171 n.18
Gener, Randy   91, 95
Gerard, Jeremy   22, 39
Gerber, Tony   91, 159
Glab, Keith   22
Green, Jesse   122–3, 170 n.26
Guare, John   4–8, 10, 12, 144, 163 n.1, 168 n.18
  A Free Man of Color   8
  Gardenia   4, 8
  The House of Blue Leaves   5–7
  Six Degrees of Separation   4, 6–8, 163 n.1
Gurtler, Camilla   22
Gussow, Mel   40, 81, 164 n.15

Helms, Jesse   51, 77, 165 n.6
Herren, Graley   68, 71–2, 80, 83, 138
Holmberg, Arthur   62–3, 69, 95
Hudes, Quiara Alegría   79–80, 84, 87–90, 93–4, 104, 107, 115, 140–54, 159, 167 nn.11, 15, 171 nn.5–7, 13–17, 172 n.20
  Elliot, A Soldier's Fugue   88–9, 147–53, 171 n.6
  In the Heights   88, 90
  My Broken Language   141–2, 145–8
  Water by the Spoonful   87–90, 146, 151–3, 171 n.17
Hull, Deborah   62, 64–5

International Arts Relation (INTAR)   10, 82–3, 144
Isherwood, Charles   114–16, 122, 131, 170 n.25

James Earl Jones Theatre. *See* Cort Theatre
Jarry, Alfred   112–13
  Ubu Roi   112–13
Johnson, Katie N.   116, 124
Jones, Cherry   22, 40, 48–50, 77, 138, 165 nn.3–4, 166 n.17
Jory, Jon   24, 164 n.5
Joyce, James   9, 34, 53, 55, 170 n.18

Karinthy, Fridges   6
  "Chains" or "Chain-Links"   6
Kimbrough, Andrew   69–71
Krasner, David   8, 42
Kubler-Ross, Elizabeth   42–4

Lahr, John   85, 129
Le Petomane   102, 112
Levenson, Steven   79, 90, 94–5
Lincoln Center   7, 79, 86, 93–4
Lorca, Federico García   16, 96

magical realism   39, 80, 82–3, 120, 124, 132, 138
Mamet, David   5, 23–4, 61, 73, 75, 101, 165 n.3
  American Buffalo   75
  Duck Variations   23
  Oleanna   61
Mansbridge, Joanna   2–3, 5, 12, 16, 18–23, 26–7, 29, 31–5, 37, 39, 43–4, 49, 53, 57, 59, 61, 67, 72, 78, 142–4
metadrama/metatheatre   35–7, 111, 118, 152
Miller, Arthur   10, 26–7, 108
Miranda, Lin-Manuel   84, 88, 90, 97, 115, 148, 169 n.12
Modern Family   32, 40
Morse, David   65, 72–6, 78, 166 n.23

Nabokov, Vladimir   5, 13, 17, 53, 62, 66
  Lolita   17, 53, 55, 57, 62, 66, 166 n.19
negative empathy   13, 17–18, 35, 62, 66, 75–6, 102, 143, 156
New Ohio Theater   40, 93
New Plays Festival   3

Index

Nottage, Lynn   4, 79, 80, 90–4, 104, 107, 115, 121, 123, 126, 140, 145, 155–61, 167 n.15
   Intimate Apparel   90–1, 93
   Ruined   90–3
   Sweat   79, 91, 93–4, 107, 115, 121–3, 167 n.13

Obie Award   4, 6–7, 12, 15, 48–9, 74, 79, 92, 104, 107, 166 n.17
O'Neill, Eugene   34, 110, 119, 170 nn.16, 20

Parker, Mary-Louise   1, 68, 72–8, 163 n.17, 166 n.23
Paulson, Michael   74, 121–2, 126, 170 n.23
Pellegrini, Ann   34–5, 142
Pinter, Harold   19, 104–5
   Old Times   19
Plunka, Gene   6
Polin, Sophia   40
Pollack-Pelzner, Daniel   115–16, 135
Pound, Ezra   17
Provincetown Players   108, 118–19, 170 n.16
Pulitzer Prize   7–8, 74, 77–80, 84–6, 88, 90–4, 107–8, 110, 123, 125–6, 140–2, 156, 165 n.4, 166 n.20, 169 nn.3, 13–14, 170 n.23

Rainbow Theatre Project   31
Reagan, Ronald   23–4, 29, 33, 46, 77
Reed, Carol   5, 42
   The Third Man   5, 42, 46, 102, 168 n.24
Rich, Frank   48
Ritvo, Max   138–9
Rooney, David   30–1
Rosenberg, Isaac   116
Roth, Daryl   121, 123–4
Roudané, Matthew   34, 38
Rousuck, J. Wynn   48–9, 60, 80, 94–6, 165 n.12
Ruhl, Sarah   4, 32, 79–80, 85–6, 90, 93–4, 99, 104, 109, 129–40, 144–6, 159, 166 n.1, 167 nn.8, 12, 170 n.1, 171 n.11
   Dear Elizabeth   136–7
   Dog Play   85, 131, 171 n.2
   Essays I Don't Have Time to Write   129–30, 138, 171 n.4

   For Peter Pan on Her 70th Birthday   132–4, 136
   In the Next Room or the Vibrator Play   85–6, 134, 136

Savran, David   4–5, 8–9, 15–17, 29, 41, 51, 72, 78, 95, 107, 134, 140, 143, 164 n.4
Schildkraut, Rudolph   111
Shakespeare, William   3, 5, 13, 16, 18–19, 21–2, 37–8, 40, 44, 53, 60, 66, 81, 97–100, 103, 107, 112, 139
Shepard, Alan and Mary Lamb   25, 27, 29, 37, 39, 46, 52, 55, 59, 63
Shklovsky, Viktor   17, 115
Signature Theatre Company   10–11, 30, 32, 59–60, 88, 164 n.8
Silverstein, Marc   104–5
Smith, Molly   59–60, 77, 165 nn.11–12
Soloski, Alexis   12, 114, 116
Stasio, Marilyn   75, 114
States, Bert   97, 101, 108, 125, 168 n.28
Stewart, Zachary   40
Stonewall   2, 33
Stoppard, Tom   19, 87
   Rosencrantz and Guildenstern Are Dead   19, 22

Taichman, Rebecca   75, 86, 93–4, 107, 109–11, 114–15, 123–5, 138, 166 n.1, 169 n.5
Theatre Network   15
Tichler, Rosemarie and Barry Jay Kaplan   50, 80–2, 84
Tony Award   5–7, 32, 79–80, 86, 88, 93–4, 112, 122–3, 165 n.4
Topol, Richard   115–16

Ubu Roi   112–14

Vineyard Theatre   8, 72–4, 79–81, 83, 85, 93, 96–104, 107, 110, 114–22, 154, 166 nn.21–2, 169 n.13, 170 n.20
Vogel, Carl   1–2, 41–4, 47–8, 64, 102, 130, 132, 165 n.2
Vogel, Donald   1–2
Vogel, Mark   1
Vogel, Paula
   And Baby Makes Seven   2, 5, 13, 15–16, 32–40, 46, 48–50, 52, 61, 93

193

Index

The Baltimore Waltz   4–5, 15, 22, 40–52, 61–2, 70, 83, 130–2, 138, 142, 145, 165 n.9, 168 n.24
A Civil War Christmas: An American Music Celebration   4, 107
Desdemona: A Play about a Handkerchief   3, 5, 13, 15–23, 30, 32, 40, 49–50, 52, 61, 74, 163 n.1, 164 nn.4–5
Hiding Scenes in Restoration Comedy   3, 16
Hot 'N' Throbbing   48, 51–2, 55–61, 124, 164 n.13
How I Learned to Drive   1–2, 4–5, 17, 49–50, 61–79, 83, 100, 107, 126, 130, 132, 142, 165 nn.4, 9, 169 n.13
Indecent   2, 4–5, 8, 75, 79, 93–4, 107–12, 114–26, 138, 160–1, 166 n.1, 167 n.13, 169 n.2, 170 n.22
The Long Christmas Ride Home   5, 130, 132–3, 142, 146
"Loose Screws" episode   1–2
Meg   3, 5, 15, 18

The Oldest Profession   3, 5, 13, 15–16, 22–32, 40, 52, 167 n.2
Vogel, Phyllis Bremerman   1–2, 61, 76

Walker, Jeffrey   31
Warner, Sara   3, 15–16, 120
Washington, D.C.   1–2, 31
Wellman, Mac   80, 95, 156
Wilde, Oscar   16
Wilder, Thornton   5, 98, 116, 169 n.14
Williams, Tennessee   16, 28, 37, 75, 101–2, 135
  The Glass Menagerie   28, 71, 73, 75, 102

Yale University   2–4, 79, 87, 90, 93, 95, 107, 109–10, 121, 138–9, 147–8, 156, 158, 169 n.5

Zaks, Jerry   6–7
Zinoman, Jason   60, 92
Zunshine, Lisa   62, 66

www.ingramcontent.com/pod-product-compliance
Lightning Source LLC
Chambersburg PA
CBHW052117300426
44116CB00010B/1704